Advance Praise for Between the Sheets

"This is more than just a book on curling. Guy and Cheryl capture the psyche of the high-performance athlete and the beauty of sport in general—and that sport teaches leadership principles and personal skills that apply to anyone seeking to lead a successful life."

—Claire Carver-Dias
2000 Olympic Bronze Medallist,
Four-time Gold Medallist, Commonwealth Games

"This is the first book written specifically on the mental game of curling. Bernard and Scholz went the extra mile in tapping into the minds of the top curlers in the world. The stories are great for fans of the game and the lessons are invaluable for the competitive player. Curlers of all levels will benefit but so will athletes aiming to go beyond their personal best."

—Gerry Peckam
High Performance Director
Canadian Curling Association (CCA)

"Packed with priceless wisdom, Between the Sheets is likely to be a must-read for every curler from novice to professional for many years to come."

—Claudia Church
Singer/Songwriter and Model
Author of Discovering the Masterpiece Within

"Unique for curlers and fans alike, who will be provided with more insight into the sport of curling. Great reading."

Neil Houston
ip Services
an Association,
Formei Men's Champion

"Wonderful ideas on the training and mental aspects of our great sport, and some great hints from many of our elite curlers on how 'they do it.' A must-read for all curlers and fans as we can all learn from each other!"

—Cathy King
Six-time Alberta Champion,
1998 Canadian Champion, World Bronze Medallist

"Fascinating, wonderful, and full of great ideas that reflect passion, commitment, and love for curling. A must-read for all curlers and fans of the game."

—Arnold Asham
Founder, Asham Curling Supplies,
Coach and Curler

"A winner! Fascinating insight into an aspect of the Roaring Game that we know little about. To paraphrase Yogi Berra, curling is 90 percent mental—the other half is physical."

—Allen Cameron
Sportswriter, *Calgary Herald*

Between the Sheets

Between the Sheets

Creating Curling Champions

Guy H. Scholz
with
Cheryl L. Bernard

Hillsboro Press
PROVIDENCE PUBLISHING CORPORATION
FRANKLIN, TENNESSEE

Copyright © 2005 by Guy H. Scholz and Cheryl L. Bernard

All rights reserved. Written permission must be secured from the publisher to use or reproduce any part of this book, except for brief quotations in critical reviews or articles.

Printed in Canada

09   08   07   06   05   1   2   3   4   5

Library of Congress Control Number: 2005934816

ISBN-13: 978-1-57736-358-3
ISBN-10: 1-57736-358-2

Cover concept by Dean Joanisse, Art of Curling
Cover design by Joey McNair

The illustrations on page 204 are copyright PHYSIGRAPHE (www.physigraphe.com); used by permission.

HILLSBORO PRESS
an imprint of
Providence Publishing Corporation
238 Seaboard Lane • Franklin, Tennessee 37067
www.providence-publishing.com
800-321-5692

Carla-Jayne! My best friend, wife,
lover, and catalyst (check out chapter two)!

You make me believe I can
write like a Stephen King or John Eldredge,
preach like a Billy Graham or Tony Campolo, and
curl like a Randy Ferbey or Al Hackner!
(Hey, you gotta aim to hit the broom, even if you don't always hit it!)
Somehow you convince me anything is possible and following my dreams
is worth all the effort. I love you!

For the serious curler:
this book will be of no value unless you read it!

Contents

SECTION FOUR—The Motivational Game

Observations of an Anxious Armchair Curler

Excerpt from the *National Post*, October 23, 1999:

It's hard to believe how worked up I can get over it.

I'm right on the edge of my seat.

I get nervous. I start sweating.

I'm watching curling.

Some people will laugh, but a lot more won't. Curling's much more of a sport than most people realize. The thinking required, and the strategy, absolutely capture me. You'd be surprised how many National Hockey League players can be found sitting in their hotel rooms in the middle of a road trip watching curling somewhere. I've been hooked on the game since I played for the Edmonton Oilers.

Hockey players were thrilled to be staying in the Olympic Village. It was like being a kid again or off to a tournament and billeted. I like to think some of those other athletes got to know a completely different side of hockey players. We got along wonderfully with everyone else, whether they were skiers or snowboarders or speed skaters.

Or curlers, of course—with me leading the cheering in that department.

—Wayne Gretzky

Foreword

I am always looking for ways to train and improve. Even though I am thirty-eight years old, I want to push the envelope and see how good I can become and for how long. I want to keep an edge on the competition, even though the competition keeps getting stronger. Excellence in performance and in life begins with a vision of where you are heading and a commitment to do the things required to get there.

The goal of *Between the Sheets* is to provide you with the strategies champion curlers use to excel in their sport. From there it's up to you to provide the commitment required to apply these strategies to your own life and sport, and empower you to live and perform closer to your peak potential.

We also hope that *Between the Sheets* will be a fun and inspirational read for those sports fans who would like to get a glimpse into the minds of their favorite curlers. The many lessons and stories in this book cross over into the principles of life that can lead one to success in whatever endeavor a person may aim for.

The vision for this book materialized when Guy Scholz interviewed me for the January 2004 issue of *Sweep!* magazine. Our love of the game and desire to understand what it takes to make champion curlers drove us to see it through to completion. In the many discussions we had, Guy's exceptional writing talent brought my ideas and thoughts to life with a style that smoothed out my verbal offerings without turning them into something unrecognizable. His patience, sense of humor, love of sport, and most important, friendship, made this journey most rewarding. I am very grateful to Guy for all he has given me.

To my mother, thank you for giving me the most amazing human gift—unconditional love. And to my father, for showing me the gifts of desire, perseverance, and belief in myself. To my wonderful brother Don for his support and love, and to Terry Meek for twenty years of friendship and the uncanny ability to understand me so well. Special thanks to Karen Ruus, who loved to talk about the game as much as I did. She was my teammate for twelve years and a friend for life.

And to my best friend, Darilyn Fortuna, for listening to me continually talk about curling from the age of thirteen through thirty-eight. You have the ability to make me understand how fortunate I am to have the passion, desire, and talent for something I love so much.

Finally, to all those athletes, coaches, and friends who allowed us to consult with them on this book. The following quote by Theodore Roosevelt reflects the respect and admiration I have for them and their dedication to the sport of curling:

It is not the critic who counts, not the man who points out how the strong man stumbled, or where the doer of deeds could have done them better. The credit belongs to the man who is actually in the arena: whose face is marred by dust and sweat and blood; who strives valiantly: who errs and comes short again and again; who knows great enthusiasm, the great devotions and spends himself in a worthy cause; who at the best knows in the end the triumph of high achievement, and who at worst, if he fails, at least fails while daring.

—Cheryl Bernard

Acknowledgments

This was a dream project for me to research and write. Since 1995, I have been fortunate to interview well over one hundred world-class curlers, coaches, and other athletes, creating the bulk of the material for *Between the Sheets*. To these warriors of pebbled ice, gridiron, arenas, and swimming pools—thank you! Curlers are among my favorite athletes to interview. No, they are my favorite! They are like the Yodas of the sports world.

Curling has always fascinated me. One of my earliest memories as a child was watching my **mom and dad, Herb and Arni Scholz**, playing in a mixed league or mixed bonspiel sometime around 1960. It could have been in Langenburg, Marchwell, Churchbridge, Esterhazy, or Spy Hill, Saskatchewan. All I remember is the bigness, the brightness, and the awe of what these big people were doing. A curling club seemed bigger and better than I could dream Disneyland could ever be—and still does. I could not wait to play the game in earnest.

The Brier, the Canadian men's curling championship, to me was on par with the Grey Cup, Stanley Cup, or the World Series. My only regret (and it's slight) is that the vocation I felt called into took me away from pursuing this game in a World Curling Tour (WCT)-type of fashion; however, it never pulled me away from the game or being able to play seventy to eighty games a season. I believe I am one of the ultimate tweeners in the game of curling (read on to find out what a tweener is).

Cheryl Bernard is my new favorite femme curler—no, make that new favorite curler! I've always enjoyed watching her curl because Cheryl plays with moxie. Her coach Dennis Balderston says, "Cheryl is one gutsy curler and has a knack for making the big shot in the big game. Not many can do that."

Thank you, Cheryl, for making the sabbatical possible to write this book that you so wanted to get published on the mental game of curling. And thank you for trusting me to put all these thoughts and ideas to print. Girl, I have had the time of my life. I have learned so much more about the inner game of curling and life in general since meeting you. You are one of the best bosses I have ever had. Thank you! From now on when I am in a tough situation on the ice I will say to myself "WWCD: What Would Cheryl Do?"

To the team at **Providence Publishing Corporation** in Franklin, Tennessee—welcome to one of the most popular sports north of the border. *Thank you* for your belief in this project and expertise in putting this whole package together. We have enjoyed the process and we have really enjoyed getting to know our new friends in Music City. I'll bet *y'all* didn't know when you were first approached about the possibility of publishing *Between the Sheets* that the Nashville Curling Club was about a two-minute walk from your parking lot, *eh*?

Thank you, my good friends and colleagues at *Sweep!* magazine, **Bob Garvin**, and **Jim Henderson**. Jim kept bugging me to do a story on Cheryl. This is how the *Between the Sheets* rock got rolling. Thank you for giving me a six-year history of writing features and the infamous *Alberta Page*. Good thing I saved all my notes, eh?

Jackie Brown (aka—Jackie Chapman-Brown), my proofreader, editor, and one of my favorite people in life—what would I do without you? Thank you for always making *Between the Sheets* a priority as well as the care and time you devoted to it. The Grande Marnier big gulp is on the way!

Darlene Reid, managing editor of *In the Rings*, one of my favorite regional curling publications. Thank you for thinking my curling rantings are worthy to publish. Many of my rantings were inspiration for *Between the Sheets*.

Thank you, **Chinook Chapel**—my day job! Could a pastor ask for a more generous and supportive congregation in allowing someone to pursue a dream outside of the ministerial norm? How many congregations give their pastor two Sundays a year to curl, just in case one of my teams makes a bonspiel final? They have more faith than I do, but I am thankful I have been able to use up some of those Sundays.

Thank you to my **curling buddies** from the 2004–2005 season. **Andy Jones** has not only curled with me since 1997 (there is a man who deserves a medal), but has often Googled up information for me to set the record straight. **Jim Brooks**, **Bob Boschee**, **Jim Perry** (son of the famous Mel, check out the 1963 Brier and Worlds), **Shawn Gorniak**, and **Jeff Sinden** and **Gerald Shymko**, the skip for the Prairie Warriors in Curl for a Cure—you guys helped the writing process in subtle ways more than you'll ever know.

Sandra Block, my skip at the Nashville Curling Club, got me the Alberta Peace Country connections needed for this project. You just may be the best femme curler in the entire Southeast U.S.

Finally, to my **Friar's Briar** teammates **George Budd**, **Stephen Hambidge**, and **Dan Eagle**. There was a lot of *Between the Sheets* philosophy happening out on the ice as we connected as quickly as any team I have ever been a part of. This stuff I have been writing about works.

Curling with all the above mentioned friends needs to be acknowledged. Being around people who love this game and give it their all keeps me in the grass roots of curling, which is the foundation of this sport. I was continually inspired, motivated, and challenged by being with you all this past season. Many times just before or after writing a certain chapter, our experiences on and off the ice gave me the words and thoughts to write. It helped! (Maybe it's a George Plimpton thing!)

Bill Tschirhart, for your enthusiasm and belief in this project. Thank you doesn't seem appropriate enough to convey appreciation for all your time and your generosity in sharing your wisdom and resources. You are truly a coach in the John Wooden, Vince Lombardi, or Scotty Bowman league.

Bob Comartin and Billy Lee, for your fine contributions for chapters 21 and 22. Your expertise and generosity has helped make *Between the Sheets* a more well-rounded project.

Jim Timson, the media director for the CCA. A very sincere thank you for all the media guides and access you got for me this past curling season. Those media guides got as much use as any preacher who uses their Bible.

Jack and Pia Biensch—my Medici friends. Your generosity, friendship, and prayers prove to me there is not only a God but that a project like this truly is a community effort.

To the gals down at **Timothy's** at the Crowfoot Center in Calgary. I think it would be safe to say that 50 percent of this book was written in the best coffee shop and lunch place in Calgary. **Kuldeep**, **Shannon**, and **Hazel**: you have restored my faith in customer service.

Claudia Church—my co-writer on my other book project, *Discovering the Masterpiece Within*. I have learned so much about the creative process through our time together. Thank you for your ongoing friendship and flexibility when Cheryl came calling. You throw a pretty good curling rock for someone born in North Carolina and living in the heart of Tennessee. Thanks for chasing that truck down that stopped right in front of Providence Publishing Corporation. And please tell Mr. Crowell we will get our book finished . . . one day soon.

My family—Carla, **Anah**, **Reed**, and the canine comic relief of **Jazz** and **Wallace** the Westie. **Reed**, you're my hero. You not only live your life with a passion and never-ever-give-up Saskatchewan DNA-way, but you are the most patient of the bunch when my writing freak-out times occur. **Anah**, you are the true writer in the family, and you inspire me to get better and better. I never will achieve your level, but you inspire me. You have set the bar high, and you don't even know it. And thank you for your patience as well. Proceeds of my share from *Between the Sheets* will go towards my *children's therapy fund* to compensate for the sometimes blundering parenting job I do.

Carla—you got the dedication, but that was about as hard a pick as saying David Nedohin has been the best shot-maker on the planet since the new millennium began. You are my muse because of your unbelievable belief in me. What the heck do you see in me? I love you!

Between the Sheets

SECTION ONE

The Team Game

Chapter One

A Delicate Mix—Developing Team Chemistry

"The biggest difference between winning and losing at the highest levels of curling is the mental game. Every world-class curler is a technically good player but not every player or team has mastered the mental game. Our team's goal is to create the best mental toughness we can achieve combined with team spirit that gives us the edge over other teams."

—Peja Lindholm,
Three-time World Curling Champion from Sweden

Curling is a team game! In order to become a curling champion on a sheet of ice, a minimum level of team chemistry must occur. This is similar to a satisfying or, dare I say, spectacular encounter between the sheets with a man and a woman. The romantic encounter between the sheets will be satisfying and spectacular only if the couple has developed a certain minimum level of romantic chemistry. Now, if we all waited for everything to be perfect before becoming romantically involved with someone, planet Earth would have ceased to exist a long time ago.

Just as becoming a Romeo and Juliet or a David and Heather Nedohin will take a lifetime of care and maintenance, becoming proficient at the mental game and cultivating team chemistry takes a lifetime of learning, re-learning, and constant concern and attention.

Paying attention to developing the mental game and team chemistry is fundamental to success. A fundamental truism (or "core major thing," as Cheryl likes to say), must be worked on, reviewed, and applied on a constant basis. Harvey Penick, of Austin, Texas, considered one of the top golf teachers in history, sought to master golf's mental game. He emphasized over and over again to his golf pupils the importance of mastering a truism, whether technical or mental, over the course of their careers. He wrote four golf books based on notes he kept in a little red book for almost sixty years as a golf teacher. Penick taught right up until his death in April 1995, the week of the Masters Golf Tournament.

One of his prize pupils, Ben Crenshaw, was struggling with his game heading into the Masters and was given a short lesson by Penick only a week before Penick passed away. Crenshaw, who was on the downside of his career, went on to win his last major at Augusta. In one of the most poignant moments in sports history, Crenshaw collapsed on the 18th green in joy and sorrow because of his mentor's passing only a few days earlier. Crenshaw had considered withdrawing from the Masters because of Penick's death and desire to be a pallbearer at his friend's funeral.

Penick's first published book, *Harvey Penick's Little Red Book*, hit the market when he was eighty-six years old. He published three more over the next three years. *Harvey Penick's Little Red Book* is still the number one selling sports book of all time. While in his eighties Penick wrote, "I must review the basic golf fundamentals at least every other day because they are so easy to forget." One of the great masters of the mental game never felt like he had arrived. He was still committed to reviewing what he knew, and he was constantly looking to learn something new that would give his students an edge.

Developing the mental edge and team chemistry in curling or in any endeavor in life will happen more in the preparation and practice than before the actual games. Curling, which is very similar to baseball or cricket, is one of those unique sports where individual talent can stand out and reap many personal accolades; if that talent is not combined with a supporting cast, however, championships will be few and far between. Curling is such an individual-oriented game as far as the technical part of the sport is concerned that it is very easy to overemphasize individual training over working together as a team.

The dynamics of professional baseball make it much easier to gel as a team because the players are paid to spend significant amounts of time together. In curling, even though it is an Olympic-caliber sport, there are very few curlers who can afford to play the game full-time without having a day job to support themselves. So much of the practice time curlers do have is spent alone rather than working on team dynamics or chemistry. But mental training and building chemistry are critical to success. Bill Tschirhart of the Canadian Curling Association's (CCA) sponsored National Training Center (NTC) for Olympic-caliber and high-performance curlers based in Calgary, Alberta likes to say, "The majority of successful curling seems to happen on the warm side of the glass in order for a team to compete at its best on the cold side of the glass."

Between the Sheets is written primarily about mastering the mental game of curling, but it is written in the context of building a strong and mentally tough team that has chemistry. Developing team chemistry is a delicate process and takes time, effort, and the realization that it never stops. This first chapter is key to setting the tone throughout *Between the Sheets*: curling is a team game. Each individual player must take responsibility to master the mental game, yet a player doesn't have to develop the mental game alone. To be a championship team takes all the players on the team being highly committed to working on the mental game and all the players dedicated to working on team chemistry.

What are the key truisms or major core principles in developing team chemistry? From Cheryl's work and involvement with the NTC, and my interviewing of well over one hundred curlers who have competed at national and/or world events (and close to fifty athletes from other major sports), we have distilled down to seven essentials for building team chemistry. Think of these keys as creating a gourmet meal for your favorite people in life. Down through history the most respected teachers, sages, and philosophers—from Aristotle to Socrates to the Buddha to Christ—have all built unity around the dinner or supper table. Maybe curlers and rugby players know this instinctively with their traditional get-togethers for a cool drink or meal after a game. Bonds are built around eating and drinking.

E.A.T. W.E.L.L.

Learning to E.A.T. W.E.L.L. is the key to creating team chemistry. Building team chemistry is an ongoing process. Trying out one of these truisms on a one-time basis will never create a healthy team. Eating a good nutritious meal every now and then will never create a healthy body. We must eat well every day in order to be healthy, and as curlers we must practice these truisms on a consistent basis in order to have the chemistry needed to find that edge. Building team chemistry is work and it is sometimes a tad messy. Just as eating from the four basic food groups is not always enjoyable when we have a craving for chocolate pie or we are having a fast food chemical reaction, but the more we eat healthy or practice team chemistry, the easier and more enjoyable it becomes.

Cheryl's current team has been together for almost two years. Cheryl and her lead, Karen Ruus, have been together for over a decade. Cheryl, Karen, and third, Susan O'Conner, have been together for three full seasons and second, Jody McNabb, is in her second year on the team. Two years ago the team got together in the summer to team build and do some exercises we will talk about in the next few paragraphs. Included in this mix is the involvement of their coach Dennis Balderston. Cheryl said:

> We never got it all together that one summer. So often teams get fooled into thinking that if we do these things once or twice it will be enough or we tried something once and it didn't work. The initial meeting or initial exercise is only a start. It took us all summer, and it's still ongoing. And it will be ongoing as long as our team is together. If we want to have sustained success, we will have to practice these major core exercises all the time or, at the very least, use them as mechanisms when things break down or to maintain the good we have.

Encouragement

Believing or knowing your teammates are on your side and pulling for you is crucial to playing at your best. If you feel your teammates are doubting you or talking behind your back, the focus can go from the technical and mental process to destructive thought processes where your concentration may be on what your teammates are thinking rather than what you can do to help your team win.

The late Sandra Schmirler (who died of cancer in March 2000, at the age of thirty-six) felt one of her keys to success was the positive, encouraging energy Joan McCusker brought to her game during their glory years together. After winning two straight Scott Tournament of Hearts ("Scott" or "Hearts") and World titles in 1993 and 1994, the team finished third in Calgary at the 1995 Scott. After qualifying for the 1998 Olympic trials in Thunder Bay in a best-of-three playoff versus

Winnipeg's Connie Laliberte in late 1995, Joan took the last half of the season off to have a baby.

The team used two different "spares" in their journey all the way to the final game of the Saskatchewan playdowns. Sandra said, "It wasn't the same for me without Joan. Our two spares we had to pick up were very good players, and Jan and Marcie tried to be a Joan to me but it wasn't the same. Joan somehow had a way of getting into my head in a good way where I almost felt I could make every shot regardless of how I was playing."

The team came very close to going back to the Scott, but there seemed to be something missing for Sandra. Walter Betker, the father of Jan Betker, Sandra's third said, "That may have been the best skipping job Sandra ever did, considering she had to use two new players at provincials with Joan being pregnant and Marcie getting sick. They had some missing parts yet only came within a couple of shots of winning Saskatchewan." The chemistry was different and moving in a good direction with the new temporary players; but this example shows how it takes time to build chemistry, how an encouraging component is so vital, and how smart a skip Sandra Schmirler was.

Accountability

Accountability, or honesty, lays the foundation for being coachable. How can players learn, grow, and improve if they are not willing to be honest with themselves or with their teammates? So often pride gets in the way and players would rather be right in their thinking than take steps to improve their game or do whatever it takes to build team harmony. Cheryl feels that it is important for each player to hear from each other that the overall goal is to win and to do whatever it takes to get there. She also feels that well over 90 percent of team conflict is based on misunderstandings that could easily be clarified if teammates would simply share their hearts' intent.

Honesty does not mean sharing every thought in your head with teammates. Hurting someone unnecessarily is never conducive to building team unity. Maintaining a sense of dignity is always at the root of constructive accountability. Gordie Howe may have had the best approach to being honest with fellow hockey players when he said, "Whenever I felt I needed to confront a player for whatever reason, I always went to him with one or two positive statements or thoughts first before sharing the negative one."

Being accountable as a team is clarifying the major values and goals the team agrees on and then holding each other responsible for carrying them out. Major values and goals could include the commitment to practice on an individual basis; the promise to eat properly; exercise; make time for bonspiel or league play; or to put in the time to strengthen the mental game through reading, team building, or accessing resources such as coaches or sports psychologists. Cheryl says:

I wouldn't change a player because of skill level, but I would let go of a player who has a lack of commitment towards the agreed on goals and values of the team. Yes, there is a minimum level of skill I look for as a skip, but if a person of this required skill level goes into a slump that is something that can usually be worked through with practice and coaching.

Trust

Trust is closely related to accountability, but it should be the natural follow-through in building a team. If a coach or a teammate has to constantly check to see if teammates are following through on the values and goals the team has set, this can cause dissension in the ranks. Morale, according to General Dwight D. Eisenhower, was the key to having an effective army that would go the extra mile in combat. Morale was strongest when soldiers could trust each other without having to worry about other soldiers doing their duties. Trust became part of their DNA, so to speak.

Trust is built in a team setting when each person understands the important role he/she fills both on and off the ice. The people in power positions (i.e., coaches, skips, or CEOs) must communicate in whatever way connects to the rest of the team and establishes how valued and important individuals are to the overall mix of what it takes to be successful.

Trust is associated with the business concept of ownership. The strongest businesses or volunteer organizations have people in place that feel if they don't do their part—no matter how big or small—the business will suffer. Curlers need teammates who all believe that if they don't do their part on and off the ice, the team will suffer. All the members of Team Ferbey, the current Brier and World Men's champions, from Edmonton, Alberta, feel this way.

During the KIA Cup (Alberta men's provincials) in 2005 in Innisfail, Alberta, Scott Pfiefer and Marcel Rocque were interviewed and asked about the strength of their team. They answered by saying, "We feel as a front end that if we do our job and out play the other team's front end we will set it up for Randy [Ferbey] and David [Nedohin] to simply come in and finish things off. We want to make things as easy as possible for our back end." That is ownership by each player. Many times in curling some players feel that if they don't pull their weight, the skip will come through and straighten out any misses that occurred before he came to shoot. The strongest teams have the Team Ferbey mentality that each player is the difference-maker.

One of the best slow-pitch softball teams in Alberta in the 1990s was the Provost Shooters. Provost is a town of only fifteen hundred people, but this team won the majority of the tournaments they entered. Brent Olson, a former Alberta high school curling champion and multi-participant at the Alberta Northern playdowns, was one of the key players on this team. Their pitcher, Al Murray, said, "It's a great team to play for but we have one major problem. Everybody on the team wants to bat clean up! [The clean-up batter is the number four hitter in the line-up and is usually considered the best batter on the team.] What a nice problem to have though, because everyone on the team feels that they are the one who can make the difference."

Wholeness

Team chemistry deepens when players feel they are growing as human beings because of their involvement with the team. This is probably not overt, but one of those underlying dynamics of what strengthens team chemistry. Dr. Viktor Frankl was considered one of the most influential psychologists in his field. He survived the horrible Nazi concentration camps of World War II. He wrote about his experiences and developed what is called Logo Therapy. The premise of his work is based on people's search for meaning and purpose. He believed that people function best when they believe they are making a difference with their lives, contributing to the human race, and growing as individuals.

Curling is a game and meant to be fun. However, high-performance curling is a game with more at stake because of the emotional invest-ment being made by each player. When someone makes an emotional investment or commitment to a competitive curling team, the intuitive hope is that other benefits will kick in. If a person sees growth in other areas of his life because of his involvement with a high-performance team, the loyalty towards each teammate will grow. Trust grows deeper, accountability is more natural, and the willingness to encourage is more intentional.

Without getting bogged down in psychological terms, Peja Lindholm articulates the overall benefits of curling to his life the best when he says, "To me one of the most important words for my life is balance. To have balance in my whole life, family, job, team, friends, training, exercise. Curling reminds me that I must put in 100 percent quality in everything I do. You will be how you live, and you will be how you think."

Claire Carver-Dias was Canada's number-one ranked synchronized swimmer from 1998–2000 and won a bronze medal at the 2000 Olympics. Claire is much in demand as a motivational speaker. She understands a lot about team chemistry, team dynamics, and how your sport can teach so many valuable life lessons. Before the 2000 Olympics, the team got together at the beginning of the season to do team building exercises and to create a team mission. Here's what the 2000 bronze medallists came up with:

> Our purpose is to be a team that is strong and true;
> A team of complete women who are centered by their
> physical, emotional, mental and spiritual well-being.
> We choose to constantly pursue new heights in our quest for a
> Gold Medal performance at the 2000 Olympic Games and beyond.
> We believe in honesty, trust and hard work.
> We know greatness will result from our passion.

Exhortation

A great team that sustains success is a team that continually wants to get better even after significant accomplishments. "Complacency," as every coach worth his or her salt says, "is the major enemy of success!" Exhortation by implication means to challenge yourself or teammates to keep improving and seeking that edge.

Exhortation to the ancient Greeks meant encouraging others to become the best they could be because you have their best interests at heart. Exhortation comes in many forms. Some people respond to a verbal challenge, some respond better to a set goal, and some respond best to seeing the road they need to take to improvement.

Exhortation is somehow finding that inner switch to keep alive someone's love and passion for the game. During 1998 and 1999, I spent a significant amount of time researching *Gold on Ice: The Story of the Sandra Schmirler Curling Team.* One of the many team insights that stood out for me during their interviews was their knowledge and keen sense of history and what their team was accomplishing. They seldom talked about this in public, but they used history as one of the carrots to chase after, which kept *complacency* out of their team lexicon.

This was a team of great confidence, but they reminded or exhorted each other constantly and naturally about not taking teams for granted; of past success and failures; of "baby steps," their mantra from the Olympic trials in Brandon in 1998, that curling is indeed one shot at a time, one end at a time, one game at a time, and one event at a time. A cliché maybe but a cliché that works when applied.

Loyalty

Cheryl is a pretty darn good businesswoman. She ran her own insurance company for almost a decade before selling it. One of the accomplishments of which she is most proud is the very low turnover rate she had with her employees; they showed loyalty to her and shared the overall goals of the business. Cheryl says, "I treat curling as I would running my business in many ways. With both my business and curling team, goals are important but equally as important are that my employees or teammates know that they are valued more than the goals. I want them to know that I care about them as human beings."

Loyalty has to do with knowing each teammate is loved and appreciated. The tough and gruff Vince Lombardi, the Hall of Fame National Football League (NFL) coach of the Green Bay Packers dynasty, believed passionately that love was the glue that kept a team unified and strong. Love in the sense that a person knows the players' best interests are at stake and that the team is dedicated to providing an environment for players to succeed to the best of their abilities.

Cheryl says:

I really want my teammates to know that we are trying to give each other every possibility for them to succeed. This is the underlying motivation of what we say, do and plan. One of the main questions we ask on our team is what do you need from the team on and off the ice to succeed? As an example, when someone misses a shot or has a string of misses, we ask what do they need from their teammates? How do they respond to affirmation, what kind of affirmation, what kind of constructive criticism, can we joke, what kind of joking? Do they need to be alone for a spell or do they need to talk it through?

The team also needs to know from my perspective what my expectations are on and off the ice. When a player misses a shot from throwing badly, I like to at least hear from them an acknowledgment or affirmation of that miss so as not to appear to treat it lightly. I like the player to come down and talk to me for a second to see if I noticed a hitch in their delivery or whatever. Sometimes it's good for them to hear from me that there was nothing wrong and that I'm still figuring out the ice, or it was a new spot in the ice.

Similar to the famed Mr. Lombardi, Cheryl values loyalty as one of the key core principles in building team chemistry. She understands that loyalty is not built by a one-time meeting or one-time encounter or a few get-togethers in the off-season. Building loyalty is a constant ongoing process throughout the life of a team.

Life

A team needs a pulse. A team needs goals to give it life. Henry David Thoreau must have been a closet curler when he said, "In the long run we only hit what we aim at." This principle works on the ice when we go to deliver our rocks, and it works for teams striving to be champions.

Mark Dacey skipped the 2004 Nova Scotia champions to a Brier title and bronze medal at the Worlds. He feels that his team bonded best because they had similar goals and commitments towards trying to win a Brier. John Morris, the two-time World Junior curling champion in 1998 and 1999 and Ontario Brier representative (rep) in 2002, says, "I approach team building from a work analogy. We are trying to build a good working relationship among the players. If we become best friends that is a bonus, but as long as we can play/work together in harmony we'll have success. Each player must be on the same page in terms of striving for the same goals, and, if we are, that will alleviate a lot of misunderstanding."

Teammates can agree to the same goals, but living out those goals doesn't always match up. This is where team chemistry can obviously break down. Resentment or bitterness can creep in and cause distrust or disloyalty. Cheryl has read tonnes of business books, attended many seminars, and is bullish on implementing the principles she feels will benefit her business ventures or curling team. One of the key business truisms she understands and practices is that goals and mission statements are useless unless implemented. One of the ways to implement goals is to creatively remind each other of what they are and to do this on a constant basis. Having realistic goals like loyalty can be the glue that keeps teams together. As Morpheus in the *Matrix* trilogy said, "Let's move with a purpose."

Team chemistry or team spirit is as crucial to overall success as a team developing mental toughness. These seven team chemistry dynamics will only come alive and benefit a team when they are used as the instruments they are intended to be. Integrity or the use of the instruments will create team chemistry. In other words, having the knowledge of the seven team chemistry instruments is good information, but learning to use these instruments will create team harmony that will more often than not give your team the edge against equal or superior opponents.

> "One day you will understand, Neo. There is a difference between knowing the path and walking the path."
>
> —Morpheus from *The Matrix*

Chapter Two

The Catalyst

"You gave me the greatest gift of all—you believed in me."

—Rodney Copperbottom
to his dad Herb in the 2005 film, *Robots*

*W*hat ifs and woulda, coulda, shoulda scenarios can teach us to learn from our mistakes, but can be annoying if we get a little too caught up with them. It is easy to use them only for making excuses rather than learning for the future.

Would Team Schmirler have won seven major events (three Scotts, three Worlds, and the Olympics) without the positive energy of Joan McCusker? Would Al "the Iceman" Hackner have won his four majors (two Briers and two Worlds) without the seemingly quiet steadiness of Rick Lang? Would Kelley Law have won the Scott, Worlds, Olympic trials, and Olympic bronze without the fire of Georgina Wheatcroft? Would Kevin Martin have led the first million-dollar curling team without Newfoundland's best export to Edmonton's curling fraternity, Don Bartlett, and his upbeat and resilient spirit? And was Kim Kelly the final piece to the Colleen Jones Nova Scotia juggernaut with her never-say-die faith in her teammates?

Every successful curling team needs a spiritual or emotional leader to sustain chemistry, to keep attitudes in a positive direction, and to help each player to keep the faith in themselves and the team in trying times.

Seldom, if ever, is this player the skip and probably shouldn't be because the skip needs someone around to cheer him or her on for moral support, or to reinforce that he or she is the best person for the job. It is virtually impossible to skip successfully if the skip senses from his teammates dissension or second guessing behind his back. This player is a complement to the skip, and, often, the high-level skip can be this person when not skipping. This player, regardless of the position on the team, is the glue which keeps that particular team's chemistry together; he or she somehow directly, and most often indirectly, makes this team go beyond the limits outsiders could ever have guessed possible. This player is the catalyst.

The catalyst is often the final piece or missing element that somehow creates this elusive formula we call chemistry. Similar to the elements we learned about in high school chemistry, there are certain key elements that make up formulas that benefit the science community. The catalyst brings those elements together, which will create a highly competitive curling team. On most teams, only one player fills this vital role. Some people seem born to be this emotional leader, and, at other times, players step up and fulfill it very well. On rare teams when there are one or two emotional leaders, it seems to work better if one player either assumes the role or is challenged to fulfill this role. When two emotional leaders are on the same team, one will almost instinctively play a lesser role. And, in the rarified situation where a team has four catalysts that seem to feed off each other, such as Team Ferbey appears to have, you have history in the making!

As important as McCusker, Lang, Wheatcroft, Bartlett, and Kelly were to the chemistries of their championship teams, would the techniques they brought to their teams work in other scenarios? Perhaps. Being a catalyst on one team doesn't guarantee that being a catalyst will work on another team. Curling teams are like a marriage to a certain degree. Some couples click and others do not; yet when they find the right mix, it could be a marriage made in heaven. The bottom line is that teams need at least one player who gets the team to believe in itself and creates a passion for the game that makes the game fun and the sacrifices worthwhile.

Phil Jackson coached the Los Angeles Lakers to three consecutive National Basketball Association (NBA) titles from 2000–2002. He is convinced that without Canadian Rick Fox on the team there would have been no titles for Shaquille O'Neal and Kobe Bryant. Fox was the catalyst within that highly explosive mix of personalities. Fox somehow got the Lakers to keep their focus on turning their passions towards titles and reminding teammates that they were sacrificing for something they had all dreamed about since being tall, little boys. Yet, when Fox played for the greatest organization ever in basketball (in my opinion), the Boston Celtics, NBA championships were only a mere fantasy.

A catalyst's primary function is to keep the passion level of the team at an optimum level, which allows the team to function at its best. They seem to have this knack to make players and teams believe in themselves beyond their own expectations and to keep the team on the same philosophical page.

Catalysts come in all shapes and sizes, and in all personalities and temperament types. Being loud and/or vocal rarely, if ever, works if the person doing the yelling and screaming is not accepted as the team's catalyst. This will only lead to resentment and teammates becoming annoyed. The catalyst—whether a quiet or extroverted soul—oozes passion and belief, has the respect of his teammates, and somehow does what he does in an infectious kind of way.

Cheryl has said to me on more than a few occasions that she believes a team cannot win without a sense of passion—healthy urgency—and a belief in themselves. Yet, all four players may be as passionate and talented as Mr. Catalyst himself, Mark Messier, was in his prime with the Edmonton Oilers and the New York Rangers. However, these teams may lack the one person who somehow ignites the passions and talents of his teammates in a way that enhances team performance. Maybe the "C" in hockey should stand for catalyst rather than captain.

As we all know and have probably been part of, many teams have talent galore, but never mesh together as all the experts would have predicted. There probably were catalyst types on those teams, but they never felt they had the green light to fill that role; maybe there were no catalysts to be found. Sometimes, but rarely, the catalyst role is naturally filled. At other times, the role needs to be earned because respect is a factor, and, at other times, the role simply needs to be addressed and permission granted. Now I ask the billion-dollar question—can a team win at the highest levels and win big without a catalyst? Perhaps—maybe if the moon is blue and the planets line up in exact perfect alignment and other rarities occur all on the same day.

John Morris's dad, Earle, is the only player in Brier history to skip three different teams from three different provinces to the Brier. This feat is worthy of a Hall of Fame consideration. He likes to use a historical example to remind John, two-time World Junior Champion and Brier rep, of the importance of team chemistry and having a catalyst type on the team.

In 1987, the CCA decided to experiment with picking the teams to represent Canada at the 1988 Olympics in Calgary. This was an important Olympics because the sport was still at the demonstration level, lobbying for full-medal status. The CCA invited eight teams on each of the women's and men's sides to play a round-robin to determine playoff teams to represent Canada. The bulk of the teams were recent Brier and Scott winners, some teams were voted in by a select group of experts, and a couple of these teams were selected individuals who had never curled together but formed all-star teams. The selected all-star dream teams struggled. Their records were abysmal, and none of them made the playoff round on either the men's or women's side. Lesson learned.

From now on, teams representing Canada were to be proven teams that had a successful history together at the highest levels of our sport. Dream teams work in some sports and occasionally in curling if they have sufficient time to find the chemistry and have a catalyst come to the forefront. The classic Canadian example in sports is the leadership shown by Phil Esposito in 1972 when Team Canada faced off against the former Soviet Union in hockey. Our last what if—what if Number Seven didn't step forward as the catalyst and wasn't respected enough by his peers to assume that role? Perhaps, September 28, 1972, would have been remembered for different reasons!

Ray Turnbull of Brier and curling broadcasting fame shares this very transparent story about his former Brier championship team from the 1960s:

> There are hundreds of stories that illustrate the importance of team chemistry, and, with a game that moves slowly like curling and builds the tensions so gradually, the mix of personalities is unbelievably important. Once you develop strong mechanics, the game is played in your head, and your ability to work together in a positive fashion with the other three members of your team is very critical key to success. The example that hits home for me so clearly, why one combination works and the other one doesn't, was way back in 1966.

> We, Terry Braunstein, Don Duguid, Ron Braunstein and myself, had just won the Canadian Championship, the 1965 Brier. Ron Braunstein left our

team in 1966 to complete his medical studies in Los Angeles, and we replaced him with a terrific young curler by the name of Rod, "The Arrow," Hunter. . . . Rod was probably a better thrower than Ron, and Rod was certainly a great guy, but the combination of personalities was different. Ron was the key to our team as Don Duguid and I were very explosive personalities (especially me), and Ron was the catalyst. His strength and, I guess you could say his control over Donny and I, really was the key to our skip, his brother Terry, and with Ron out of the picture, we did not work well as a team. Even though Rod Hunter was a better curler, it was different chemistry, and I might add a very frustrating year; we couldn't win a thing! Rod Hunter and Donny Duguid went on together in 1970 and 1971 to win two Briers and two World Championships, but the combination of Braunstein, Duguid, Hunter, and Turnbull just didn't work, and we are still very close friends to this day—it was no one person's fault, it was just a different chemistry. Team combinations, because of the importance of communicating, are imperative for success in the greatest game in the world.

Team chemistry—believe in it!!! The game is in the head, so all four heads have to be in the game. Acting as one—not separate identities. This is just one of the elements that is imperative to success.

In being interviewed for *Gold on Ice*, Sandra Schmirler said on more than a few occasions that she needed someone like Joan McCusker on her teams. When Joan was around, she felt like she could make any shot in the book and that they always had a chance. Joan came across as believable and connected with Sandra's personality. When Joan took maternity leave and Jan Betker tried to stand in for Joan, it just never worked. Ironically, Jan and Sandra were the absolute best of friends. What was missing was the catalyst in terms of the emotional and spiritual leadership that Joan brought to this mix of four athletes.

Cheryl said Judy Pendergast was the catalyst for her team when she went to the Scott in 1996 (where they finished second in Canada to Marilyn Bodogh and her Ontario rink). Judy was her lead and had a fire inside her and a determination that came out in both actions and words. Cheryl says:

Judy has that way about her that we were not ever going to give up and that each of us had the ability and talent to make all our shots regardless of the circumstances. I always felt with Judy on the team that we could take it to the next level and beyond. If we ever got complacent Judy seemed to nip it in the bud right away. Judy had a way of getting me, and I believe the others, to play with a passion or urgency. And almost every team she is on, whether in women's or mixed, she is the catalyst.

The following represents a weekend warrior or curling club version of the catalyst. My favorite curling season was in 1998–99. We won ninety-one games that season with a .790 winning percentage, won two bonspiels, won two more consolation events at bonspiels, and finished in the top four in A-Block in two men's leagues. We qualified in everything or made the playoffs in everything we entered but zone playdowns. Even there, two of our three losses were on last rock to teams that qualified for the Southern Playdowns in Alberta. Most of this was accomplished with our first-year lead Benjamin Fell. Our second, Andy Jones, was in his fourth year of curling but only in his first year beyond recreational mixed. Luckily, I scored a seasoned curler/preacher by the name of Grant Rodgers to play third. He was one of Regina's top juniors in the 1970s before he answered the pastoral call and wound up in Calgary. We just kept winning when I thought we should have been toast.

Benjamin is a competitive soccer player (with a hockey mentality) turned curler and was the catalyst for this unlikely bunch. My expectations were to drop no lower than B-Block in the men's leagues and to at least win a game or two in bonspiels. Benjamin was the type who got ticked off at us for shaking hands after six ends when we were down by a bunch. One night, we did shake early with an end to go when we were nine down after giving up a big end. Benjamin was good at math. He would be in our faces if any of us talked negative or snipped at each other. Benjamin would be the type who curled 20 percent in the first half of the game and always knew he was one shot away from turning it around. His motto seemed to be, "Screw the percentages, we can win if we make enough of the right shots, and, if I make enough of my two shots every end, we'll win."

He swept like he played for the New Jersey Devils—like a man possessed. Benjamin oozed passion, and he had a nice knack of holding the rest of us accountable to playing that way—we didn't want to shake early because we'd get phone calls and e-mails the next day hearing about it. He believed that any curling team on any given day could be beat by the worst or possibly get hot enough to beat the best.

Benjamin lived for the comeback. We counted twenty-four games that season where we were down at the halfway point, came back, and won. Just having Benjamin on the ice made the whole team believe we had a chance.

What does a team do that doesn't have a catalyst? There is no easy answer to that question. But living *Between the Sheets* is about experimenting and taking certain risks at times. Maybe your catalyst is already on the team and simply needs permission to take on this role. Maybe your team needs another season together to see who could best fill this role. Maybe your team needs to make a change and bring in a new player, or old player, who has the knack for making your team believe and play with passion. Maybe your team needs to bring on a coach, team psychologist, or curling consultant who can help you work through this process of identifying the catalyst. Maybe your team in whole or in part needs to disband and part ways. Maybe you and your team need to pick the brains of successful teams or players you admire and they could give you some sound advice. Maybe you need to pull someone out of another sport or find someone in a curling league who is eager to learn but is a Benjamin-catalyst type. Just as in real life, success and finding that catalyst for a meaningful time together is not always a neat and tidy adventure.

Remember that the catalyst has a way of keeping the belief and passion levels of the team at levels necessary to keep the team competitive. The catalyst is the spiritual leader in the sense that he or she holds the team accountable to its values. The catalyst is also the emotional leader who keeps the team accountable to playing wholeheartedly— with passion. The catalyst has a way of keeping the team focused on the things necessary to be successful and doesn't allow the team to be distracted by inward pettiness or outside distractions. The catalyst is the conscience of the team.

"Man only does great things when he acts from great passion!"

—Benjamin Disraeli

Chapter Three

Cool Mad!

"The notion of some players appearing to play angry is really about building intensity. Some players need more intensity and some need less to achieve their ideal performance state. It's up to each player to determine their ideal performance state and alter their emotions and thoughts to achieve that ideal state."

—Brenda Bohmer,
Five-time Scott, Eleven-time Alberta Provincials,
One-time Worlds, and Two-time Olympic Trials Participant

am Snead coined the phrase "cool mad" during his heyday as one of the best ever Professional Golfers' Association (PGA) golfers. Snead felt he played best when he played with passion and even a little anger. But he also strongly believed that his anger or passion needed to be managed, controlled, or balanced. He felt that if he played with misguided resentment or bitterness, this would cause him to focus on humiliating an opponent or trying to prove a point to a critic at the expense of concentrating on the necessary skills. Snead, like many of the world's greatest athletes, felt that when he played with a healthy anger it enabled him to focus on the fundamental skills that he needed in order to compete at his best. Rather than trying to get even with someone who offended him, he learned to take his anger out on people or situations by throwing all his energies into performing well and playing at the peak of his abilities. He also realized that not all anger was negative in its roots, and he could conjure up something to get himself going. Maybe it would be an old newspaper article that criticized his play or a comment he overheard in the dressing room from months or even years earlier that he had worked through, but it would help him get in the right frame of mind to concentrate. Snead would use whatever things in his life stirred him up and got his blood boiling, so to speak.

As a Canadian, I can sure understand his reasoning from our other winter sport of hockey. A team that is enraged or intimidated by an opponent has one of two choices: Fill the penalty box up with stupid penalties or become even more disciplined and beat the other team on the scoreboard. When an athlete is filled with high intensity, his powers of concentration are often at his peak.

To stick with the hockey theme, I need look no further than my hometown senior hockey team, the Warriors of Langenburg, Saskatchewan. During my growing up years of the late 1960s and '70s, I used to enjoy watching the exploits of the Warriors' *Slap Shot* version of play in the Yellowhead Hockey League. The team usually led the league in penalty minutes and lived near the basement of the standings because of its lack of discipline and misguided anger (but we went to support them because you just never knew what might transpire out on the ice). Then the late 1980s and 1990s kicked in a new era of hockey. A new Royal Canadian Mounted Policeman (RCMP) transfer who once played in the Quebec Major Junior Hockey League (QMJHL) now coached the local Warriors. The team still played with an edge and the talent level seemed much the same, yet they ran off a string of over a one dozen straight league titles and were a constant threat during the provincial playoffs. Instead of filling up the penalty box, the new coach emphasized special teams and filling up the stat sheet with goals and assists. He somehow got these passionate players to focus their energies on something positive—like winning—rather than getting even. Cool mad at its finest.

Brenda Bohmer probably captures the essence of this key mental element as well as any curler I have interviewed. Brenda articulates well what **cool mad** really is—intensity. She says, "The notion of some players appearing to play angry is really about building intensity." This intensity can be motivated from anger but also from other emotions such as pride, fear, or love and enjoyment of the game.

Wayne Gretzky and Joe Montana said their intensity was primarily motivated from a fear of failure to live up to their own expectations or even those of their teammates and fans whom they didn't want to disappoint.

Bill Russell, the great Boston Celtic, took almost a blue-collar work-manlike approach of simply wanting to do a job well or taking pride in weaving a masterpiece out on the court.

Sam Richardson in his book, *Say It Again Sam!*, said the famed Richardson curling team got its intensity from pride and natural competitiveness. He said:

I wouldn't swear on a stack of Bibles, but I don't think we ever lost an exhibition game. Most teams, when they get home from the Brier, Silver Broom (former name of the World Championship) or a big cashspiel, they've become soft wood to whittle. But when we'd come back and walk on the ice, we didn't want those four guys to beat us. We didn't have letdowns, and that's hard to do. If a guy beat us fair and square, made more shots than us, well then, fine. But he had to do that.

Dordi Nordby, the two-time World Women's Champion from Norway, simply likes the challenge the game has to offer. She has almost a childlike innocence or love for the game, which is enough to get her to that intense place she needs to be to perform.

Brenda Bohmer goes on to explain her views of the importance of building intensity into her overall game:

Emotional control is one part of my mental tactics and training related to curling. In order to use my emotions to my advantage, I must be very self-aware. Armed with a high level of self-awareness, I can sense when emotions are impacting my performance. When I need to bring my intensity up, I use pre-planned cue/mood words and self-talk to do so. And, when things are getting tense, I try to let any negative energy flow out of my body as stress and tension will cause tense muscles and, in turn, have a negative impact on my delivery. I use a combination of deep breathing techniques and thought control to alleviate negative tension and stress. My ideal performance state is inspired and energized, mentally confident, and calm.

As for remaining calm in key situations, such as sweeping a draw to the four foot for a Canadian championship, the key is confidence and focus on the task and not the potential outcome. As sweepers, before the shot is thrown, we know the kicktime required on that particular line in the ice (that comes from mapping the ice throughout the game). At release, we make the initial judgment of the weight that has been thrown (using short kick time as a guide) and use our eyes and senses to judge the weight all the way down the ice. When the draw is to win the game, the situation can suddenly become chaotic when the skip and/or third starts yelling their advice to sweep or not to sweep. They usually don't judge weight, but, when it's the draw to win, you have to be ready for that distraction. If you make the shot and win, it sometimes takes time for the win to sink in as you were so focused on the details of the task you've just completed.

Cool mad, or controlled intensity, is one of the most important keys for the curler or any high-performance athlete. As Brenda explained, intensity is the trigger for playing at a high concentration level, which helps keep your attention on doing all the little things needed in order to find that edge. High intensity can only hurt when the overall objective becomes slightly skewed. Sometimes unmanaged intensity can hurt, especially in the early part of a big game or late in a game where every little miscue is at a heightened peak. A person or team can be so emotionally charged that they can actually forget what the purpose of the game is—winning or focusing on the process of what it takes to win.

Football, because of its violent nature, is one of the most emotional games on the planet and has many stories and advice on how uncontrolled emotional intensity can cost a team. Richie Hall, the assistant head coach of the Saskatchewan Roughriders and a curling fan, says:

I don't worry about our players being ready and up for a big game. Our job often is to calm them down a bit so they don't lose focus. It frustrates me when the press or a fan says a team or player comes out flat in the biggest game of the year when the reality is they are too hyped up. . . . Players can lose perspective on the little things, which create success and opportunities when the emotions aren't channeled properly. And what often happens when a team gives up early points or is losing the field position battle because of this lack of focus is they can get down on themselves by swinging the pendulum the other way. Either way the proper focus can be lost and players can lose sight on the task at hand.

John Madden, the former Oakland Raider coach and Emmy-award winning football commentator, has said many times in his broadcasts and in his books that sports must be played with what he refers to as "controlled fanaticism." In his book, *One Knee Equals Two Feet*, Madden explains what he means.

> *I like the word fanaticism. So did the players, especially those with that wild look in their eye, the kind you need running around out there on kick-offs. The trouble was, they took me at my word. In trying to prove their fanaticism, some guys were flinging their bodies into the wedge with reckless abandon. But they were forgetting to tackle the ball carrier who was sometimes running it out to midfield. To make it worse, we were getting too many penalties. We got so many clipping penalties—hitting from behind—that I told my players, "If you can't read the guy's name on the back of his jersey, don't hit him." But in their frenzy, I wondered if they could read those names.*
>
> *That didn't help much either. I finally had to tell my players. Special teams* breed *controlled fanaticism. I still wanted them to run down under that kick-off as hard as ever, but then they had to get themselves under control and try to make the tackle. After that they kept their fanaticism in perspective.*

Cheryl often talks of how her best games are when she feels really intense. Sometimes it is fueled by anger, but most of the time it's fueled by the carrot at the end of the stick, like a Scott berth or an opportunity to play in the Olympic trials. Cheryl is usually motivated by the goals she and her teammates have set at the beginning of each curling season, and a simple reminder to herself is often all she needs to create the necessary intensity to perform.

She says she once went through a very short-lived phase where she felt she had to express her intensity out on the ice to get her teammates going and to intimidate opponents. The outward expression of this inner drive actually threw her teammates off and caused them to play below their skill level because they felt they weren't measuring up to whatever standard Cheryl was trying to convey. She began to realize that her teammates could sense her intensity whether she verbalized it or not because they knew her heart. Cheryl began to understand more fully that intensity is an inner quality of high concentration and focus on the fundamental skills and strategies needed to compete at your best.

Everyone's personality or temperament is different, and outward intensity will be expressed in a myriad of ways. Yelling and screaming may work for the odd person, but yelling and screaming is usually a sign that someone is in over his head and not properly prepared. Often, the quieter a player becomes, the more intense he or she is feeling. The key is in the eyes.

My "decent" Calgary club team met the Kevin Koe team (consistently ranked in the top twenty on the WCT, former Canadian junior runner-up in 1994, and Canadian Mixed champion in 2000) in the Calgary district playoffs in 2003. We were on a bit of a roll and were scheduled to play Koe, who was ranked number eleven on the WCT at the time, on the very early Saturday morning draw. Since we were slightly older than Team Koe and probably got a little more sleep, we found ourselves one up after the first five ends and playing well over our heads. Koe missed an opportunity in the fifth end, and it seemed to wake him up and/or piss him off. When I said my niceties to him after his miss, Koe was polite, but it's like the switch went on after his miss.

His eyes became curling's version of the famous Mark Messier look. In the next end we had an opportunity to maybe steal a point if I made an almost perfect freeze. I didn't make it perfectly enough and thought Koe had a chance for only two to go up by one. He saw an angle raise double opportunity for four. Now down at club night league play at the Huntington Hills Curling Club, I would have bet on our steal and wagered the family John Deere dealership on it. Even my teammates said, "No way! If anyone has a chance Kevin does, but not the way he's been curling this morning." I thought to myself, *You guys haven't seen the look in his eyes since the fifth end break.* I was worried and, at this stage, wouldn't have wagered a whole lot of anything other than Kevin probably making the shot. Kevin made the shot and never missed a thing from that point on. Needless to say, we dropped down. Koe never lost another game and earned a spot in the Southern Alberta playdowns, the next step towards a provincial berth.

Cool mad is finding that balance of managing intensity. Winning big cannot occur unless there is some fire burning deep within. Hollywood knows this, and, as corny as some sports films can be, they tend to make money. The *Rocky* film series and its memorable song *Eye of the Tiger* captured Rocky Balboa's needed motivation or fire within to overcome all odds. How often in arenas and stadiums around the world do we hear that song? And how often do the hometown team and its fans get into it? In the movies *Miracle, Slap Shot, Bull Durham, For Love of the Game, Hoosiers, Bend It Like Beckham, The Longest Yard* (both versions), and *Men with Brooms,* the story line or turning point is when teams or players regain that fire or intensity which takes them over the top. They start to play with a controlled passion, which heightens their levels of concentration and helps them focus on the fundamental skills that lead to success.

Becoming a cool mad curler will never guarantee you or your team's success on the curling ice, but, if you or your team don't cultivate cool mad into your mental game arsenal, you will never see success at the high-performance level. The key is in your mental game preparation. Kevin Koe, generally, is ready to go for most of his curling games. When he faced my Huntington Hills powerhouse, I'm sure the thought crossed his mind that Scholz meant "bye" in Inuit. His wake-up call came when his caffeine kicked in during the fifth end break—or when he realized the oldest of all curling truisms—that anybody really is capable of beating anybody in curling. But Kevin Koe, who has nurtured his game with sports psychology, paying attention to WCT-level curlers he has faced, and picking the brains of high-performance teachers through the National Training Center, knows that building intensity starts well before the first rock is thrown. Intensity is something to be worked on daily just as being in top physical shape is a daily commitment.

John Morris was the 1998 and 1999 Canadian and World junior curling champion. He represented Ontario at the Brier in 2002, won the WCT Tour Championship final in 2004, and has been a constant threat to represent Alberta at the Brier since his move to Calgary in 2002. Morris is one of the best shotmakers to hit the scene since the days of Paul Gowsell in the 1970s. He is known for his intensity on the ice and entertaining antics. John shared many of his thoughts on intensity and the importance of sustaining it.

> *I think I was born with intensity in my DNA. My dad, Earle, and myself are competitive in almost everything we do. But I know intensity is the key if a team puts in the necessary time to complement it. My dad used to have a saying about a fellow junior competitor that we couldn't seem to beat at first and always battled with. He would say, "That guy just refuses to lose." My motto for curling has become "refuse to lose." To perform at the highest of levels you have got to want it, to have that burning desire to win, the internal fight that no one can beat you. Determination to refuse*

to lose. You won't always be successful, but, if you can maintain this determination, you will have your fair share of success.

When I lose that sense of intensity, I take a step back to when I was younger. I would have given my left arm [John is right-handed] to play at the highest level and especially a Brier. I used to just crave to play against the best. I remind myself how lucky I am to be playing at this level.

A lot of intensity comes from wanting to prove to yourself and others you are capable of playing against the best. I love the simple challenge of trying to go out and beat the top teams. My favorite role is the underdog role because I am not intimidated by playing any of the teams out there. Being the underdog is a natural motivator for me.

I really liked Sandra Schmirler's approach to sustaining and developing cool mad into her game. If something ticked her off, the focus was not on getting even or gaining revenge. She would acknowledge or vent with her close friends the hurt she may have felt, but her overall approach was, "To kill them with kindness and beat them on the scoreboard." It's amazing how often the doubters, naysayers, or gossips will change their tunes when our attitude takes the high road and our skill on the ice speaks for itself.

> In your anger do not sin, search your hearts and be silent . . . do not let any unwholesome talk come out of your mouths, but only what is helpful for building others up according to their needs, that it may benefit those who listen . . . the Kingdom of heaven has been forcefully advancing and the forceful men lay hold of it . . . build your house upon the rock.
>
> —Ancient wisdom from the Bible:
> King David, the apostle Paul, and Jesus

When applied to curling, the point is that anger is a healthy emotion when directed in a positive direction. We have to do something with our anger because we simply can't just let it go into some kind of a vacuum. We have to either direct it **forcefully** or with great effort into a positive direction like focusing on the process of what makes us competitive.

Schmirler would also try and come to the rink prepared emotionally or have her intensity at the level she knew she needed it to be by getting her mind to focus on the thoughts, strategies, or helpful self-talk that would fast track her to being on top of her game. Sandra knew this switch couldn't just be turned on without previous efforts of mental training practiced throughout the season and off-season.

Adrian Bakker has won more than his share of Southern Alberta zones and had the opportunity to go onto compete at the Provincials. Individually he would be in the top twenty lifetime winners of zones in Alberta. Adrian can't remember exactly how many southern zones he has been to, but it is somewhere around fifteen or sixteen. He has also qualified for a good handful of Alberta provincials. Adrian also holds the record for leading his midget hockey team in Claresholm, Alberta, in penalty minutes—as a goalie. That just may be a record at any level. Adrian is a very honest and transparent man and shares his thoughts on cool mad:

I was born with a bit of a temper. I might not like it, but that's the way it is. In terms of curling success, I believe it has held me back. So, I have no problem having enough intensity for an important curling game. The challenge for me is controlling that intensity in a way that my teammates and I can benefit from.

Mistakes by a teammate don't typically bother me, unless it is a stupid mistake resulting from a lack of concentration or the effects of too much booze the night before. However, I am very hard on myself. I have high expectations of myself, and, when I do not perform at the level I feel I am capable of, my natural tendency is to get angry, and often even confused, and lose confidence. That's pretty much anytime I make a mistake, such as missing a shot.

So in preparing to compete, it is important that I relax and try to get into a mental state where I take a lot of pride in my performance, but will accept myself for a great effort and not become too hard on myself when I err. Sometimes early in an important game I will feel nervous and uncomfortable, and not play well. In these situations it is often good to let myself get a bit angry—but not destroy-my-broom-mad. The butterflies usually leave, and I can refocus and start playing well. Actually I haven't destroyed a broom in years. They are too dog-gone expensive these days.

Chapter Four

"They Don't Do Complacency"

"Complacency will kill you."

—Kevin Martin,
Multiple Brier Winner, Olympic Silver Medallist, and
All-time Money Leader on the World Curling Tour

K athy Fahlman was one of Saskatchewan's best curlers in the 1980s–90s and is in the process of making a competitive comeback. She skipped a team, which included Sandra Schmirler and Jan Betker, that went to the Scott in 1987 in Lethbridge where they finished a very respectful fourth. Fahlman remained friends with Jan and Sandra as they went their separate ways and formed what many consider the greatest women's team of all time. Kathy not only played with two of the best shot-makers in the history of the sport, but continued to do battle with them on the WCT circuit and in the Regina Superleague. She also was a fan, and continued to observe this championship team that dominated the curling scene like no other from 1992 to 1999, until Sandra's untimely death from cancer in 2000 at only thirty-six years old. I asked Kathy what was the key, or keys, to Team Schmirler's dominance. Without hesitation, she said simply but firmly, *"They don't do complacency!"*

Human nature is to feel content after a great accomplishment or two, regardless of the level of competition. The greatest players or teams in sports find a way to deal with complacency. Five of the greatest North American coaches had absolutely no tolerance for complacency.

Pat Riley, the great NBA coach of the Lakers, Knicks, and Heat, and his rival Phil Jackson of the Bulls and Lakers each called it a **disease**. John Wooden of UCLA basketball fame and voted the greatest coach of any sport of the twentieth century by ESPN called it a **very destructive attitude towards winning.** Vince Lombardi of Green Bay Packer coaching fame referred to complacent players as **hinky dinky**. Don't even get Scotty Bowman, the most successful National Hockey League (NHL) coach ever, started. Bowman's approach towards even a sniff of complacency was to get in his players' heads in such a way that they would feel a healthy amount of insecurity.

Whether it's Riley, Jackson, Wooden, Lombardi, or Bowman, complacency was a dirty word that had to be dealt with immediately. These five men coached their teams to forty-three championships at the highest level of their sports. All of these coaching legends said pretty much the same things in various ways when talking about complacency. And they were all in agreement that the biggest hindrance towards sustained success or individual consistency is when complacency sneaks into a player's psyche or a team's mindset.

In my many interviews with Sandra Schmirler, this was a topic she became very passionate about discussing. She hit on five major areas of prevention necessary to minimize—or dare I say, eliminate—complacency from a team's psyche: cultural upbringing, humility, history, fun, and healthy pride.

Cultural Upbringing

Sandra was a very driven person who appreciated and understood her prairie roots. Phil Jackson is much the same in his approach. Of the five aforementioned coaches, he verbalizes or writes as strongly as Sandra about this disease. Maybe it's his upbringing by western Canadian parents born in Saskatchewan and Northern Ontario and his Williston, North Dakota, roots (about an hour from curling's heartland of Saskatchewan) that makes him so adamant about the dangers of complacency. Growing up on the prairies is not very conducive to the "we've finally made it" mentality. This mindset is awfully hard to adopt when raised in or around agriculture. Enjoying a bumper crop one year can be followed by trying to survive on a hail-insurance check the next.

Sandra never seemed fooled by her team's success of three world titles and Olympic Gold. Her team knew that to sustain success would be an enormous task. Complacency was a potential obstacle of which they were very much aware and they were willing to go to great lengths to manage.

Sandra strongly felt that her cultural roots and those of her three teammates brought their team's awareness to the subtle, and not so subtle, issues around complacency. Now, this doesn't mean every curler has to spend time on the Canadian or American Great Plains to overcome complacency, or that prairie folk never suffer from this disease. But, when one acknowledges their roots, the appreciation will bring awareness.

Scotty Bowman was a Montrealer, which is one of the world's great cosmopolitan cities. He grew up in a family of blue-collar workers and was around people who knew the value of hard work and how easily affluence or success could be taken away from someone. Warren Buffet is one of the wealthiest people on the planet, yet he is proud of how his children have adopted a blue-collar attitude towards life and work. Buffet challenged his children to earn their ways as much as possible, and he put them in situations where they had to learn the value of hard work rather than looking for a handout. Good parenting and good coaching! In studying people who know how to deal with complacency, the common attitude seems to be one of hard work and taking nothing for granted.

Humility

Curling itself can be a huge deterrent to complacency. All four members of Team Schmirler grew up with and observed the uniqueness of curling, which unmercifully exposes the pitfalls of becoming satisfied with one's accomplishments.

Early in the 1993–94 curling season, the team entered its first bonspiel of the season in seeking to defend its first world championship. A local warm-up spiel in Regina, Saskatchewan, the bonspiel would be the equivalent to other sports' preseasons. Winning was more of a side benefit; working on basic fundamentals was the team's primary concern.

Jan Betker, the team's third, explains how this particular bonspiel was later used as a key motivator to enter every game or a spiel with high intensity.

I guess everybody wants to say they beat a world champion. I know I would. We didn't curl particularly well, but it was good to work on our deliveries and just get back out on the ice. This bonspiel had every level of curler from Brier and Heart champions to your average club curler right from A-level to D-level (recreational). Some of these teams would never win a zone and aren't highly motivated to anyway. To some of them it's just a fun game to play, which to me is the beauty of curling. We played three games and lost them all. We weren't brutal, but just weren't sharp. You could see the intensity in the eyes of the teams we were drawn against. It might be their only time to be on the same sheet as a world champion team, let alone beat one.

It reminded all of us very quickly how an average club team could knock off the best team in the world on any given day. Any decent team is capable of curling 80 percent to 90 percent every now and then. The secret of course is to sustain high averages over the course of the season. We realized after that fun spiel that every team we would play from now on wanted to say, "Hey, we beat a world champion." This experience seemed to be a healthy wake-up call for us. You must maintain the elements that make your team successful because, if you don't, your chances of contending forsake you pretty darn quick.

That bonspiel and its lesson for complacency are another reminder of how curling is possibly the only sport in the world where a semi-competitive team could conceivably win a game versus the number-one seeded team. What makes curling even more unique is that followers of the sport are not shocked when it happens.

Ernie Richardson, of that other Regina-based world championship team, used to acknowledge:

The toughest part during our era of getting back to a Brier was often winning a berth in our own local club to move on to the next level. Everybody at the club knew us and weren't intimidated by our team. They'd all seen us lose a few club games. We lost our share of games to teams that couldn't advance out of their own local clubs.

A healthy respect for one's opponent and the game itself can help keep complacency at bay.

History

If there is anything Team Schmirler had a clear grasp of, it was its sense of history of the game and its place in it. The members seldom, if ever, talked about it publicly, but they were very much aware of what they were accomplishing or had a realistic chance of accomplishing.

Bill Walsh, the coaching architect of those great San Francisco 49er teams of the '80s and '90s, was also a huge believer in studying history and using it as a motivator and teaching tool. He also despised the word **complacency** with a passion. He felt that if a team tried to create even a little history this would filter down into his players' lives and make them more responsible citizens and make a difference in society. He saw the game as a teaching tool to learn valuable lessons in life.

Walsh would have enjoyed working with Team Schmirler. This team was willing to look at the past and would quite often pick the brains of curling greats such as Sylvia Fedoruk, Vera Pezer, and Lindsay Sparkes—all former Canadian champions.

Team Schmirler was so impressed with Lindsay Sparkes that they would fly her out to Regina from Vancouver to use as their complimentary coach along with full-time coach Anita Ford, who was also one of Canada's best shot-makers in her prime.

As a child, Jan Betker was fortunate to observe her neighbor in this regard. George Reed, arguably the Canadian Football League's (CFL) greatest player of all time, lived practically next door, and he would sometimes barbecue with the Betker family. The one lesson Reed taught to any CFL fan, devoted or casual, was the importance of never giving up and playing through whatever adversity one encountered. Reed's experience impacted an observant Jan. If there was ever a player that fought to the end, it is Jan Betker.

Becoming the first three-time world champions and the first Olympic gold medallists were the carrots that this team would consciously dangle in front of themselves. History can be a terrific motivator to guard against complacency. Innately we all want to leave a legacy or to know we have made a dent in the historical annuals of life. This can be on a world or national scale, or simply at the regional level.

Fun and Joy

All four Schmirler players had and have a genuine love for the game. It was their competitive outlet from work and family. They seemed to have a pretty good grasp of where curling fit in the big picture of family and values; therefore, curling was deeply rooted in the love for the game. They would be the first to admit that they could lose perspective with curling. It could affect their self-esteem and take a higher priority than they knew it should. But when push came to shove, they played the game because they enjoyed it immensely and it brought a certain amount of therapeutic value to their lives. Jan Betker once said that even after her competitive days, she would probably keep curling because of how much she loved the game.

When something is fun, and it is your passion, and it brings enjoyment, and you are extremely competent at it, the natural desire is to do well. Reminding yourself of why you play the game helps to keep things in perspective and brings the necessary emotional drive a player needs to play at his or her best. Complacency kicks in when one loses enthusiasm or priority necessary to compete effectively.

Dordi Nordby from Oslo, Norway, has been to more World Championships and Olympics than any curler in history; at the time of this writing, she is only forty years old and still going strong. We asked her why, and how she keeps her motivation so high? It wasn't so much the wins and losses, Dordi said.

Curling is a living game; it is never static. Curling is similar to chess in that it is always different and seldom the same. Every end, every game is a new experience, and I like that challenge.

Wayne Gretzky was asked during a television interview on TSN at the 2004 World Juniors in North Dakota what advice he'd give the Canadian Juniors before the final game versus the Russians. This is an insight into number 99's love for his favorite sport and how he never flirted with complacency. Gretzky said:

I told them to treat this final game like a game seven we all dreamed of playing in as kids while playing street hockey for fun. We'd all pretend to be one of the best NHL'ers, and we all felt as kids that we would be the star player scoring the big goal. I told them to remember those times and see this as an opportunity to be seized and not to be afraid of. Their dreams have come true, and they needed to go out on the ice and enjoy the opportunity, because as kids this is what we lived for.

The great athletes all remind themselves of the fun their sport brings, and this prevents complacency from being a part of their personal lexicons. Gretzky, Michael Jordan, Joe Montana, Mickey Mantle, Gordie Howe, Sandra Schmirler, and Dordi Nordby all cultivated this childlike quality into their adulthood. Complacency implies that one doesn't care about the outcome of an event. If a talented curler is complacent, somewhere along the way he or she lost love and passion for the game.

I was once driving across northern Alberta in -30ºC weather to lead a workshop in Edmonton. I tuned the radio onto John Short of Edmonton who used to have one of the best sports talk shows in North America. That night, he asked a panel of guests what made the greatest athletes the greatest. Was there any specific quality that stood out? The panel concluded that the greatest—and they listed Gretzky, Jordan, Steffi Graff, Mario Lemieux, and Joe Montana as the best of the best—took **initiative** in their sport. These athletes all took control and **initiated** the flow and tempo of their games. They were all creative athletes at the top of their games at the time. And then the panelists pontificated on where this creativity and **initiative** came from. They concluded these athletes all had fun, loved their sport passionately, and had a childlike quality to them.

Carl Jung, the great Swiss psychologist, said this about the importance of play or fun:

> The dynamic principle of fantasy/pretending is play, which belongs also to the child, and as such it appears inconsistent with the principle of hard work. But without this playing with fantasy no creative work has ever yet come to birth. The debt we owe to the play of the imagination is incalculable.

Healthy Pride

Sandra Schmirler had a tremendous amount of pride (or competitiveness) in her ability to perform at her best at all times—or, at the very least, to make something good out of an off-performance. Her mom, Shirley, described Sandra as possessing a fiercely, competitive drive. She had very high personal standards. She was good at keeping losses in perspective, especially at the non-playdown levels, but she still expected herself to play at a certain level to sustain her consistency. Competing against one's own expectations can be healthy if the curler is constantly trying to improve or find that competitive edge. It's having that personal pride in striving to do your best. Creating or maintaining the hunger necessary to compete with full emotional energy will naturally keep complacency at bay.

Sweden's Peja Lindholm, Europe's first three-time World Curling champion, is Mr. Intensity in this department. He takes pride in maintaining his high standards. He says, "I will never throw a rock if I am not focused, whether it is a practice or a game. I can live with misses from my teammates or myself, but I have very little patience if one of us misses from a lack of concentration. I firmly believe that you will be how you live and you will be how you think." Peja's attitude is that if you are on the ice you may as well go full out and do your best at all times. He believes that by continuing to have high standards you are always reinforcing the good habits needed technically, emotionally, mentally, and spiritually (meaning the values you and your team believe in).

The curler needs to build his own lexicon of important words or terms to incorporate into his game. Cultural upbringing, humility, history, fun, and healthy pride are non-negotiable ones. Complacency must be whited-out, deleted, and treated like a terminal disease.

When Kevin Martin recruits new players, he tells them right up front.

I am pretty straightforward with my expectations. I tell them complacency will kill you. Almost all new players will work hard for the first year on a new team because they want to impress their teammates. I want someone who has drive, who will keep it going. I don't bug guys to see if they are practicing or working out because you know if they are cutting corners because their edge starts to go. They aren't at the gym as much, they aren't practicing as much, little things like that, and it shows up out on the ice. This just might be the main quality I look for in a player is their drive and lack of complacency.

"Complacency is the enemy of growth."

—U.S. General Colin Powell

Chapter Five

Creating a Sanctuary

"A team is meant to be a sanctuary."

—Phil Jackson,
Former Chicago Bulls and
Los Angeles Lakers Coach

hil Jackson is one of the more interesting case studies of a successful coach. He is tied with Red Auerbach of the Boston Celtics dynasty with nine NBA championships as a coach plus another couple as a former player with the New York Knicks. Jackson's primary skill (among many) seems to be to take MVP-caliber players that haven't won championships and teach them that basketball is a team game. Michael Jordan, Shaq, and Kobe had never won titles before Jackson came along, and they probably never would had he not entered the picture. It is well documented from both M. J. and Shaq how they feel about Jackson.

Jackson has deep curling roots, geographically speaking. His mom was born near Swift Current, Saskatchewan, and his dad was born in Northern Ontario close to where the great Al Hackner grew up. Phil mainly grew up about an hour's drive from the Saskatchewan border in Williston, North Dakota, which for years was the only American city that had a Canadian Football League (CFL) ticket office (for the Saskatchewan Roughriders). In 2004, Phil wrote a one-page article for *Sports Illustrated* during their fiftieth anniversary year. His story was on growing up in North Dakota and his impressions of the sport scene there. The center-piece article on North Dakota focused on curling. Jackson says his coaching values are a direct reflection of his upbringing, love for the Great Plains, and passion to build cohesion into his teams.

I read everything I can that Phil Jackson has written, as well as the dozens of articles about him. His latest book, *The Last Season: A Team in Search of Its Soul*, is one of the best case studies of a team trying to find its identity. Jackson's candor is refreshing as he notes the mistakes, failures, and experiments of trying to lead his L. A. Lakers back to the NBA finals in the midst of Kobe Bryant's then-pending criminal trial. During that season, Jackson may have done one of the best coaching jobs by anyone in the history of pro sports. I'm intrigued by his method of building a team atmosphere, as covered in that book.

Basketball only carries a roster of twelve players, which is about as close to a curling roster of a team sport one finds in North America. When I discovered his prairie roots, spiritual journey, and Canadian heritage, I became hooked. Jackson is often perceived as "the basket-ball Zen master," which he lets the public run with because it often bleeds into misconceptions by his opposition. Yes, he is Zen-like, but no more than any curling, philosopher junkie you'd find in Vernon, British Columbia; Edgerton, Alberta; or Baie Verte, Newfoundland. His prairie upbringing also makes him incredibly pragmatic and practical. He can speak a Zen-kind of language and come back to you as down-to-earth as a farmer discussing grain prices at the local coffee shop. Jackson is like a blue-collar renaissance man.

B-Ball Wisdom That Works in the Arena

A team that is successful and sticks together creates a sanctuary, or safe haven, for its committed players to grow as players and people, to develop their skills to the maximum, and to be allowed to make mis-takes in an atmosphere of minimal judgement.

Creating a sanctuary is never easy. Jackson is very intentional but in such a way that many of his players don't realize he has a set agenda or plan. He is fully aware that some of his players and people he wants around for the long haul don't always buy into team building program. But as Jackson has said on more than one occasion, "Throw enough manure at the wall, and some of it will eventually stick." How many Zen-masters have used that phraseology?

The following are samples of Jacksonisms that could benefit any curling team.

#1 Every Player Has a Vital Role To Play

Jackson understood that M. J. or Shaq were the go-to guys. However, he also would communicate one-on-one with his players the vital roles they would play. Sometimes he would recommend specific books for players to read to build their confidence or motivate them. He also wanted every player ready to make the key shot when the game was on the line.

Jackson tried to emphasize to each one of his players that they needed to take ownership in the process of winning. One of the ways he would do this was to challenge players in critical situations in the regular season to get their mindset ready for similar scenarios in the playoffs. This could involve setting a role player up for the winning shot or keeping a second stringer on the court in a close game in the dying seconds.

This philosophy has benefitted many of the greats in curling as well, such as Debbie McCormick. Her American team won the Women's World Curling Championship in 2003. She had never skipped competitively before that season and very rarely at the club or recreational levels. When Debbie skipped her team to World gold she was still only twenty-nine years of age, but she had been to more than a couple of Nationals and nine major International events at Worlds, Junior Worlds, and the Olympics as a third and second. Debbie said:

> Throwing the last rock in a pressure situation didn't faze me a whole lot because I always had the mentality that if I make my shots they could be the difference between winning and losing regardless of the position I am playing.

Her dad, Wally, a competitive curler himself who had gone to Worlds a few years before, had always stressed the importance of every team member being able to make a difference on the ice.

This is not always the case with all four or five members of a curling team. In many cases the non-skips can have the mentality that if they don't play up to their potential, the skip will bail them out.

#2 *Nous Sommes Famille!* (We Are Family)

Jackson is very coy with the press or outside world when it comes to delving into stories on his teams. Not that it always works, but he stresses to his teams that what goes on within the team stays within the team, especially the family fights. He understands that in healthy families disagreements are part of the norm and need to be treated as such. Certain things are meant to be private, and some things can be shared in the public forum. He wants his players to feel a sense of safety within the atmosphere of the team, and he has gone so far as having at least one of their practice facilities totally closed off to the public.

Again, he uses the manure metaphor when sharing the various team building exercises he has the team doing. Throw enough stuff at the team and maybe something will catch. He fully understands that not everyone will buy into his team building ideas no matter how brilliant he thinks a player may be. He gives each player one or two books a year to read. Not the same book for every player; he goes out and buys a specific one for each player.

The team has a meditation room, and often the team will have a joint quiet time to focus on upcoming games or situations involved with the team. The meditation can vary from player to player, because not every player will embrace similar spiritual convictions. The purpose is to get the player into a positive mind-set going into the upcoming game. Michael Jordan loved the meditation room and for him it was more about getting centered on correct game thoughts and minimizing the distracting negative thoughts. The Bulls would meet in the meditation room as often as three times a week, but, with the Lakers, it was much less because the dynamics were so different.

As most good coaches do, he encourages his team to socialize together to create the necessary bonding and pulling together when adversities or opportunities present themselves. Jackson also understands the concept that relationships are the key to accomplishing successful ventures in life. He knows he can't expect players to be best friends, that is a bonus, but he wants to create a loyalty and trust where players will go the extra two kilometers on the court for each other. Theodore Roosevelt, former president of the U.S., military leader of the famed Rough Riders in the Cuban-American War, and face on Mount Rushmore said, "The most important single ingredient in the formula of success is knowing how to get along with people." Families don't have to be best friends, but, to be functional, they must be loyal.

Currently, Team Larouche from Quebec City is Quebec's most successful women's team to date. They are also one of the most popular young women's teams in curling, and they probably will be for a long time. Each one of the team members has said that one of the major keys to their staying together and being so successful is that "we are family" or, in French, "*nous sommes famille.*"

#3 The Triangle Offense or the Beauty of the Free Guard Zone

Jackson incorporated an offense called the triangle offense that involves each player requiring strict discipline, sharing of the ball, and sacrifice. This particular offense is ideally suited to creating a team concept, especially in an era where the NBA gets hammered for a lack of fundamental skills and selfish individual play. Many basketball pundits believed this shortcoming was finally exposed at the 2004 Olympics in Athens where the American men failed in their quest for gold. Jackson can sound like a broken CD with his constant harping that successful teams play like teams.

Part of Jackson's genius as a coach is to incorporate a style of play that forces his players to play as a team, much like curling teams who embrace the Free Guard Zone (FGZ). Many of the Chicago Bulls have said that before Phil Jackson came along, they often felt like spectators on the court when Jordan was doing his thing. Now that they all felt like part of the team, they felt like they were contributing.

Randy Ferbey, along with David Nedohin, Scott Pfiefer, and Marcel Rocque have captured this concept as well as any of the great curling teams in history. The FGZ has forced teams to have very competent players at each position. Before the FGZ, it was understood that a team might get away with a weaker lead or second as throwers if the back end was quite strong. Each player on Team Ferbey is content to try and be the best at his individual position. They enjoy playing their positions and the nuances each brings to the game. During the 2004 Alberta Provincials in Innisfail, Scott said, "Marcel and I really believe as the front end that if we outcurl the opposition front end we will seldom if ever get beat, and this makes the job easier for the back end of Nedohin and Ferbey."

Marcel, as the lead, understands that if he gets his first two stones into a good position in each end it makes Randy's job that much easier in dictating the remainder of the end. One can see as a spectator that when Marcel doesn't make his shots he really feels like he let the team down. Marcel and Scott, Huffin' and Puffin' as they have been tabbed, take a tremendous amount of pride in their ability to time rocks and to make a difference in sweeping their team's rocks. They know that a well-swept stone often makes that very fine line between winning and losing.

#4 Have a Yoda Hang Out with the Team

There is a well-known African proverb that says, "It takes a village to raise a child." Jackson appreciates wisdom of elders, both from his upbringing and from his love for the Sioux Nation and their history. Jackson loved and respected his father, the preacher, yet he disagreed with some of his father's beliefs in later years. However, he always admired his father's passion and integrity. Tex Winter, one of Jackson's assistants for almost his entire head coaching career, is much the same. Winter has coached well into his eighties and has coached at almost every level of basketball. Jackson says in *The Last Season*, "Tex focuses on principles and fundamentals. We call him the voice of the basketball gods." Having a Yoda-like, wise soul near your team can be a calming effect and a voice of reason when things get a little dicey. Wisdom, as the ancient Hebrews used to say, doesn't have to do so much with age but with experience at applying the truisms of life on a consistent basis.

The Sandra Schmirler team had Anita Ford as their full-time coach and for awhile as their fifth. Anita is considered one of the smartest players on the Saskatchewan curling scene, and she isn't threatened by additional wise people being added to the mix.

One of curling's most respected psychologists, coaches, and players is Vancouver's Lindsay Sparkes. She is employed as the CCA's coach at international events. When Team Schmirler first went to Worlds in 1993, they realized the wisdom behind the CCA's choice. From that time on, Sparkes was considered part of the Schmirler team, and it used her skills on many occasions apart from the World Championships. She flew into Regina on more than one occasion to sit down with the team, hash through issues, and to set goals for upcoming seasons.

In 1976, Jack McDuff and his young Newfoundlanders won Newfoundland's first and only Brier. A humble and teachable team, they realized in advance that their driver for the Brier had a little curling wisdom stored up, since Sam Richardson had won four Briers and four World Championships with his brother Ernie. Jack was quick to acknowledge how Sam's influence was an integral part of them winning the Brier. They were constantly "picking his brain" for tips and secrets to gain an edge. He taught them everything from pacing themselves for the week to treating the Brier as a serious business trip and not getting caught up in the party atmosphere of the week. Sam was a calming and humorous influence that kept this team from The Rock focused.

#5 Love

You often hear members of champion teams (at any level) yell, scream, and cry out that they love each other. To be honest, one never knows the sincerity level of these ecstatic players, but there is a truism on which they are touching. Whether the love is seasonal or long-term is hard to discern, but for that dream bonspiel victory or dream championship season, there is an intense **like** or **affection** that teammates seem to have for each other. When teams have gone to battle together, lasting friendships are often formed. Not to overstate this point or devalue what veterans endured in war times, but I have often heard World War I and World War II veterans say that the most alive they ever felt was when they were young men or women fighting together for a cause. Many of their longtime friends came out of these battles together.

Jackson's strength (and perhaps legacy) is his ability to create a family atmosphere on his teams. Everything from his style of play, to team meetings, and to creative methods used to get players to think and bond is motivated by a desire to create a safe sanctuary where players feel they can experiment with their game, be themselves, and fully live in their potential. Jackson knows each player started out with a common love for the game, and he knows that deep within the human psyche is a desire to be great and accomplish incredible feats.

Jackson knows the key to a team game is to play as a team, and that it involves more than what goes on the court or on the ice. When teammates have a loyalty for each other, the team has a definite advantage that creates a stronger and more sincere bond. Love cannot be forced, but a wise team will bond on the things they love. This creates ownership, responsibility, and sacrifice on the ice.

Maybe words like "fun" or phrases like "we enjoy each other" is what coaches like Jackson are trying to create. Teams like Schmirler, Lindholm, Ferbey, Trulsen, and Colleen Jones seem to genuinely enjoy each other and are able to get over the personal statements we sometimes hear over the microphones on television. To get to this stage as a team takes a lot of thought, planning, and intentional effort to get to know each team member—just like what families try to do.

Final Thoughts

Maybe the best definition of team I have ever come across is Phil Jackson's: A team is a sanctuary! Throughout history, a sanctuary has had three primary uses.

One is that it is where sacred objects are kept. For a curling team this could easily imply a place where the awards and accomplishments are remembered. This could be a trophy room or a team journal to recall the moments.

Second, a sanctuary is to be a place of shelter from danger and hardship. Curling is competition, and for the high-performance team, there needs to be an atmosphere and a place of letting your hair down where a player can feel safe in being himself or herself. We all need a place to vent, share our excitement, and our insecurities. Understanding a team as a shelter frees us up to focus on the game or event and does not allow our minds to drift off to distractions that can take us away from being fully present emotionally while on the ice.

And last, a sanctuary is a **place to be taught, encouraged, and filled with hope**, developing the ability to go out and live up to our full potential. A healthy functional team hitting on all cylinders is to function as one unit. As Dordi Nordby, the all-time winningest female skip at Worlds, has said, "A curling team that is very successful must be four players who play as one and if they achieve this it is as though they have become like five versus four on the ice."

Chapter Six

No Rest for the Champion

"They will be working very hard through the summer—if they are smart."
—Bill Tschirhart,
NTC Development Coach, 2005

In a *Calgary Sun* interview by Angela MacIsaac on April 5, 2005, she queried Bill Tschirhart on what Olympic qualifying teams could do to prepare for the Tim Horton's Olympic trials in Halifax eight months later in December. Bill has worked with dozens of the world's best high-performance curlers, and he has studied what champion teams and players do to get to that level. He doesn't limit his coaching to Canadian players, as he has his door open to players from around the world. The New Zealand men's team has come to train under Bill more than a handful of times. South Korea, Japan, America, Australia, and many of the top European (Euro) teams have come to the NTC in Calgary to take advantage of Bill's insights and wisdom.

Bill shared these thoughts with MacIsaac:

They will be working very hard through the summer—if they are smart. They have to make sure that when they hit the ice in September to be ready to really hone their skills. They need to make sure they are on a nutritionally sound program and that they'll be physically ready to be the best they can be.

Team dynamics are also a homework project, but by the new season, those issues should be behind each squad. The key is why they qualified for trials in the first place. Curling teams generally don't do that enough. They don't identify the factors for their success and concentrate on these when things get a little difficult.

It is all about peaking. There was a time when I didn't put much stock in that but certainly in our sport, you do have to play well when the chips are down and everything's on the line. And there is nothing more on the line than the Olympic curling trials.

The teams will have to build on that through the summer, make sure they put everything in perspective. Sometimes they can get on a roll a little too early come September and October. I'm not suggesting that's the case here but a lot of the times, you can't choreograph that. You just play as well as you can.

Tschirhart touches on a key ingredient for championship curling—learning to keep the spark alive in the off-season. When one studies the Euro curlers and the new wave of Asian curlers and professionals of other major sports, the top athletes are maintaining their edge throughout the season.

Randy Ferbey, who has curled in six Worlds ranging from the late 1980s to the mid 2000s, made the following observation about the international curlers and their commitment level to becoming the best. In an April 1, 2005, Terry Jones column in the *Edmonton Sun* during the 2005 Worlds in Victoria, Ferbey said:

These teams are using our resources—resources we're not even using ourselves—to beat us. The Europeans are doing more progressive things in the sport than Canadians now that curling is an Olympic sport. They're using all the modern sports training methods, video, sports psychology— all those things elite athletes in other Olympic sports use.

They're using us, when it comes to coaching, to beat us, too. They're taking coaches from Canada and using them to beat us. That's not new. But now they're taking it to another level. When they lose, they go back and look at the video with the coaches to learn how it happened. They're training their guys to beat us.

Learning to eat properly, working out, staying mentally sharp, tapping into sports psychology, and working on team dynamics in the off-season can help a team come out of the gate sharper than ever before. This is not to suggest that curlers shouldn't take some serious time off away from the game or even each other for a spell, because that can also be healthy in maintaining perspective and keeping the passion to perform alive. However, not allowing yourself to slip mentally, emotionally, spiritually (from the team's core values), or physically, is vital. Allowing oneself to become drastically out of shape in any of these four areas can hinder a team's momentum and ability to compete against the top teams entering a new season. As most high-level athletes know, if a negative tone is set early in a season, it is sometimes very hard to reverse the trend. The opposite is also true that if a good tone is set early, it can snowball throughout the entire season.

Becoming drastically out of shape in the off-season in one of these four critical areas means that we have become lazy or fat to the point where trying to get back into shape when the season begins takes away from the team's expectations to achieve on the ice. The key to staying in shape in the off-season or not suffering burnout during the season is balance. Burnout is not just a sexy term Dick Vermeil came up with when he took his almost two-decade sabbatical between National Football League (NFL) coaching gigs. When one talks with the extremely passionate and focused Peja Lindholm, balance is a phrase he is constantly throwing out because it is so easy to go to extremes in either taking time off or playing to the point of exhaustion.

John Morris and his Calgary-based rink qualified for the Olympic trials almost a full two years before the event. His team was the WCT champion for the 2003–2004 season. The team made a decision to go hard on the circuit in 2004–2005 in preparation for the trials and Brier playdowns. They played in a WCT event every single weekend leading up to the Alberta playdowns. John said, "It was too much. This was the only curling season where we never won at least one event. Zero! I think we may have got a little burned-out. Our plan for the 2005–2006 season leading up to the Olympic trials in December is to scale back and go every second weekend at the most. We will still practice when we are at home because I have every intent of living every day down at the curling rink in preparation for Halifax, but to somehow balance out the intensity level."

Conventional wisdom suggests to go as hard as a team can during the season in entering as many spiels as possible, but this may not be the best way to go for every team. There is no easy answer other than finding what works for your team. In 1997, when I started to work on *Gold on Ice*, I underestimated Team Schmirler and its chances for winning the Olympic trials later that year in Brandon, Manitoba. The book was to be based on the team becoming the first ever three-time women's world champions. To me that was the story. I thought the fact that three of the women had babies in 1997 would hinder their chances. Most of the other teams who had qualified for Brandon were committed to bonspiels almost every weekend leading up to the trials. Team Schmirler committed to half the amount but committed to throwing rocks almost every day between events.

Was the way they chose to enter the trials the template for all other teams in the future? We would say no, because what works for one team is no guarantee that it will work for another team. On the flip side, Team Ferbey won its record-setting fourth Brier in five years in 2005 and had an approach almost opposite to the 1997–98 Schmirler team in preparing for its record-setting attempt. Every team has to find what works best for its players.

Balance is something you will have to discover for yourself and your own team. The important thing is doing whatever it takes for your team to stay sharp and to peak for the events you have made a priority. The Europeans and Asians love playing in Canada as much as possible to stay competitive, but the reality for most of them is that they can only play in Canada on a limited basis. Generally speaking, they play less competitive games a season than do North Americans but they throw as many rocks as North Americans because they put a premium on practicing as much as possible. But, when one observes and researches the top international curling teams, they are also in great physical shape, work with sports psychologists, practice, and continue to work on all four elements (body, emotion, mind, and spirit) to achieve on-ice success.

So what can a player and team do in the off-season? "In order to come out in September or October like you have been playing all summer, what can a team do that doesn't have the resources or access to WCT teams on a weekly basis?" Cheryl asks. "What do Kurt and Marcy Balderston, who continually put teams together that compete for Alberta Brier berths or go to Scotts on a regular basis, do while living in virtual curling isolation in the Peace Country of Alberta?"

Kurt Balderston and his wife, Marcy, were the 1992 Canadian mixed champions out of Sexsmith, Alberta. Marcy has been to three Scotts and two national mixed events. Kurt has been to the three national mixed events and has been to almost fifteen Alberta men's provincials, making it to the final game to go to the Brier on four occasions. All-totaled, Kurt and his teams have appeared in eight provincial final games, having the opportunity to go to nationals in junior, mixed, and men's, winning all three mixed finals.

Kurt may be the best curler in the world not to win a major (Brier, Olympics, or Worlds). For you older readers who followed curling on the Canadian prairies from the 1950s to 1970s, Kurt is the 1990s and 2000s version of Saskatoon's Merv Mann and all his success and heartbreak. Kurt is the Brooklyn Dodgers, Buffalo Bills, and post–Bobby Orr Boston Bruins all rolled up into one. The Dodgers had to get past the dynastic Yankees of the 1950s. The Bills had to get past the Cowboys' run in the 1990s. And the Bruins had to face the Canadiens and Oilers dynasties of the 1970s and 1980s. Kurt Balderston first had to face the Lukowich–Ryan rinks of the late 1980s and 1990s and then had to go head to head against curling's first million dollar team, the Martin Express, and all-time Brier winners Randy Ferbey and company.

Kurt and Marcy find a way to compete against the best year after year. How do they do it? Kurt explains:

We love the mental game and know how important it is so we make every effort to mature in this area throughout the year. We have used sports psychologists off and on for a number of years to improve this aspect of our game. We read a lot of motivational books: self-help, inspirational, business, leadership, sports psychology, and books on communication or team building. I love studying the mental aspects of the game. I'm learning that communication is so important and am trying to make more of an effort to deal with things much quicker with teammates than in the past. It's a team sport, and we have to learn to work together and know that we are all supporting each other.

We have also learned the importance of having realistic expectations and keeping things in perspective. This has evolved. When I was in my twenties, I took some losses pretty hard, especially losing two provincial finals; well, three actually counting juniors versus teams like Ryan and Lukowich. We came so close. Having children and winning the mixed in 1992 has helped me realize that curling isn't a life or death proposition. When we won the mixed in '92 my reaction was, "This is nice but not life altering."

I'd love to get to the Brier and win it, but I can live without it too. Since '92 I have become much more relaxed on the ice and have kept my expectations more in perspective, and I think it has made me a better player.

Team building in the off-season is becoming more of a high priority for us as well. We'll get together every now and then over coffee, golfing, barbecues. I'll often get together with my third to talk over strategy or philosophy towards calling our games.

We have started to work out in the summers as well because we find that if we are physically fit, our mental game is so much stronger when we are playing these mentally draining games against the top playdown teams.

Kurt and Marcy remind us of the type of player NFL and CFL Hall of Fame coach Marv Levy looked for. He wanted players with balance in their lives. He found that players who were solely focused on gaining their worth from their sport were the ones who tended to wilt under pressure when the game was on the line. Those players who made family a priority, had healthy outside interests, and were well-read tended to cope with pressure situations much better because of the balance they brought into their lives. Players who realized it was only a game and not life or death, yet still treated their passion with respect, performed at much higher levels when the stakes were highest. These players still grieved after devastating losses but were able to recover much quicker and get on with life.

Cheryl's curling dream is to get back to the Scott, become a Canadian champion, win the Worlds, and go to the Olympics. Life will go on if this never occurs (and, if it does, life will still go on), but it's a worthwhile pursuit because she knows she'll learn much along the journey to benefit her in other parts of her life.

She echoes the comments of Randy Ferbey in the beginning of this chapter that Canadians would be wise to learn from our international curling friends and rivals in how they approach curling as a year-round pursuit and to be more intentional in training and training techniques.

She cites the example of English soccer post–1966 and Canadian hockey post–1972. History has taught us that in their home nations, English soccer and Canadian hockey teams were expected to be world champions, as if it were a divine right. Since 1966, England has never won a World Cup and has hardly threatened to win. The belief is that the rest of the world caught up with England, and the English had been reluctant to learn about the advances other nations have discovered and taken to new levels. They now have mechanisms in place to improve their game and to catch up with the rest of the world.

The year 1972 marked the famed Canada-Russia hockey clash of the titans. Canadians, generally speaking, thought of themselves as leagues and years ahead of the European nations. When Canada barely won the series by one game in the eight that were played, we received a cold slap in the face and the realization was that we were barely hanging on. Canadians reacted in a positive and pro-active way and started to reevaluate their approach to hockey to a degree seldom seen in sports. Canadians may have taken a step backwards for a handful of years but learned from emerging nations and became trendsetters in making the game even better. As a result, Canada has held a steady reign on the bulk of the major tournaments over the last thirty years.

Cheryl takes an Olympic-mentality approach to her curling career in the off-season that she has seen in the international teams. At the end of each season she is glad for the time off, but after a month she is raring to get back on the ice again. She has a fitness regime of working out at least six times a week, using weight training, biking, running, and swimming. During the curling season, she works out three times a week as more of a maintenance program to sustain her off-season conditioning. She stretches every day throughout the year to maintain flexibility and prevent muscle pulls. She cites that most of Canada's top curlers such as Colleen Jones, Kelley Law's former world champions, the Schmirler team, Team Ferbey, Kevin Martin, Gushue's Newfoundland team, and John Morris and his rink all have workouts built into their list of priorities.

Cheryl also tries to eat well. She has gone to nutritionists to learn what would work best for her and her team. She emphasizes that she still enjoys certain sinful foods every now and then, as long as she doesn't overdo or abuse them. She is far stricter during the season so as not to lose needed energy.

The mental game, of course, is huge for Cheryl, and she works on this aspect throughout the year. She is a voracious reader of books similar to those that the Balderstons talked about. She watches tapes of both men and women's games from the previous season to see what strategies teams use. She finds the break from games in the off-season good for regaining objectivity in her approach to calling games and being more open to make adjustments.

Cheryl also does a lot of visualization in the off-season and will often play out game scenarios in her mind while driving or enjoying a hot tub. Like many players, she often finds herself practicing her release with her arm and hand while driving down the road or walking through her house. She laughs about teammate Karen Ruus whose neighbors tease her about how they know she's a curler. Often while walking her dog down the street, Karen practices her delivery and release motion.

For champions, curling is a year-round passion. Breaks are needed, even during the season, but for champions, the game is never too far away from their thoughts. The city of Corinth in ancient Greece had the Isthmian Games, which were considered the next major event after the Olympics. Winners of events would win a wreath and have a gate in their city constructed and named after them for posterity's sake. The apostle Paul of the Bible loved to attend these games and used an analogy of these highly trained athletes to emphasize the importance of commitment and passion in his writings. He uses the Olympic-caliber boxers and track athletes as examples. Allow me a little literary license to scrap the track star and boxer and use a winter games example to close this chapter:

> "Do you not know that in a curling game all the curlers participate, but only one team gets the prize? Curl in such a way as to get the prize. Everyone who competes in tournaments and bonspiels goes into strict training. . . . Therefore I do not curl like a man curling aimlessly; I do not compete like a man with no goals. No, I beat my body and make it my slave so that after I have taught others, I myself will not be disqualified for the prize."
>
> —1 Corinthians 9:24–27
> (If Paul had been a curler)

Chapter Seven

Coaches' Corner

The question asked at the Media Bench at the 2005 Brier in Edmonton, "Who's the best curling coach in Canada we should consult with for the Coaches' Corner chapter?" And without a word of hesitation:

"He's right under your nose. Bill Tschirhart of the National Training Center in Calgary. There are a lot of good coaches in curling, but he's the best we have come across. If you are going to sit down and pick someone's brain, you need to sit down with Bill."

—Bob Garvin, editor of *Sweep!* magazine
and Jim Henderson, publisher of *Sweep!*,
curling's number-one read international magazine

*L*iving in Calgary, I have sat down with Bill Tschirhart on more than a few occasions to interview him and talk curling. The *Sweep!* expert opinion was no surprise to Cheryl and me. Cheryl volunteers her time at the NTC as its competitive consultant and knows Bill and his current assistant, National Development Coach Paul Webster very well. Paul is also the coordinator and National Coach of the CCA's La Releve program, which is an Olympic training program looking towards the 2020 Olympics in Vancouver. Bill is the co-coordinator of the NTC and is the CCA's National Development Coach.

Bill and Paul have worked with countless players, coaches, and teams over the years that have gone onto Briers, Scotts, and Worlds. Bill and Paul listen to what the best curlers and instructors discover is working in curling. They are also fortunate to work with many high-level players and coaches such as Ron Mills, Marcel Rocque, Russ Howard, Jim Waite, and Pat Reid who volunteer their time at various CCA high performance camps across Canada.

We asked Bill and Paul a number of questions:

1. What are the characteristics of a championship player?
2. What are the characteristics of a championship team?
3. What are the key dynamics that destroy teams?
4. What makes a good coach?

In this chapter, we will let Bill and Paul do most of the talking. Dick Irvin wrote a wonderful book on the oral history of the Montreal Canadiens a few years ago, recording the insights and thoughts of many of their great players and coaches. This chapter follows that format.

Characteristics of a Championship Player

Attitude

Paul calls this dedication. He says, "Something I have learned is that good curlers do about 10 to 15 percent of what is required to be a champion, but great players do 75 to 90 percent of what is necessary." Too many players try and get by on talent alone. Talent may take you far at the junior level and it may get you out of your district playoffs at the regular level, but that's about as far as it will get a player on a consistent basis.

Brain Balance

Bill refers to Tim Gallwey's sports psychology books a lot in his interviews. Gallwey emphasizes the importance of brain balance.

Bill continues:

If a player doesn't find a way to balance his left brain-right brain he will inevitably suffer from a syndrome that we refer to as a competitive breakdown. Our left brain is the analytical part of us that needs to logically think things through to understand the process of how to do something. Our right brain is the more artistic, feeling side of who we are; the part of us that creates and performs. An effective curler will learn to rely more on his right brain in competition than his left brain. The ideal state for an athlete to get to is when he or she can unconsciously perform the necessary physical requirements without over-thinking the process.

When the left brain dominates the thought processes in competition, competitive breakdowns will occur. Gallwey calls the left brain, Self One, and the right brain, Self Two. The brain works best when it balances technical thoughts and the "just do it" impulses. If Self One dominates, there could be information overload that leads to competitive breakdown.

So many curlers ignore this key element to performance and concentrate almost exclusively on the technical aspects of the delivery. If all that an athlete takes into competition is a sound technical delivery, he really doesn't have very much because it's unprotected and unsupported. Competitive breakdown, sometimes referred to as pressure, will take hold sooner or later.

We videotape athletes' deliveries at the NTC, which is not uncommon with today's elite curlers, but I find it interesting that some of the most important aspects of what it takes to make curling shots, I can't put on videotape. I can't tape the curler's **attitude, mental image, delivery thought, brain balance**, and most importantly, the level of trust that he has in his delivery.

I see so many well-intentioned coaches spending countless hours on the ice trying to turn a 75 percent shooter into a 76 percent shooter with absolutely no time spent on the aspects of the delivery outlined above. The result is an athlete who you will send into the fray with little or no support for the technical advances the two of you have worked so hard to achieve. The good news is that those **intangibles** [listed in the preceding paragraph] can be learned just as much at the placement of the sliding foot, grip, or any other physical aspect of the delivery. These things take time, effort and practice, again, just like the bio-mechanics of the delivery. Frequently, following a great performance, an athlete will claim that they didn't think about anything, they were so much in the zone. Don't be fooled by that statement. What the athlete is really saying is that he is so well practiced that they bring the intangibles into play so automatically through directed practice that they are not even aware they are doing so.

Dealing with Distractions

Paul says the way players deal with unnecessary distractions is critical to success.

The best players I have come across know how to deal with distractions, not that they never get frustrated with things but they keep their poise. I find there are two types of players. One is a constant blame-shifter at heart and looks for or uses excuses to explain their lack of success. The other learns to deal with distractions or adversity and rolls with the punches.

A couple of recent examples were the 2005 Women's Worlds in Scotland where the ice conditions were less than ideal. The teams that made the playoffs began to deal with the circumstances they were dealt and tried to adjust. A second example was witnessing how Team Ferbey handled themselves at the men's Worlds held in Victoria, British Columbia. I have been able to observe them a lot this year, and they gave me an open invitation to sit in on team meetings to learn how they go about their business. I can bet you when they were on the verge of elimination and had to win eight straight games to win it all, there was no yelling and screaming in the dressing room before or after games. I can't see a team like that getting flustered. They knew what they had to do. There was no panic.

Mental Toughness

Bill adds that great players have mental toughness.

This is one of those characteristics that can only develop over time. You don't see it fully evolved at the junior level although for many it is developing. You look at the elite teams, especially in Canada, where the road to the Scott or Brier is so long. How do the elite teams go to all these WCT events trying to qualify for the Olympic trials, then hit the playdown trial, go to a Brier or Scott, and then sometimes throw in other WCT or Trials events in between playdowns, a Nationals or Worlds and perform well? Mental toughness can only develop by experience and being committed to mastering the mental game.

Passion

Passion's paramount, Bills says.

The great ones love to compete and play. If they are just in it to compete, they tend not to last that long. There must be a love for the game deep down inside. I saw this in Marcel Rocque just after they had won their third Worlds (Victoria, British Columbia in 2005). I mean they had just won the Brier, went to the Canada Cup, and off to Worlds all within a month of each other. Most know that he and his teammates had taken the competitive season away from their jobs to devote to curling, and Marcel was slated to return full-time to the classroom. He traveled to Ontario to actively participate in a national coach's conference. He had every right to stay at home and rest, but he didn't. Marcel simply loves the game and loves to give back to it.

Bill and I talked about Wayne Gretzky and his love for the game. During his playing days, it was often documented how number 99 would play street hockey in Edmonton, Los Angeles, or New York with kids in the middle of a hectic hockey season. Joe Theisman used to do the same with the kids on his block in Toronto and Washington during his CFL and NFL playing days. Love for the game!

Practice

Paul says practice *does* make perfect.

I think it's safe to say all the high-performance players play or practice at least six days a week on average during the season. You can't downplay the importance of throwing rocks. The best players practice to the point where their game becomes an unconscious act, similar to a toddler developing into a confident child or adult walking down the stairs. As adults we think nothing of walking down a flight of stairs because we have done it so often. This is the point where curlers want to get to and stay at where playing the actual games almost becomes an unconscious act. Where they can focus on the process of competing and not worry about technique at all.

Quiet Eye

Bill says the concept of the "quiet eye" has tremendous merit for curlers. Quiet eye is in the process of being researched and developed primarily by Dr. Joan Vickers of the University of Calgary. The premise of her extensive research is that the eye should focus on what the body is trying to accomplish, especially for the last few seconds before the act is being performed. This study is based upon those actions in sports that are not spontaneous but take time before occurring. Trying to make a putt, kick a field goal, attempt a free throw, or hitting a brush in one's curling delivery all have eye-hand coordination skills involved that take place over an extended period of time. Her well-tested theory is that the last thing an eye focuses on just before doing the intended task will bring about a higher degree of success.

Dr. Vickers has also discovered that if an athlete takes too long in focusing on the task at hand, distractions can actually take over and the process of focus can become cluttered. Vickers has calculated that if an athlete focuses for three seconds or longer just before attempting their requirement, distractions in one's thinking can begin to occur. In curling she calculated from the beginning of the delivery in the hack until release is usually seven to eight seconds of intense concentration on the broom. But, for most curlers, it is only three seconds from when the player is in his full slide until release. This means the final three seconds of release must be intense focus on the skip's brush and nothing else.

Thought Processes

Bill elaborates on how thinking matters:

Skills don't change! So much of success is how we think and balance our thinking. Ninety percent of the game is between the ears. "Are we," as Dr. John Dunn likes to say, "Functional perfectionists or dysfunctional perfectionists?" The elite athlete aims for perfection but must be realistic that none of us will ever get there.

When it comes to championship players having the correct thought processes, I asked Bill how he worked with Team New Zealand. The Kiwis have made numerous trips to Calgary to spend time with Bill at the NTC. The Kiwis are easily the most improved team on the world-curling scene, having just qualified for the Olympics for the first time ever. The team is skipped by Sean Becker, a native Kiwi, and his three Canadian-born teammates. There is only one full-time curling facility in New Zealand and only a handful of high performance players. A casual observation says there is no way this team should be competing, let alone qualifying for an Olympic medal. Over the last couple of years, this team has seldom, if ever, gotten blown out by the favorites.

Bill shares what he feels will help the New Zealand team:

First off, we got the New Zealanders to identify their strengths and commit to playing to them regardless of the opposition. This is the key to Team Ferbey. They know they throw down weight shots better than most every other team they face, so they constantly work on perfecting this strength.

We work a tonne on the intangibles that we are talking about right now under this heading. I remind the team that they can make all the shots with the deliveries they have developed. Their deliveries are adequate enough to perform at a high level. They have strengths in their game that can help level the playing field. We try and clearly convince them of these strengths and develop a game plan they can use to take advantage of their strengths and minimize their weaknesses.

One of their advantages is that the four of them are the best curlers in New Zealand and they are stuck together regardless, so they are forced to play together and develop as a team. It's almost by default in a sense. One of the things we have talked about over the course of time is that they do not have to be afraid of their opponents. They know the reputations of the best curlers in the world.

My advice to them is play your game in such a way that regardless of who you play, make the opposition prove to you they can do it, or play at their best. So much of their success depends upon each one of them thinking correct thoughts before, during, and after games.

Trust

Don't overlook the value of trust, Bill says.

So much of this game is trust. Learning to trust your own game, your own delivery. Does a player hope to make a shot or expect to make a shot? Does a player trust his teammates and have enough confidence in them that he feels they can have success together?

Cheryl would add:

Does a player trust his own preparation was adequate enough to prepare him for actual games? Does a player trust the skip? Do I, as a skip, trust my play calling? So much of what we do on the ice is determined by what we focus upon as a team. If we don't trust what we are focusing upon in terms of our game plan or philosophy, we will probably fail because we are not fully committed to what we should be trusting. When we trust the process or ourselves or the skip, our focus is on those things and we tend to perform up to our abilities or beyond.

Visualization

Bill Tschirhart likes the story of Major James Nesmeth as told in *A Second Helping of Chicken Soup for the Soul.*

In the book, Nesmeth is described as an average golfer until he was imprisoned as a prisoner of war in North Vietnam for seven years, during which he lived in a cage approximately four feet high and five feet long. In his long, lonely, and cramped confinement, Nesmeth realized he had to exercise his mind or he wouldn't survive. So he started playing imaginary golf games daily, visualizing the course, the fragrances, the changing seasons, the sounds, the feel of the club in his hand. He pictured the swings he made, and he was able to always place his shots where he visualized. He spent as much time playing his imaginary games as it would have taken him to play eighteen holes in real life. When Nesmeth came home, he was able to finally play a golf game for real. And he shot a seventy-four his first time out.

Bill goes on to say:

What Major Nesmeth had done was put his skills into the hands of the power of his mind. And, what he called visualization was actually three things: Visualization—the ability to see in the mind's eye. Imagery—the ability to use the other senses such as smell, touch, auditory, acuity, and even taste. Mental rehearsal—the ability to practice in the positive domain of the mind.

Keys to his success were:
a.   the loyalty to his regimen in that he played golf every day,
b.   positive feedback in that he never missed a shot,

c. real time in that he took the same amount of time to play his imaginary golf as he would have to actually play

Characteristics of Championship Teams

Bill likes to tell the story of Herb Brooks picking his American hockey team for the 1980 Olympics, as portrayed in the film *Miracle*. Craig Patrick, Brook's assistant coach says, "You're missing the best players." Brooks replies, "I'm not looking for the best players, Craig, I'm looking for the right ones."

Bill continues:

> Choosing the right players who can become greater than the sum of its parts is the key to a championship team.

> I wrote an article for the NTC Web site on what makes a championship team. The list I have is from Lindsay Sparkes, one of the best world champions our country has ever produced and one of the top coaches, period. To hear Lindsay say it, no team has ever won a championship without most, if not all, of these characteristics.

Lindsay's points make up numbers one through nine. Number ten is contributed by Paul Webster, from his observations of championship teams. Paul comments on numbers five and ten; Bill expounded on all the others.

#1 Have a Steadfast Belief in Each Other

Believing in each other is what makes a team greater than the sum of its parts. One of the teachers in my school has the saying in his classroom that the hardest thing about reaching your goal is to start! It's believing that you can that makes it possible, and in team sports, each player must have the belief not only in himself, but in his teammates as well. A very wise person once said, "When we lose trust in one another, the seas engulfs us and the lights go out." When things go badly and losses start to build, teams begin to lose faith and then look to assign blame. When you are at the blame stage, the wheels will soon come off. When things begin to go badly is precisely the time to restore faith and trust, not to abandon those attributes.

#2 Promote Honest Communication

So often in curling, the word communication surfaces as either the cornerstone of a team's success or its Achilles' heel. Notice that according to Lindsay's observations, the adjective honest describes the quality of the communication. Hey, if you mess up, admit it! Trying to cover your sins by blaming them on bad brush placement or a fall in the ice that you know is not there only hurts the team! It's only when the communication is based upon what everyone feels is the truth can the communication become the cornerstone of your success! But, that being said, be sure that you don't inadvertently make the communication brutally honest. I sometimes quote the theologian who said, "One of the main tricks of the devil is to get you to do the right thing in the most obnoxious way possible." Remember that the way you say something is part of the message you wish to convey!

#3 Have a Satisfaction with the Position on the Team

Successful teams exhibit daily the treatise that the team can only have one skip and must have a third, second, and lead who know how to play the position, understand its significance, and want to be the best there ever was at that position and believe their teammates feel the same way. I believe the best example of this to be Neil Harrison, career lead for the Wrench, Eddie Werenich. Has there ever been a more dedicated lead, or one who understands the position and its significance? I don't feel that there would be too much argument that Neil has the fire to be the best lead in any competition he plays. I believe the same is true for Marcia Gudereit, lead for Jan Betker and formerly Sandra Schmirler, or when Christine Jurgenson was lead for Kelley Law.

I see this strength in all the championship-caliber teams. I used to like how Kate Horne knew her role when she was with Cathy King (Borst at the time). She was the lead on the team, and one of her roles was that she was very good at seeing the big picture. Whenever Cathy and her third, Heather Nedohin (née Godberson) would get tunnel vision, which is so easy for back end players because their job obviously is to set up the ends, Kate would come in and say, "Maybe it's time to redecorate!" In other words maybe it was time to bail out or to try an alternative strategy with what was taking shape. Cathy and Heather expected this out of Kate because this was one of the strengths she brought to the team. Marcel Rocque fulfills a very similar role with Randy Ferbey, and his role is understood. Not that Scott Pfeifer never has any input, but it will usually come from Marcel because he is wired this way in his ability to step back and see the big picture.

#4 Have an Openness to Coaching Input

Being open to coaching input is a quality that is near and dear to my heart. Ladies, take a bow here! You are light years ahead of the guys in this respect! Enough said. (That'll get me in trouble, eh?)

This may be the shortest explanation, but it's equally as important as all the other points. Russ Howard once said to Bill, "Imagine how much more successful our teams could have been if we had had some good coaching." This necessary emphasis on coaching hasn't always been there. And look what the all-time Brier winning skip has accomplished in his stellar career without coaching. Scary thought!

#5 Establish Clear Goals

Goals are what so many teams *don't* have. I have an acronym called S.A.M.M. I use for goal setting. Goals must be Specific, Achievable, Measurable, and Mutual. A team must have long- and short-term goals as well. These goals must be recorded and revisited frequently and, in the case of the truly committed team, verified with a signature by each member of the team.

Paul Webster says he has an exercise he will often use with teams as well:

I have a list of thirty to thirty-five performance factors I will present to teams and will ask them to prioritize what six or seven they should focus on during the season [to] improve their overall performance. Some of the items on the list include brushing, ability, draw weight, brushing judgment, confidence, comfort with rocks in play, big weight, goals, line calling, placing of the brush, shooting ability, angles, sense of timing, communication, weight control, defined game plan, patience, resilience, ice reading, team dynamics, strategy, hitting ability, mental toughness, physical fitness, passion. Every team is different, and, if they can focus their attention on a handful of these items over the course of the season or part of the season, they should become better in these areas.

Setting goals and making priorities are critical to individual and team performance. The words of the late NCAA and NHL coach Robert "Badger Bob" Johnson are apropos here: "You achieve what you emphasize." Johnson said that if a team had high focus on a handful of important performance areas, those were the areas in which a team either excelled or became better. Johnson loved for his teams to be in the top third in the league in special teams and always made it a very high emphasis because he felt this kind of discipline would take his teams deep into the playoffs. Check the records of his University of Wisconsin Badgers, Calgary Flames, and Pittsburgh Penguins and you will see that his teams were always at the top or near the top in special team stats, and his teams usually went deep into the playoffs.

#6 Adhere to Established Routines

Routines established for team effectiveness are the pathways to success. I had the pleasure of coaching the Patti Lank team at the U.S. Olympic trials. On their own, with very little urging from me, they established a routine. Beginning one hour before game time, everything was choreographed to the second. The mental toughness and role definition it established was clearly evident to anyone who observed the team in its pre-game preparation. In the on-ice, pre-game warm-up, I was told precisely what my role was and what I was expected to do! That's the attitude!

#7 Adopt the Attitude That the Team Comes First

And now the spot where the rubber meets the road. Team comes first! We're talking commitment here, guys. This is where the five or six of you (don't forget the coach and fifth player) sit across a table, look one another in the eye, and state your case. Remember those goals that Lindsay referred to earlier. Now is the time to test the mutual part! Not only that, it's time to state the degree of commitment. I believe I hear the word sacrifice in the background. Notice how closely team first is allied with the initial characteristic, a belief in each other.

#8 Show Unity and Fearlessness

Have you ever played an elite team? Did you notice how confident they are? They're not cocky or arrogant, but confident! This confidence is especially displayed in time of crisis in a game or competition or when something adverse happens such as when a crucial shot picks. There's no gnashing of teeth or flailing of brushes or cursing, not among the truly championship teams, just the also-rans! Champions have an inner conceit. They truly believe they can win every game. The secret is the word *inner*. The conceit stays there while the confident presence shows!

#9 Pay Attention to Detail

Every championship team pays attention to detail. Leave no stone unturned. To teams who attend CCA high-performance camps, we quote Pat Reid, "If you want something you've never had before, you had better be prepared to do some things you've never done before." This applies to all teams.

I can't stress this one enough. The truly great teams all have this characteristic. Always looking for an edge or a way to improve the team's chances no matter how small.

Randy Ferbey invited John Morris and Brent Lang to a spiel in Switzerland in 2004. David Nedohin and Scott Pfiefer had to decline. Randy still called the game and had John throwing the last two stones. Team Ferbey doesn't use stopwatches and, to be clear, it's not that they are against the stopwatches, but for them they have learned to time rocks by observing carefully each other's deliveries. On one shot Randy seemed to throw perfect split-time weight, and Brent thought they would hardly have to brush it. All of a sudden Marcel starts hammering it, and they barely get it to the spot where Randy called for it to stop. On another stone by Randy a few ends later, it looked from the split time that they would have to brush like crazy to get it there. Marcel called the brushing off and the rock glided unaided to the pin. Brent wondered why his split times weren't consistent in judging the stones.

Marcel explained to Brent and John that they study releases, and, on that first stone, Marcel was watching Randy's release all the way and at the last moment he squeezed the handle ever so slightly to take a little speed off. Marcel said if he was watching his stopwatch, he never would have noticed Randy's adjustment.

On the other rock that confused Brent, Marcel knew from Randy's speed coming out of the hack that Randy was really close to the desired weight of the called shot location and gave the stone a slight push right at the split second of release so they'd probably not have to brush at all other than cleaning the path even though the split-time seemed to indicate sweeping was needed. This team had been together so long that they began to know just how much brushing or lack of brushing a rock would need from observing each other's releases.

Paul finishes up the list of characteristics of a championship team with this:

#10 "Whatever It Takes" Attitude

We encourage teams that work with us to have the attitude at an event that says, "We want to leave this event knowing we can say that there may be teams that have worked as hard as we have, but there shouldn't be a team that has worked harder." Championship teams will try and find a way to do whatever it takes in the areas necessary to compete to the best of their abilities. I saw this with Cathy King's 2005 Alberta champions. Raylene Rocque had an extremely busy work schedule, and the team called a practice for a certain day and time that worked for three out of the four players. Raylene had a scheduling conflict, but her attitude was that I'll do whatever I have to, to be there. The team and its priorities came first. Raylene found a way to be at that practice.

Key Dynamics That Destroy Teams

Lack of Commitment

Paul expands on one thing that wrecks teams:

This seems to be the downfall of so many teams. Three out of four players are on the same page and one player isn't. Granted, in some cases, family and work priorities can interfere, but that is usually caused by lack of communication by the team itself with its goals and being open and clear with work and family.

Bill adds:

Players and teams must learn the delicate balancing act of being amateur athletes with jobs and families. Sometimes a player may be taking on more than he can handle, which isn't fair for anyone. Honest, clear communication is key in this area. Each player needs to know how deep the commitment to the team is by each teammate.

Lack of Communication

This is an ongoing theme throughout *Between the Sheets*. Paul tells the story of being around Randy Ferbey and his team talking about team issues. One of the funnier, but very true, statements was when Randy said; "Maybe what our team needs most is not a coach but a marriage counselor."

Team Dynamics Breaking Down

Bill outlines what he feels is a major problem.

This is the most critical of all things that can destroy a team. If teams don't work on chemistry and all these other intangibles, things can fall apart quite quickly. Curling is a team sport, therefore the key is to develop a strong team. The list that Lindsay Sparkes put together on studying championship teams must be a priority or the chances for success will become so slim.

Qualities of a Good Coach

In answering this question, Bill focused on one concept and Paul focused on another, as well with many variations of the same concept.

Empowerment

Bill saw one key quality that allows coaches to do all they need to successfully.

Coaches have many hats that they can wear in working with teams. I was once asked how many different hats do you think you wear for this one particular team? I counted twenty-three, and they ranged from coaching, delivery clinician, sports psychologist, nutritionist, exercise physiologist, manager, travel agent, social worker, family counselor, driver, teacher, statistician, computer scientist, event co-coordinator, media relations, officer, journalist, on-air analyst, fifth player (who'd have thought that?), legal advocate (in player grievance), facilitator, parent, and friend.

However, I believe the key role of a coach is to empower the athlete. In a sense, we need to work ourselves out of a job, even though that may never happen, but that is the coach's goal. So much of coaching at the elite level is helping the athletes realize their potential they already have within themselves. The elite athletes have the technical skills mastered in most cases, and our job is to create an environment for them to do what they already are capable of doing on a consistent basis. A coach should try to work with what is already there and tweak the technical if the situation arises or is necessary. And facilitate or point them in the direction of the characteristics which athletes need to possess in all the intangibles. As Nike says, "Just do it!"

Humility

Paul saw one characteristic as the key to being a good coach.

This involves a few things. A coach should be someone who has been coached. This, of course, helps them to identify with the athlete. A coach should be coachable, willing to keep learning, and to use other resources at their disposal to help make the team better no matter what it involves. And, in some cases, a team can either outgrow its coach or, in special circumstances, he may have to step down because of the personality dynamics.

An example of this is a team I helped coach in Ottawa. We had three dads on this junior team who were all level-three certified curling coaches. It is sometimes hard to coach one's own children, not always but sometimes, and these men felt their teenagers would learn more effectively without overt parental involvement. These dads were so good in stepping back and supporting me and cheering me on as I coached their children, and these were people fully qualified to coach at this level, not just because of their certification but also their track records. They truly wanted what was best for this team.

> "The primary role of a coach is to make the team greater than the sum of its parts."
>
> —Bill Tschirhart

SECTION TWO

The Mental Game

Chapter Eight

Dealing with Disappointment

"Fight on my men;
A little I'm hurt: but not yet slain;
I'll just lie down and bleed awhile;
And then I'll rise and fight again."

—Sir Andrew,
Fourteenth-century Scottish Warrior

*I*n the NHL, NBA, NFL, and MLB (Major League Baseball), there are only thirty to thirty-two teams vying for a league championship. Thirty or thirty-one teams will end the season in disappointment, if one views winning it all as the final criteria for success. Dennis Green, the former head coach of the Minnesota Vikings and now current coach of the Arizona Cardinals, would be the equivalent of the Territories' entry at a Hearts or Brier in terms of championships.

He usually has a pithy way of summarizing a game or a season. After his first season as head coach and rebuilding the Vikings, the team made the playoffs for the first time in a couple of years and then lost their opening round playoff game in a nail-biter. After the game, a very disappointed-looking Dennis Green was interviewed. He was asked to put his first season coaching the Vikings into perspective before leaving for the locker room to console his players. Green simply said, *"unfulfilled success!"*

Curling at the regional or local level has a bittersweet way of dealing with championships. Usually there are three or four events at each bonspiel with a first place winner in each event, but there are also prizes or cash for the second to fourth place finishers in each event. Professional sports leagues also have money for each of the qualifying playoff teams regardless of how far they advance along the playoff trail. But for the teams with great expectations, even if they place in the qualifying spots whether in curling or any sport, disappointment can be a huge issue. We're number two or we're number eight can have a pretty hollow ring to it.

Going onto provincial playdowns leading to a Heart or Brier leaves the curling path full of disappointed players and teams. In Canada it varies from province to province, but in most cases each province begins with a minimum of forty entries to as many as two hundred or more vying for that coveted Purple Heart or Scott Tournament of Heart Ring. Multiply that by twelve because of the Northern Ontario and Territories entries, and we have a minimum of 480 to well over 1,200 entries for Canada alone. Granted, there are probably only fifteen to twenty legitimate contenders in each region or province, but still there are close to 2,400 teams on both the men's and women's sides that have a shot at winning Canada each curling season. Additionally, there is always the darkhorse entry who seems to win at least one of the provincial spots each season, and that team is not included in the top one hundred favorites.

That is a lot of disappointed curlers. NHL players will often pat themselves on the back and say the toughest trophy in sport to win is the Stanley Cup because of the potential of twenty-eight games played in a two-month period. Usually twenty-two to twenty-four games will win a Stanley Cup. Being a Canadian, I will give them this honor at the pro level.

If a Canadian curling team gets hot at the playdown level, they may play as few as twenty-eight games in order to win a Heart or Brier championship. But in most cases these teams will play thirty to forty games, needing at least a 75 to 80 percent winning percentage along the way, with no best of seven chances to give more opportunities to advance. The mental and emotional strain for the highly competitive is as demanding as any professional or amateur sport.

I have talked with many curlers who have either given up playing the game or have settled for purely recreational enjoyment because the disappointments just added up much too high to continue on pursuing a Purple Heart or Hearts Ring. The time, effort, sacrifice, and broken dreams along the way were too much to handle.

Many curlers will take a competitive leave of absence or a curling sabbatical after a heartbreaking loss or disappointing season. Mark Dacey was going to take a one-year hiatus after three or four near misses of gaining his first Purple Heart in Saskatchewan in the early '90s. As fate would have it, he got two calls to play third for a competitive men's team and second for a mixed team. Mark had a choice to make. Say no and take the year off, or try something different and not skip for a year or two to see what happened. Mark, of course, chose the latter.

Mark went on to win his first Purple Heart in 1995, throwing third stones for Brad Heidt, and they went on to finish second at the Brier. His mixed team also won the provincials and went to Sarnia, Ontario; placed well; and he met his future wife, Heather Dacey-Smith. She happened to be curling third on the team from New Brunswick that won New Brunswick's only mixed title to date. Mark eventually went on to win the 2004 Brier and a Canadian-mixed with Heather in 2002.

But not all curling stories have ideal happy endings. One of Calgary's best is Frank Morissette who has knocked on Alberta's Purple Heart door for close to thirty years. In the mid '90s, he lost the provincial final in Calgary in an extra end to the Kevin Martin team. Many curlers in Alberta would give their tucked left knee to come that close. Frank was so disappointed that the second place silver tray his team won was placed in his shoe closet at his front door entrance and sat there for months hidden away.

Disappointment is part of life and definitely part of curling. From a purely mathematical perspective, our chances of winning a Brier, Scott, or World title are extremely slim at the best of times. Randy Ferbey may have put it best—after winning his third straight Brier with David Nedohin throwing skip stones—when he said, "I have been fortunate to win five Briers and three World Championships. Some very good curlers have never won a bonspiel." So how can we minimize the negative effects of disappointment and learn to view it as a stepping stone to improving ourselves and improving our game?

Consider the Life-Lessons Disappointment Can Teach

We learn best from metaphors, movies, music, and memorable moments (the "M" thing just came out). How often in our daily lives do we get good ideas that make a difference in our thinking, from recalling a line from a song, a film, or a lesson from the pebbled ice on a previous Thursday night? If curling doesn't do anything else but entertain and give you a social life—fine. But curling can teach us that, as in real life, progress always coexists with obstacles and problems along the way.

One of the best chefs in Edmonton told me he plays chess to get his mind working in a problem-solving way so that he can better work with fellow colleagues and clients. Curling teaches us not to panic and that life is full of variables and obstacles. Life and curling are seldom a smooth ride without setbacks. I like what Hall of Fame PGA golfer Sam Snead used to say about life and golf, "I became a better golfer and person when I learned to scramble from the first tee right onto the 18th tee. There is never a smooth round of golf, ever." The same is true for curling.

In the film *The Legend of Bagger Vance*, the main character is taught life's most important lessons through his passion of golf. He learns how to forgive himself and to get back to his "authentic swing" in both golf and life. Playing a game he once loved and paying attention to its life lessons were the major parts of his healing process after he survived World War I. How often have we as curlers used our own ice experiences in making better life choices at home and at work? And how often have those lessons been from a disappointing experience and learning to never give up?

Time is the Balm Which Heals and Restores

After the Buffalo Bills lost their first Super Bowl bid to the New York Giants on a last-second field goal, head coach Marv Levy called a morning-after meeting with his fragile players. Posted on the white board entering the meeting room was the quote from Sir Andrew which opened this chapter. Levy said he only posted quotes on that board twice in his career in Buffalo. This one became ingrained in the culture of the Bills during Levy's tenure and, to a degree, continues to this day. The Bills are still the only four-time reigning AFC champions, and they are still also the only NFL team to lose four straight championships.

This version of the Bills was known for its resiliency and ability to bounce back from disappointment after disappointment. People often forget that in the next three Super Bowls, the Bills were significant underdogs in meeting very powerful

Washington and Dallas opponents from the NFC. As Chris Burman of ESPN says of that Buffalo team and its ability to regroup and fight, "No one circles the wagons like the Buffalo Bills!" One of the keys to the team's resiliency was Levy's insistence that the team take some time before making any drastic decisions.

The deeper the disappointment the more important it may be to take a mini-sabbatical and regroup. Although this comes from my weekend warrior perspective, I have semi-seriously considered giving the game up on only two occasions. The first instance was in 1993, after a tie caused by yours truly almost cost our team a chance for our club championship. The second instance happened in 1997, after a heart-breaking come-from-behind loss in a bonspiel final at the Avonlea Curling Club in Toronto. Life just didn't seem fair! Sir Andrew was the key to perseverance on both occasions. (I keep his poem in my wallet.)

That 1993 loss was followed by a lot of soul-searching, one more loss, and a thirteen-game winning streak. This helped us win two club championships, two A-event bonspiels, and a B-event bonspiel win over a three-week period of time. Then, 1997 was followed by two years I'll never forget: ten finals and eight wins. On both occasions I had long talks with my therapist (wife) and consciously took some time to regain perspective. Sometimes there is a light at the end of the tunnel. We can learn from our disappointments if we choose to hang in there and remind ourselves that curling **is a game**, especially when it may have temporarily lost its true meaning and the fun it brings.

In Marv Levy's book, *Where Else Would You Rather Be?*, he asks the question, "What do you say to a team that has just lost the Super Bowl? . . . There was a five step formula I adopted to help us get back on track." His first point is to **allow oneself some time to mourn**. Time heals as we step away from the event for a set time. The other four steps he mentions are to **own up, recognize the good, make a plan**, and finally **go to work on that plan**. Levy's whole purpose in stepping away and letting time heal restores us emotionally and mentally; the commitment and expectations we make for something we care deeply about can drain us to the point of losing perspective on overall life.

Disappointment Develops Determination

Determination is often the one attribute that separates the very good athlete from a great athlete. Every high-level curler will tell you that there was a lot heartbreak along the journey both before and after winning significant events. Winnipeg's Gary Ross skipped one of Manitoba's top teams for almost forty years. In both Winnipeg and Manitoba, he was one of the most respected players on the circuit, yet he may hold the record for disappointments in provincial final games at a national event.

In both men's and senior men's play, his teams were zero and ten in finals heading into the 2000–2001 curling season. His team finally won the big one in the Manitoba Seniors. Ross represented Manitoba well at the 2001 Seniors hosted by the Calgary Curling Club. They fought their way into the playoffs to eventually meet Edmonton's Tom Reed in the final. Reed's Alberta team went into the final with a perfect undefeated record. Team Ross beat Alberta in the final on last rock, which was set up by a Tom Reed shot that picked to set up the national championship. Curling justice or karma—perhaps. Ross is one and ten in provincial finals and now one and zero in national finals. Tom Reed, who would easily echo these comments on disappointment, hung in there and with his exact same line-up of players, won the 2003 Canadian Seniors to go along with his three Purple Hearts.

In referring to the lessons disappointment can teach, the apostle Paul said, ". . . we rejoice in our sufferings, because we know that suffering produces determination; determination produces character, and character produces, hope. And hope does not disappoint us . . ." We should not forget that Al "the Iceman" Hackner, one of the greatest curlers ever, was once labeled as someone who couldn't win the big one.

Hackner and his Northern Ontario rink went to two straight Brier finals in 1980 and '81 only to lose to Rick Folk and Kerry Burtnyk. The 1981 final may have been one of the most painful of any final in history. Hackner finished first in the round-robin portion of the Brier and earned a direct berth to the Brier final versus the youngest-ever skip to win a Brier, Manitoba's Kerry Burtnyk. Hackner was two up coming home, and his rink had curled an unbelievable, almost flawless, week. Their defense was almost perfect that entire week until the tenth end of the final game. The only time all week his team gave up more than a deuce was in that dramatic final end versus Burtnyk.

Hackner never gave up. He came back for his third straight Brier appearance and third straight Brier final in 1982, winning both the Brier and the Worlds. Then in 1985, his team won it all again. Rick Lang, Hackner's third, said of that 1985 season that he could count fifteen or seventeen times during their Brier run and down the playdown trail when if Hackner hadn't made his last shot in certain games, they would have been eliminated from going on. Those earlier set-backs and disappointments only served to deepen the team's level of determination and to mature them as players. Lang doesn't know of many other players who could have skipped and played as well under pressure as Hackner in that 1985 season of dramatics.

The Brier final alone versus the undefeated Pat Ryan team is still talked about as perhaps the most dramatic final in Brier lore. Hackner's thin double for two in the tenth to force an extra end is still revered as the greatest shot in Brier history. Ian Tetley, his second man in 1985, went on to win two more Briers and Worlds after hooking up with Eddie Werenich and then with Wayne Middaugh.

The Iceman is still talked of in almost reverent tones by those who watched his teams through the '80s and into the '90s. He was, and still is, known as a wily veteran who gives his teams a sense of hope whenever he stands at the tee-line or sits in the hack ready to throw. Bertie C. Forbes may have put it best when she said, "History has demonstrated that the most notable winners usually encountered heartbreaking obstacles before they triumphed, this was because they refused to become discouraged by their defeats."

Be a Big-Picture Person—Gain Perspective

Actor-comedian Steve Martin says, "The problem today is that the only success is a total success. And a lot of things don't fall into that category." If we view ourselves as curlers/athletes first, regardless of our talent level, and not as growing complex human beings, disappointment on the ice will color our lives in a very myopic, or narrow, way. It may be important to remind ourselves that seldom, if ever, will people be drawn to us as friends or support system because we can draw the four-foot almost any time under any circumstances.

The legacy we leave in life, the influence we have on others, and how we love others are actually more important than the outcome of a big bonspiel or provincial, state, or regional championship.

Whether you like Dr. Phil, Dr. Victor Frankl, Mother Teresa, or David Letterman, they will all tell you that character is still the drawing card for friendship and that it is leaving a legacy, not performance in work or sport, that matters. Gaining perspective is easy to say but hard to practice for all of us, especially after a huge disappointment preceded by huge expectations.

In 2000, Brad Gushue of Newfoundland lost the Canadian Juniors on last rock. His team psychologist reminded Brad that he would probably only make 80 percent or so of his last shots because he was about an 80 percent shooter. He asked Brad how many last shots he thought he had made? Brad thought for a minute and said probably about 80 percent. So why should it be different on last rock or in overall shooting with all the factors involved? Brad said, "This talk with our team psychologist brought me into perspective. I still probably make around 80 percent of my last shots, but in the 2000–2001 season when we won both the Canadian Juniors and the Worlds, I never missed one last shot all season."

Gaining perspective may be the most important factor in dealing with disappointment. My guess is you started curling because the game was fun. You continued in the sport because it was fun. Somehow we must keep the joy in our passion for curling to continue through the disappointing times. When we lose perspective, we can lose our desire to compete, and it can filter down into other areas of life.

Claudia Church, my co-author on another project and a Top 40 *Billboard* country artist, actress, author, and model who lives in Nashville said,

> When our passions lose perspective . . . it can take away the beauty and innocence of the dream or passion we began with. When the joy is gone and it just becomes a contest, who becomes the judge in this unfair world of rating our worth? Therefore, if we don't come out the victor in wins and losses or in sales and ratings, we too often feel less than as people. . . . We must remind ourselves of the source of what is causing us to feel like failures in our disappointments. If it is just critics, or fans who don't know our hearts, we must consider the source.

Sometimes a long walk, a "perspective talk" with your significant other or a teammate may put disappointment into perspective. A trip to the soup kitchen was former NFL coach and TV analyst Sam Wyche's cure for the "small world-view disease." He said that he lived in such an unrealistic world of expectations and unreality in pro football (which he still loves) that he needed to consciously swing the pendulum the other way. Or just phone your mom, and she'll set you straight.

The roots of disappointment mean you are a passionate person who cares deeply about your expectations, whether misplaced or not. This shows that you are alive emotionally and spiritually because you have passion. Passion never guarantees success, but there are no significant accomplishments without it.

Learning to deal with disappointment on the ice can be an informal mentor because when disappointments occur and the lessons are assimilated, you will become a more tolerant, sympathetic person who will be a walking advertisement of one who never gives up.

> ". . . so you lost. At least you were in the arena of life competing. That is better than those sorry souls who didn't have the courage to at least even try."
>
> —Theodore Roosevelt

Chapter Nine

Feel the Fear and Curl Anyway

"I am the most negative human being on the planet. I thrive on negative energy."

—Anne Montiminy,
Canadian Olympic Multi-medallist in Diving

One of the many questions we liked asking curlers was who they admired in other sports. Peja Lindholm was inspired a lot by Swedish tennis great Bjorn Borg. Sandra Schmirler loved the World Series-winning Toronto Blue Jays of the early 1990s. Wayne Middaugh is inspired by the aggressive nature of his golfing hero, Tiger Woods. Every Saskatchewan-based curler wore Rider Pride stickers on their brooms, curling bags, or had the stylized "S" tattooed on various parts of their bodies. And, when we interviewed Marie-France Larouche's Quebec City-based team, two of their heroes were Olympic champion divers Annie Pelletier and Anne Montiminy.

Annie Lemay, the second of Team Larouche, and Marie-France were especially inspired by the heroic comebacks of both Pelletier (who gets my vote and that of CBC's Brian Williams for the Canadian version of the film *Perfect Ten*) and Montiminy who were both written off after Olympic failures the four years before they medalled. Montiminy maybe had one of the gutsiest comeback performances ever for a Canadian Olympian. She was ranked fourth in the world going into the 1996 Olympic Games and bottomed out in a very disappointing twenty-fourth place. Four years later at the 2000 Olympics in Sydney, she won a very inspiring bronze medal, the first medal ever won by a Canadian at the Olympics in ten-meter platform diving. She barely made it out of the preliminary round to advance to the semi-final round with seventeen other divers. In the semi-finals, she was again just adequate to qualify for the final round of dives. She was ranked near last place going into the final round of twelve divers who made it through to the semi-finals. In the final round, she was simply outstanding, moving up in the standings to win her bronze. It was one of the biggest ever come-from-behind performances in a major diving event.

Anne Montiminy explained why she thrives on negative energy in the *MacLean's* magazine 2000 Olympic special edition. The article explains how she uses this negative energy for motivation:

> Anyone who has met Montiminy knows her vibrant personality and brilliant smile suggest otherwise. But, she says she performs better when she heads into meets thinking she could finish last. Conversely, she blames her disappointing 24th place finish at the Atlanta Olympics in 1996 to feeling, well, too darned relaxed and confident. She was ranked fourth in the world and seemed a good bet for a medal. "I remember that I slept so well before the event, and that's not good for me."

> After that unfortunate day she ordered herself a five-month rest from the boards to contemplate her career. "I think the time off actually helped me get rid of some bad habits. My skills are a lot better now."

Curling Psych 101

The negative energy Anne Montiminy speaks about is based in fear, but it doesn't have to disable our performance. There are varying degrees of fear we all have to deal with, from overwhelming terror—which is usually based in being totally unprepared—to twinges of nervous excitement before an opportunity you have dreamed of or prepared for sufficiently. We all have the emotion of fear in our lives, and, if we didn't, we wouldn't be human. The great long-distance runner Alberto Salazar once said, "At a marathon start line, everyone is afraid."

However, the key to dealing with fear is learning how to manage the emotion. Fear does not have to control our choices or how we carry on with life. The influence of an emotion can be very strong in persuading us to choose a certain direction, be it positive or negative, but a healthy choice can always trump a negative emotion for the maturing athlete. Mentally strong curlers find a way to keep their minds on the constructive process and give themselves opportunities to be successful. They aren't controlled by negative emotions but are controlled by their healthy choices.

Allen Cameron of the *Calgary Herald* is one of Canada's best curling writers. He has written stories and articles on most of the top players over the last couple of decades and says:

The great ones that stand apart are mentally tough. They know how to deal with distractions and negative thoughts. I'm sure they must have them, but they sure know how to deal with them. If or when Colleen Jones gets some negative press, I'm sure she is not even aware of it. She seems to just block things out. She is so into her focus and routine. Kevin Martin's ability to bounce back amazes me. He has lost more than his share of heartbreakers at the world level but never gives up. This would shatter some curlers, and you'd never hear from them again. Pat Ryan is one of the best I have ever seen at dealing with distractions. Shannon Kleibrink never seems to get rattled. Her ability to forget is stunning. Nothing fazes her. It's as if she is bulletproof. I once asked Shannon if she visualizes. Her response was, "Nope, never! Just my next shot!" It seems that the great curlers know how to forget losses, they have short memories, and they don't dwell on the past negative experiences.

Cheryl says:

Viewing our emotions as a metaphorical weather system may be helpful. Does a curler always curl in the high-80 percentage range when they feel their mood is like a sunny clear day, and does a curler always curl in the low-60 percentage when they are feeling like a miserable, rainy, windy kind of day and it's still Monday, with worse weather forecast for the rest of the week? Any curler worth his salt will tell you they have curled horrible games on days they have felt like their mood was like a perfect Hawaiian weather system before delivering their first stones. And any curler will tell you they have shot the lights out on days that have felt like a freak Arctic-like-Saskatchewan-blizzard-was-coming-on-in-the-middle-of-May kind of mood. High-performance curlers will tell you they curl well because they have chosen to get their heads in the game regardless of their mood.

In curling, fear can be used as a positive source in our lives when we realize its ultimate purpose is to remind us to prepare better and utilize what we have already learned. As Karo Gagnon, the third for Marie-France, says:

> I think the best way to manage fear is to think about or get yourself to focus on the task you have to do. When you are prepared and have practiced enough for an event, it is important to play in the present and not to worry about the possible outcomes of a shot or a game. When you start to do that, you are thinking about things that haven't happened yet and not about the task at hand; and this is when shots are missed or games are lost. I try to not think into the future when I am playing. Because if you think into the future, you are thinking more of possible consequences rather than what you are supposed to be doing to try and be successful now.

The opposite of fear is having confidence or a strong belief in one's own ability. Biblical theological studies (it has been pointed out at all three theological schools where I have studied) show that the main negative emotion God addresses throughout the Scriptures is fear. Fear more than any other emotion, when kept unchecked, can lead to inappropriate choices or to choices we regret. And His antidote to fear is always to be strong and courageous in our choices. In other words, choose the high road or do what we know is right regardless of how we may be feeling.

Don Bartlett, the longtime lead for Kevin Martin, may have put it best: "Whenever I am in a situation where the nerves may be getting to me, I always remind myself of what would Jules say (Jules Owchar, his coach)? If I focus on Jules' advice for the situation, I seldom go wrong." When in fear or doubt, the best response is to remind yourself of your training, past experience, and preparation in order to bolster confidence.

The best choice in response to fear is courage, focusing on what we know needs to be done, taking the high road. As the late great actor John Wayne put it, "Courage is being scared to death but saddling up anyway." Fear is simply God or nature's way of warning us of potential danger or reminding us to prepare ourselves for what we are about to encounter. It is our responsibility to remember the preparation we have already done and to apply it appropriately.

In curling, if we allow our negative fears to govern our choices and how we perform, we either play in a timid fashion and play under our potential, or we try and play out of our character and we begin to beat ourselves with mental mistakes. As Cheryl says so often, "This happens because our focus is on our fears and not on our game plan or preparation. Fear becomes negative when we become paralyzed or timid in our decision-making, which can be a result of a lack of preparation. We can become cavalier and try to be someone we are not in order to compete with an opponent we respect much too much."

Cathy Overton-Clapham, one of Manitoba's most successful curlers, currently curls the third position with the 2005 Scott champions, Jennifer Jones' team. She has been to five Scotts and has been on two winning teams, the first time in 1995 with Connie Laliberte. Cathy held the broom in St. John's, Newfoundland, in the 2005 final versus the upstart Jenn Hanna and her young Ottawa-based team. Jones made maybe the most sensational looking "in-off" ever to win a national final at any level.

Overton-Clapham captures how preparation and experience trumps whatever nerves or fears one may be feeling:

I'm sure this will sound strange, but I wasn't nervous at all when Jennifer went to throw her final stone. I totally knew she would make it. If she threw it right, which I knew she would, and I called the line right, we'd make it. Part of the reason I felt so confident was that we had played on that side of the sheet earlier in the week against British Columbia's Kelly Scott and the ice was reacting in the same way. Also, we knew two shots earlier that Jennifer might have to play the in-off, so we were already thinking in that direction. We were so thankful Jenn decided to play her other shot to guard, so we were already thinking about trying that shot for the win. And I know part of the reason we had such confidence was that we were playing all week and our confidence was at a good level, we were throwing well and reading the ice very well. We just had to focus on executing what we had to do.

In 1987, I skipped a junior team to the Manitoba final to go on to the National Juniors. I missed a wide-open hit on my last rock to lose. All I had to do was make contact; I could even roll out and we would have won. I was playing third on the team from Manitoba the year before that won provincials, and I thought we were a lock to win and go back. That shot haunted me. I had a hard time dealing with that miss. After that miss my dad suggested I go for a visit to Cal Botterill, a sports psychologist in

Winnipeg. He taught me the importance of "parking situations." What he meant by parking was to put those things out of my control in a place in my mind that wouldn't influence my performance. He reminded me to focus solely on what I could control in my performance on the ice. Now in these situations I remind myself how much I love to play this game, and this is why I practice as much as I do because, when I am prepared, I tend to play well.

Cathy went on to win the Manitoba Juniors in 1989, then the Canadian title and came home with a bronze at Worlds.

Fear plays a role in many inspiring Hollywood movies. We can learn from many of them. In the film *The Replacements*, Keanu Reeves plays a quarterback named Shane Falco. The watershed moment for the misfit football players trying to make the NFL during a lockout inspired this dialogue:

Coach—A real man admits his fears. That's what I'm asking you to do here tonight. Fears . . . let's talk about them.

Shane Falco—You're playing and think everything is going fine. Then one thing goes wrong. And then another. You try to fight back, but the harder you try, the deeper you sink. Until you can't move . . . you can't breathe . . . because you're in over your head. Like quicksand.

The team galvanizes as they all realize they have the same fears of failure and not performing up to their potential. The turnaround happens as they recommit themselves to their coaching staff and to working their tails off in practice to prepare for upcoming games.

In another Hollywood flick, but based on the true story of high school basketball coach Ken Carter, Coach Carter asks each player, "What is your deepest fear?" He is trying to teach that the main hindrance to playing up to one's potential is learning to manage one's fears.

Near the end of the film his star player and main malcontent, Timo Cruz, quotes Nelson Mandela:

Our deepest fear is not that we are inadequate. Our deepest fear is that we are powerful beyond measure. It is our light, not our dark that most frightens us. Your playing small does not serve the world. There is nothing enlightening about shrinking so that other people don't feel insecure around you. We are all meant to shine as children do. It's not just in some of us; it's in everyone. And as we let our lights shine, we unconsciously give other people permission to do the same. As we are liberated from our own fear, our presence automatically liberates others.

In the great *Star Wars* film series, Yoda, says this about fear: "Fear is the path that leads to the dark side. Fear leads to anger. Anger to hate. Hate leads to suffering." If he were a curler, he'd say: "Fear is the path that leads to mediocrity. Mediocrity leads to frustration. Frustration leads to team dysfunction. Team dysfunction leads to losing."

> "It's important to remember that you have to be way out of line to make a fool of yourself."
>
> —Cathy King,
> 1978 & 1979 Junior Women's Champion
> and 1998 Canadian Women's Champion

Chapter Ten

Dealing with Pressure

"Every shot is a big shot. Every shot in my mind is a defining moment shot!"
—Wayne Middaugh,
Two-time World Champion

Everyone feels the tension, the pressure, the nerves of a big shot, or a big game, or a big event. The best players have learned how to manage their emotions.

Pressure is usually viewed as a negative word, but it doesn't have to be. Many times, pressure is the excitement of a big moment that players have dreamed of for months or even years. Randy Ferbey says, "I get excited, almost giddy when I have the opportunity to wear the crest for Alberta or Canada. It's a wonderful feeling to wear that crest. We've prepared for four or five months to get to an event like a Brier, and I want to soak in the atmosphere."

Pressure becomes negative only if we allow ourselves to be over-whelmed by the moment or the event and play below our expected potential. Sandra Schmirler admitted that her hands sometimes shook before an important shot that could win her team a Provincials, Scott, Worlds, or an opportunity to win an Olympic medal. Yet, of all the curlers that have ever played this sport, Sandra is one of the rare few that most observers and colleagues would have picked to throw that last rock to win it all when it mattered.

So how do these athletes develop what we perceive as nerves of steel? The one key word that we heard over and over again is *preparation.* Georgina Wheatcroft said, "Preparation is the key. The best-prepared teams and players do every single thing they can to be ready for a game or tournament. Under pressure situations in games, it's a normal human tendency to speed things up and get out of your routines that you do when you are playing well. I like to slow things down in those kinds of situations and remind myself or my teammates of what a great opportunity we have in front of us."

Wayne Middaugh and his cousin Pete Corner started their preparation as young teenagers in Ontario. They are only a few months apart in age and lived a couple of blocks from each other as kids. Both of them played with Russ Howard in 1993 as his front end players when they won the Brier and Worlds. Wayne talked extensively about his practice routine with Pete and how they developed a mindset that still serves the two of them well:

> When Pete and I used to practice, we threw every shot like it was a last rock of the game and that something big was on the line like a Purple Heart or Brier championship. I still practice this way. To me, every shot I throw is a big shot and potentially a shot that could win you the game, be it in the first end, third end, or an extra end. I really like to practice with another person be it Sherry [his wife], one of my teammates, or Glenn Howard, who is one of my best friends. We always play one-on-one games with something on the line. With Pete as a kid, it was the typical—chips and a pop. I find when I play a game even in practice it helps me stay in that competitive mind space for when we are playing actual games. And my practice games I plan my shots like I would in a competitive game. For me, this breeds confidence, and, when it does happen in a big game, it's like I have done it before and I can take my mind to that place in practice where I already made the shot. Every shot is a big shot. Every shot in my mind is a defining moment shot!

Besides Georgina Wheatcroft and Wayne Middaugh, Cheryl and I asked about a dozen curlers very specifically how they dealt with pressure before an event, a big game, or a defining moment shot. The following is what these players had to say.

Greg McAulay, the 2000 Brier and World Champion from Vancouver, says:

I'm nervous before every game, usually until the first rock is thrown or you're being piped in at a Brier or Worlds. I never really get nervous in the sense that I get all excited or worked up if things don't go right, because I have always seen curling for what it is—a game to be enjoyed. So I think maintaining perspective is very important.

In Saskatoon when we won the Brier in 2000, we were in the runway before the final game versus Russ Howard. His team was just ahead of us about to get piped out onto the ice. My nerves were starting to go away, and then, all of a sudden, my all-time curling hero, Ernie Richardson, whom I had never really sat down with and talked to up to this stage, was bending down over the railing and I heard him calling my name. I looked up and . . . he says, "You're going to win this game, Greg, and do it for the west because the west is the best." Then I thought to myself, holy crap, it's Ernie Richardson. *Boy, did I get nervous all over again for a second or two, but then my adrenaline went through the roof. I started to get shivers up and down my body. What a rush to my entire body and the confidence I started to feel when I knew I had the greatest curler of all time cheering for me.*

When I am about to throw a big shot or defining moment shot—if you watch closely you'll notice my routine of rubbing my hand on my pants, I probably rub my hand even more to remind myself to focus only on the shot and not the results. My routine is the same all the time. I get in the hack and clean my rock. Then I stand and wipe my sweat from my hand onto my pants (even if there is no sweat) *and then I will focus on the task at hand, visualize, remind myself of the correct weight, and go into the mechanics of delivering my rock. I never think about the possible results of the shot.*

Pete Fenson, the 2005 American champion from Bemidji, Minnesota, and representative for the 2006 Olympic Winter Games in Italy, says what so many players say:

When I go to throw my last rock to win a game or a defining moment shot where you know you could take control of a game, I simply focus on the process or my delivery basics such as my kick and weight on broom and not worry about the outcome of the shot.

Sean Becker, skip of Team New Zealand, views pressure in this way:

I try not to think about it too much. I want to get in the right state of mind, to relax and enjoy the game. When I relax and enjoy what I am doing, I play much better. I also believe that before a big game or event I need to get the right amount of sleep and take care of any nagging gripes. (Nagging gripes is a Kiwi term to take care of those things in your life that are causing you grief or getting your mind to focus on things that are distracting you from playing or living up to your potential. Nagging gripes can be conflicts with family, friends, and teammates. I like to get them talked out and sorted out because I then find that I play with much more focus and confidence because I am concentrating on what is necessary.)

When I have a big shot to make, I block out everything in my mind and focus on the broom. Then I remind myself of the line and weight I need to throw. I like when my sweepers reinforce for me what weight I need to throw as well. All of this helps me to focus on what I need to focus.

Randy Ferbey handles pressure in the Yogi Berra way. Berra, of course, played for the New York Yankee dynasty of the 1950s. He is the owner of ten World Series rings—more than any player in history. One day in Berra's rookie season of 1947 his manager/coach, Bucky Harris, asked him to bear down at the plate and think before he swung. Berra says in his book, *Ten Rings*, "With that advice in my head, I struck out. That's when I told Bucky, 'How can a guy think and hit at the same time?'" Randy says he approaches every shot in that fashion. "I want my mind to go blank and just focus on the shot. I don't really ever get nervous when I throw, but I sure do when I am holding the broom for whoever is throwing last rocks of the end."

Peja Lindholm is among the most prepared players in curling today. He practices, prepares, and has the philosophy of leaving no stones unturned. Peja believes the more prepared you are the more comfortable you will be in a pressure situation both on and off the ice:

I believe in 100 percent quality in everything you do, whether it is nutrition, sleep, practice, or the actual games. This is grounded in preparation. I strongly believe that you will behave how you live and you will behave how you think. I like the movie title, The Untouchables. *That is the mood I want to create when I am out on the ice: untouchable. If you believe this in your heart, the more you do something the more confident you will become and you can become untouchable. And I will never throw a rock in practice, a fun game, and especially in a competitive game unless I am focused. When it comes to a last rock situation, I just focus on my delivery and not think about the results.*

Warren Hassall of Lloydminster, Alberta, was the 1992 skip of the Alberta junior champions. He and his teams are continually in the top forty or fifty overall on the WCT circuit finishing as high as fourteenth overall in 2000. Chris, a real student of the game, tends to get the most out of his teams. He always seems to find a way to do well in the Northern Alberta playdowns—what many consider the toughest region in all of men's curling. Chris's thoughts on pressure include:

I try to keep my mind clear and not overthink too much. If I find myself thinking too much, that's when I tend to get into trouble. You need mental breaks during the games or else you'll become too distracted. I think that is why Randy Ferbey often looks around at other games and watches other things going on. Not that this works for everybody.

I try to empty my mind of any distracting thoughts, especially with the big shots, and just concentrate on the fine-tuning things like strategy, line calling, and weight. When we won the Alberta juniors in '92, we won on last rock with a draw and all I had in my head was to look down the sheet and remind myself of the weight I needed to throw.

When you practice something enough, I believe you get what you earn. You pay your dues, so to speak, and you'll be more successful than not. I remember reading an article one time about a high school or college basketball coach in the States. One of his players was struggling with free throws and made a free throw in practice. His coach pulled him aside and told him to shoot one hundred more and to try and make one hundred out of one hundred as his goal. I always remembered that and worked on my fundamentals in practice. I find that when you practice something enough it becomes routine and it can keep your mind clear and you are more comfortable when the pressure hits.

Glenys Bakker is one of Alberta's best shot makers. She either curls front end or third, and is currently with Shannon Kleibrink in Calgary.

Glenys was with Shannon in 1997, losing that heartbreak final to Sandra Schmirler in Brandon at the Olympic trials and appeared in her first Scott in 2005 (she was fifth in 1993). She will be playing at the 2005 Olympic trials in Halifax. Glenys offers some great advice on pressure:

> *Breathing is so important. Everything speeds up in a pressure situation. So I try and slow things down. I concentrate on my breathing; I even slow my talking down. I know I need to play at a low-key level to stay calm. For me I won't even listen to rock and roll before a big game. I visualize because I believe it is so important. I imagine the whole routine from pulling my rocks out, to cleaning them, to my entire delivery. I even imagine what the crowds may be like. I try to put myself into the game as much as I can so that when it starts it's like I have already done it before.*

> *I learned a lesson that still sticks with me from the 1997 Olympic trials in the final versus Schmirler. I had forgotten about the crowd and the magnitude of the game. I was playing third and about half way through the game made a suggestion to Shannon. It was so quiet in the arena that after I made the suggestion the crowd went nuts. I had forgotten there were over five thousand people in the arena and a huge national television audience. I lost my focus for a second and consciously stopped myself and got refocused.*

Brad Gushue was the skip of the first curling team—no, first sports team ever—from Newfoundland to win a world championship at the World Juniors in 2001. He has since gone on to represent Newfoundland at three Briers. Brad lost a very disappointing last rock decision in the 2000 Canadian Junior finals that haunted him throughout the entire off-season. Brad consulted with his team sports psychologist, Bas Cavanaugh. As discussed earlier, Cavanaugh said something that seemed to be a bit of an "ah ha" moment for Brad, "If you are an 80 percent shooter, you will probably only make 80 percent of your last rocks as well. So you aren't going to make them all." Brad goes on to explain the process of working through his disappointment that led to his dream season:

> *I also had to learn or re-learn that I need to focus on my routine and stick with it, and not worry about or think about the possible outcome of the game when I am sitting in the hack to shoot.*

Bas also taught our team the "stop-start" routine for positive thinking. Whenever a negative thought begins to dominate our thinking, he taught us this little exercise to recognize the negative thought and to quickly replace it with a positive, realistic thought. Part of this is imagining or visualizing what I am supposed to do in throwing the rock rather than focusing on things outside of my control.

Brad tested the stop-start technique in his first major men's bonspiel in the following season. The team was playing in the Don Bartlett Classic in Gander, Newfoundland, and faced Guy Hemmings in a crucial game. Brad had to make a hit and roll for the win on last rock and had the opportunity to practice the stop-start exercise. He executed it perfectly and maybe exorcised an inner demon or two in the process. Beating someone of Hemmings' caliber in a WCT event as a junior was almost as comparable to Brad as a game at the National Juniors. During that spiel, Brad had the opportunity to make three last rock shots, including a draw to the four-foot. He made all three.

As the season wore on, Brad's team won its Canadian Junior title and found itself in the final game fighting for the gold medal at Worlds in Utah. As the curling luck would have it, the final came down to last rock, a win or lose shot. Brad said:

I have to be honest; "it" was in my head. I had almost totally dealt with my last rock miss a year earlier, but of course, the media kept whispering "it" up during the season and especially at Worlds. As I was sliding up the ice for that last shot, "it" popped into my head. So I practiced the stop-start routine. I replaced the fear with the image of me making that last rock and what I had to do to make it.

As history records, Brad was perfect and captured the World title.

Sherry Middaugh has won just about everything there is to win in curling except for a Scott and a berth to the World Championships. Her team is continually in the top ten of the WCT in final earnings on the circuit. Her perfect day in curling, which shows how she dealt with pressure, happened in Kamloops, British Columbia, at the 2004 Canada Cup and earned her a spot in the 2005 Olympic trials.

The final day of the event was my perfect day in curling. I know it may never happen again, but, when I think of preparing for a big game, I will probably always think of that Canada Cup final. You can never totally recreate what happened that day, but it's a great model for me to remind myself of important things to remember when preparing for a big game.

We were about to meet Kelley Law in the final. The game was scheduled for the late afternoon, so we had a lot of time to kill. Our hotel was only a couple of blocks away from a local curling club, so we planned on going over there for a short practice. We had breakfast together at our hotel, which was very nice. We were on a first-name-basis with the server, which made things seem very comfortable.

After breakfast we walked to the curling club to practice. The ice was a lot heavier than over at the big arena where the Canada Cup was being hosted, so our goal was to throw our rocks only halfway down the sheet of ice.

The times all week for draw weight at the main arena were about the same as the half-way point of the club ice. I think the people who were curling in a regular league at the club must have wondered what was wrong with us in that we weren't even making the hog lines with our draws.

I bet they wondered how in the world our team made the final, but we wanted to play under the ice conditions we had been playing under all week. We thought there was no point in fighting the conditions at the club where we were practicing.

After practice, we headed back to the hotel for some down time. When it came time to go to the main arena, three of us chose to drive with our host driver, and Sheri Cordini decided to walk the few blocks to prepare herself for the game.

I don't know if I ever felt more energized, intense, and relaxed before such an important game. My energy level and feeling of confidence was as good as I ever felt.

Handling pressure comes down to a couple of important principles for the high-level curler. These include proper preparation and getting oneself to a comfort level where one's mind is focused only on the task at hand and releasing the myriad of distractions that can steer us away from competing at our best.

In the baseball film *For Love of the Game,* Kevin Costner plays a veteran pitcher by the name of Billy Chapel who is in the twilight of his career. His Detroit Tigers are out of the pennant race and wrapping up the season against the New York Yankees. The Yankees need the win to have a shot at the playoffs, and Chapel pitches the game of his life, flirting with a perfect game.

As the game begins, there is a great scene which shows how the veteran pitcher deals with the distractions of a hostile Yankee Stadium crowd and how he deals with his nerves. Chapel says to himself, "Clear the mechanism." As he says this statement, the movie goes into slow motion, and Chapel enters a zone where it's just him, the catcher, and the batter. Throughout the game whenever he finds the pressure getting to him, he stops himself and reminds himself to "clear the mechanism," and he re-enters the zone he needs to be in to perform.

"Clear the mechanism!"

—Kevin Costner as Billy Chapel
in *For Love of the Game*

Chapter Eleven

The Intangibles

"When will we ever learn that the most important things in life are rarely the things we can see, taste, touch, or smell? The most important things are the invisible things that make the biggest difference in getting ahead in life."

—Venus Flytrap,
Radio DJ on *WKRP in Cincinnati*

As curlers, we all know that success at any level takes more than mere talent, knowledge of the game, or finding the four best players available. There is usually one or more unseen elements, or intangibles, that will take a player or team to a more consistent level of winning. These unseen intangibles are what tend to make the fine line difference.

The intangibles that work are as varied as our personalities or as diverse as drops of pebble spray on the curling ice. These curling case studies, or vignettes, are from various aspects of the game that show how wide ranging intangibles can be. We'll explore a ceremony in a cemetery, the Los Angeles Kings' field trip to a curling club, some curling preachers, a Schmirler story, and one of my favorite senior curlers, from whom I always seem to learn something when we compete.

Our first vignette is with Cathy King (née Borst) and her 1995 Alberta women's curling champion team of Heather Nedohin (née Godberson),

Brenda Bohmer, and Kate Horne. They talked quite openly about one of the key intangible moments that caused their team to jell.

The team was in Medicine Hat, Alberta, and was on the verge of capturing its first provincial championship. The team valued chemistry and worked on developing a strong team culture. This was also the year the *Chicken Soup* book series hit the market. Team King was reading the first *Chicken Soup* book and read a story of someone going to a graveyard to deal with fears and insecurities and putting them to death—metaphorically speaking.

In between one of their games, the team ventured out to have a little ceremony at one of Medicine Hat's local cemeteries. All the team members wrote out their fears and insecurities on a piece of paper and buried or burnt them as a symbol of not being controlled by their inner fears.

The team felt that this simple exercise was one of their key team bonding moments in leading up to their first Alberta title. The exercise helped the team members focus on what they could control and not get caught up in the little mind games that could have caused fear to sabotage their chances of success. Afterward, whenever they drove by a cemetery, it became a positive reminder of putting their fears to rest.

The next example tells of a hockey story based in curling. I was quite fortunate to work on a writing project that took me on a few trips to Los Angeles in 2001. I was reading the *Los Angeles Times* and came across this gem of a story in the sports page. The article relayed that the Los Angeles Kings were going to the Calgary Winter Club to curl. This was too weird: reading about a curling club I live about five minutes away from in Calgary and drinking a latte near a palm tree in southern California.

The story focused on how the Kings were underachieving earlier in the season and in danger of missing the playoffs once again until a late season road trip took them through Western Canada. Kings head coach, Andy Murray, is originally from big-time curling country in Souris, Manitoba, and was wrestling with how to create some much-needed team chemistry to turn the fortunes of his hockey club around and get it to play up to its potential. He believed the team would start battling for one another if they could develop strong emotional bonds. Being good, healthy men with an abundance of testosterone, he knew a forced group hug would probably only make things worse.

Murray came up with the idea of taking the team down to a curling rink and getting his players to compete in something in a fun atmosphere. In the article, Murray and many of his players said the turning point of their season coincided with their curling outing in Calgary before facing off against the Flames. Was the curling the intangible that was needed for the Kings, or was their time at the Winter Club just one of a handful of dynamics the team did to turn things around? We'll probably never know for sure the full extent of the Kings' curling experience, but it definitely helped spark the Kings pulling together.

The team went on to become the second most successful in Kings' history, as they upset the powerful Detroit Red Wings in the first round of the playoffs. Maybe we curlers should have an old-fashioned game of shinny to stoke the competitive juices to improve our team dynamics when things are going a little south!

The Sandra Schmirler team's first major conquest was the Autumn Gold Curling Classic in Calgary back in the early 1990s. This team was often asked how they maintained such strong team unity and chemistry.

Whenever I cross the walking bridge from the Calgary Curling Club to the downtown Eau Claire Market, I recall a story they shared about talking through some team issues on the middle of that bridge between games at the Autumn Gold. It set a tone for their team. One of their intangibles was that whenever a conflict occurred, they would deal with it as quickly as possible. The key word here is when, not if, because this team understood that conflict was an inevitable part of life.

Their team rule was not to let a conflict go on for more than forty-eight hours before dealing with it. They made a conscious team decision to work on their relationships because they knew from observation and experience how important communication is on the ice. Playing with a heart free from unresolved conflict creates a freedom to concentrate on the task at hand rather than having your mind consumed by hurts or disappointments.

I compete in a national curling event nicknamed the Friars Briar (aka: The National Clergy Curling Championship), which is approaching its thirtieth season of declaring the national champions for clergy and church workers. The following story has merit, but I will admit also that it is a shameless promotion of my favorite bonspiel. The founder of the *Canadian Curling News*, Doug Maxwell, in his 2002 book, *Canada Curls*—which may be the most comprehensive historical and fun-to-read book on the history of curling in Canada—devotes three pages to the Friars Briar, more than any other non-sanctioned national curling event. Maxwell says, "Very few, if any, of Canada's major sports are so connected to the clergy as is curling. The first visit of Scots [Scottish curlers] to Canada (in the late 1800s) had the Reverend John Kerr, historian and curler, as its captain." Kerr published some of the earliest known curling books.

Maxwell goes on to say that clergy and curling were a natural mix, especially in the rural regions. The arena was usually the hub of the community in the winter, and, if a pastor was to be community-oriented, the arena was the place to be. The Friars Briar is one of dozens of non-sanctioned national curling events in Canada. The police, postal workers, the Legion, firefighters, and a host of other vocations and organizations have run events like this for decades.

The core of our Friars team had a major turning point back in 1996, and has gone on to win the Friars Briar four times in the last ten years. The team has earned a medal in all but one of those years since. That run started with a friendship bracelet given to me by my daughter Anah-Jayne when she was nine years old.

I was mired in a pretty good slump about halfway through the 1995–96 season and was constantly fighting myself over rotating my wrist at the point of release. Finally, while sitting in the hack thinking terrible thoughts and contemplating never skipping again or taking early retirement from the game I love, I noticed the friendship bracelet on my wrist and how the little knot was in a funny spot. So, without much thinking, I turned the little knot and lined it up with the straight part of my wrist that lines up with my thumb in the traditional hand-shake position upon release of a well-thrown curling rock. It was like my eureka moment! I stopped wristing my shots (or, let's just say I do it less and less). I told my team about it, and they all thought (or humored me) that it was a worthwhile reminder. We all started throwing with a consistency we hadn't quite experienced before.

It became the big reminder for the team to not break our wrists at the point of release when releasing our stones. I have worn a manly bracelet on my throwing hand ever since as a visible reminder of an invisible truism or delivery thought.

The little things often go unnoticed. There are certain players or teams you can play against where you can learn a lot about the nuances of the game if you choose to pay attention. A few years ago, one of the teams I played on at the club level in Calgary had a very raw front end, a rookie, and a third year curler. My third and I tried to encourage them about *good misses* in attempting to hit the broom.

One night we got absolutely killed by a team skipped by Lorne Danielson and his rink, former Calgary City Club Champions as well as regular zone winners at the Seniors level who have qualified for provincials. After the game, our team was bemoaning the fact that we had to have hit the broom more than the Danielson team and still got smoked. Why? There were two clear reasons. Their weight was always reasonably close, and, when they didn't hit the broom dead on, they missed it smart and always gave themselves a chance to at least make a half shot or better.

What a great lesson for our team that night. The mantra of our front end (which was a good reminder for us back end players as well) for the rest of the season was, "If we miss the broom, let's miss it the right way." It was a good lesson for our team that particular season as we somehow snuck into the club playoffs. The team was thrilled to death one year later when we met Danielson in a bonspiel final and defeated them with the lessons learned a year earlier.

The intangibles are the little things, the invisible things, which make a difference in improving one's game. You may never win a zone or represent your region or country at a major event, but you and your team may graduate from "C" or "D" blocks at your local club up to "B" or "A." Success is a relative term, but each little step of success builds confidence which can spill over into other parts of our lives.

"Someday you're going to find that your way of facing this unrealistic world just doesn't work. And when you do, don't overlook those lovely intangibles. You'll discover those are the only things that are worthwhile."

—John Payne as Fred Gailey in
Miracle on 34th Street (1947 film)

Chapter Twelve

Aim for Perfection—Achieve Consistency

Roy "Tin Cup" McAvoy—"Tempo is everything; perfection is unobtainable
. . . give a little nod to the gods."
Dr. Molly Griswold—"A nod to the gods?"
"Tin Cup" McAvoy—"Yeah, a nod to the gods. That we are fallible. That
perfection is unobtainable."

–1996 film *Tin Cup*
with Kevin Costner and Rene Russo

Being a Saskatchewan tuck-slider who has averaged eighty to one hundred curling games a year over the last thirty-four years, a person who played as many different sports throughout my life as possible, and who serves in a profession that claims it spends a lot of times on its knees, has taken a toll upon my knees. I landed in Dr. Gord Dewar's physio and acupuncture clinic in Calgary for some treatments a few years back.

The treatments helped immensely, but I also learned a major curling lesson that stuck with me. Dr. Gord is a competitive curler who plays on a Calgary team that has lost two heartbreaking Alberta Seniors Finals. He also donates his time for most of the major curling events that come through Calgary and offers his services to other tuck-sliders and players who suffer various aliments. Dr. Gord grew up in central Alberta and lived out a childhood fantasy with his previous job of being a railroad engineer.

"Cool job" he said, "but after doing the same runs over and over and over again, I needed a little more stimulation for my other passions in life." Thus, Mr. Dewar became a doctor and acupuncturist.

I became a victim (I mean client) of his for a few months. Every now and then he'd stick a needle in my skin in various locales, and it would send a kind of shock wave through my body. He would smile and say he nailed that one perfectly. So, in my delusional state, I asked him about the other 97 percent of his needles that didn't send these sensations through my body. He said:

> *The area I must aim for with the needle is about a dime in diameter. Every now and then I hit the spot dead center and that's when you get that feeling, but as long as I hit the target area within the perimeter of a dime, the same effect takes place regardless. I don't have to be perfect; I just have to be consistent within the area of the dime. Kinda like curling when we throw our stones at the broom. We don't have to hit the broom perfectly every time, but as long as we miss it the right way with the appropriate weight, we'll make most of our shots because we are close enough and we can use the sweepers.*

Curling, like most sports and life in general, does not need perfection to be highly successful, but we must try and achieve a very high level of consistency. Aiming for perfection but realizing consistency is one of the fundamental keys of being a competent curler. Elisabet Gustafson was at the Autumn Gold Curling Classic in Calgary during Team Schmirler's heyday. Gustafson went on to become the first and currently only four-time women's World Curling Champion with her Swedish rink. In an interview, she said:

> *The main thing I have learned from the Schirmler team was they didn't just hope to come close to making their shots, they expected perfection. They seemed to understand that perfection was impossible but because of this mindset, they make more shots than most of the other teams and it shows. We used to be pretty content with coming close with most of our shots, but against the elite teams we could only go so far because we had to be better. Our mindset now is to aim to be perfect, and with this attitude we have become much more consistent and can now play with the elite teams from around the world. And we make much more perfect shots than we ever used to.*

This principle of aiming for perfection to achieve consistency is beneficial to one's overall game and not just individual shot making. This can involve many critical items such as making an effort to create team chemistry, sweeping in sync with a teammate, learning to be on the same page with line calls, developing your team's overall philosophy, learning to broom each player as necessary, and creating the same team goals. Every high-level athlete desires perfection but not all high-level athletes have come to grips with the unrealistic expectations they place on themselves or their team. There must be some wiggle room in creating a good team atmosphere in relating to each other and allowing teammates to be human and make mistakes. There is a difference between sloppiness and making honest mistakes; sometimes in the emotion of a game this line can be blurred.

In trying to wrap our psyches around the concept of aiming for consistency versus perfection, it is important to grasp the idea that curling is not a game of justice. You can practice, develop team chemistry, bring your A-game to the ice, have your team play with consistency over the course of an event or season, and have your team do everything humanly possible within its ability to win that elusive zone, big bonspiel, club championship, or company spiel. Yet, you still find your team coming up short! Your team can out-play, out-curl, and have the higher percentages, and it may still not be good enough. Why? Because there are elements that are ultimately beyond our control.

Outside forces such as errant debris on the ice, an honest to goodness fluke by the opposition at a defining moment of the game, or a struggling skip who is curling around 52 percent but who makes that one out of one hundred shot can all throw a wrench into your game. And the list goes on. The opposition brings their A-game to the table even though they generally curl at C-level, or the ice changes by half a second at the crucial time of the game and your front end who is always on top of the timing of the rocks doesn't pick it up until after your turning point shot. Is there no fairness or justice?

As NFL coach Bill Parcells says, "At the best we can maybe control about 75 percent of the final outcome of a game if we do almost everything right in our preparation. We have to always keep in mind that there is an opposition who cares about the outcome as much as we do, weather/elements, unforced errors, and flukes because of human nature. Seventy-five percent period!"

The National Training Center in Calgary brought in Dr. John Dunn from the University of Alberta in the fall of 2004 to give two workshops to the high-performance curlers in the NTC program. John is the team psychologist for both the Randy Ferbey/David Nedohin and Heather Nedohin teams out of Edmonton. Most of Calgary and the area's best curlers attended. One of Dunn's workshops was on perfection and unrealistic expectations. After his highly educational and entertaining lecture, he concluded by saying, "If you don't remember anything else I have said tonight, please hold onto this tidbit of truth I learned from reading Bob Rotella's golf psychology books. Golf is not a game of justice! Curling is not a game of justice! Life is not just!"

Needless to say, I let these tidbits of wisdom distill in my brain for a long while after listening to Dr. Dunn. I found myself driving around Calgary and mulling over the simple but profound truth that curling is not a game of justice.

How many heartbreaking losses do we curlers go through throughout our careers? I have talked to countless curlers reminiscing over past losses that have caused sleepless nights; sometimes I realize that these losses happened thirty, forty, and even fifty years ago. I am as passionate as any Scott or Brier contender about my curling game, and I wager that you, the reader, regardless of your skill level, are as well. Maybe the goal is only to win a regional bonspiel, or contend for the local club championship. That session with Dr. Dunn has been therapeutic and has helped me come to grips in dealing with almost thirty-five years of heartbreak and success. Curling is not a game of justice!

Dunn's overall theme in learning to deal with expectations and motivating the high-performance curler was to aim for perfection while being realistic in knowing it is never attainable. Dunn reminded us all that we probably all tried curling initially because it was fun. We continue in the game because we became somewhat competent. We further advance in the game because we probably experience a level of success, which brings a certain amount of satisfaction. These are all very good reasons to compete, but it is also easy to lose perspective when we limit our self-esteem to performance in our passion for curling, or anything else in life.

Dunn's emphasis, of course, was to bring some perspective to the big picture. As he said:

Teaching this material is easy, but so hard to put into practice. It is so easy to forget all the great life lessons and enjoyment curling can bring.

*There are lessons of sacrifice, commitment, honor, and developing give
and take relationships in team building. There is also learning to deal
with disappointment, setting realistic goals, not giving up, and a myriad
of other lessons curling can teach if we pay attention.*

I have loved to read about and study two different coaches over the
years, Dick Irvin Sr. and George Lee "Sparky" Anderson. Irvin was a
twelve-time Stanley Cup finalist as a coach with Toronto and Montreal
from the 1930s to 1950s. He was a brilliant man who sired one of
Canada's best sports analysts, Dick Irvin Jr., who grew up in the curling
mecca of Regina. Sparky Anderson was the longtime Major League
Baseball (MLB) manager of both Cincinnati and Detroit, and won World
Series championships with both ball clubs.

Dick Irvin Sr. said, "In every season there are three or four games
you will not win—period—in a 70–90 game schedule if playoffs are
included. Just hope and pray they don't happen in the playoffs. Some
games your team will do everything right and still lose." He coined a
phrase that many sportswriters of his era really enjoyed. Irvin Sr. would
write off these weird losses or unjust losses "to the unseen hand!" What
he meant was that his team lost to a second-string goalie that got red
hot, to a weird bounce of the puck, or to a penalty call that obviously
was not a legitimate call. These were all outside factors that could not
be controlled.

Sparky Anderson had successful teams, often contending for league
titles, nearly his entire major league career. He was colorful, funny,
smart, and he even had the occasional cameo on *WKRP in Cincinnati*. He
never had a losing season until very late in his managerial career when
the Tigers stopped spending big money for players.

During one of his last seasons, the usually upbeat Anderson took a
short sabbatical because the losing got to him, despite how well a job
he thought he was doing. He came back refreshed and with a renewed
perspective and an insight that I highlighted and circled in my journal.
Sparky said, "Mastering the elements that lead to success won't ever
guarantee success—but unless you seek to master these elements your
chances of success decrease dramatically."

In our curling game, we must strive high with our expectations in
order to better ourselves. Aiming for perfection is acceptable in any
endeavor in life, but it must be colored with realistic expectations without compromising our standards of excellence.

Cheryl is someone who strives for perfection, but she has learned over the years to maintain equilibrium with her expectations. She would be the first to agree with Dr. Dunn when he said, "It is much easier to talk about having realistic expectations than actually having them when we don't live up to often unrealistic expectations." Cheryl hurts after big losses in playdowns, provincials, the Scott, or aiming for an Olympic trials berth, but she has ways to cope with disappointment.

In 2004, she lost at the Southern Alberta stage on last rock in the C-Final, which would have earned her team one of Alberta's final eight spots. Extra frustrating for her was that her team was having a great year, having just clinched the number-one spot overall in WCT world rankings. But after this disappointment, she did not have another major event for six weeks. She told me she grieved for at least a week, took some time off (maybe even two weeks) without any curling, visited her mom in Arizona, golfed a bit, then came back with a vengeance.

Some losses we will never get over. The key is to learn to live with them without letting them affect our self-esteem in a negative way or to lose perspective on other things in life that just may be a tad more important than curling. Because even if we do achieve perfection or come real close by our standards, there are still no guarantees we will have the continued success we expect.

In 1976, I attended my first of many Briers with my dad, Herb. We drove three hours from my hometown of Langenburg, Saskatchewan, to what I considered the huge city of Regina. It was home to the Roughriders and Taylor Field, so for me this was the big time. I still have the ticket stubs from my first-ever Brier draw. This was the year that Jack McDuff and his St. John's Newfoundland rink caught lightning in a bottle and won Newfoundland's only Brier to date.

My biggest lesson that day was watching Quebec skipped by Jim Ursel playing Ontario skipped by Joe Gurowka. The two games I really wanted to watch were my home province Saskatchewan on one sheet and this red-hot Newfoundland team playing a couple of sheets over.

Saskatchewan had a brutal Brier but won its game in six quick ends and McDuff had control of his game almost from the get-go, so the Ontario-Quebec game became my focus. This wasn't a hard transition for me because I loved Ursel's delivery and we sat right by his sheet. I kept thinking that Quebec should be putting Ontario away, but they couldn't seem to. I said to my dad after Ursel's extra end win that I thought the Ontario skip curled close to 100 percent. My dad said, "I don't think anyone has ever curled 100 percent in a Brier game, ever." The next day in the Regina *Leader-Post*, however, they reported that Ontario's Joe Gurowka might have been the first skip or player at any position to ever curl 100 percent in a Brier game. Perfection, yet he lost in an extra end.

Perfection may happen on occasion for a player or two on the same team but probably will never happen for an entire team. Regardless, the lesson here is that even if the skip who throws the final two stones of every end is perfect, there is still no guarantee that a win is assured. I'm sure Joe Gurowka would have traded his perfect game for a win over Jimmy Ursel and his extremely consistent Montreal-based team of the 1970s.

"I am careful not to confuse excellence with perfection. Excellence I can reach for, perfection is God's business."

—Michael J. Fox,
Canadian-born Actor

Chapter Thirteen

ABCs: Adversity Builds Character

"Progress co-exists with problems."

—Dr. Don Posterski,
World Vision Canada; Author; Sociologist

David Nedohin had just been part of a four-point blown lead going into the eighth end of the 2004 Brier at Saskatchewan Place Arena in Saskatoon. Throwing skip rocks for Team Ferbey out of Edmonton, Dave and team were on the cusp of winning a record-setting fourth consecutive Brier title.

The four-point lead wasn't blown all at once, but Ferbey gave up three in the final end to lose 9–8 to Mark Dacey's Halifax team. Dave missed both his shots in end number ten to set up Dacey's four-foot draw to win Nova Scotia's first Brier in fifty-three long years. This was the kind of loss that would drive some competitive players to say, "Enough!" and to walk away from the game. Dave needed time to gather his thoughts and get back on the road to perspective. He chose to rent a car and drive the five or six hours back to Edmonton in order to clear his head of the devastating loss viewed by well over one million curling fans.

Dave and his team went on to regain their Brier title in 2005 on home ice versus another Nova Scotia team, led by Shawn Adams. During the 2005 Brier, Dave said, "It wasn't so much that we lost that

Brier final [2004] but how we lost it." Meaning, of course, that his team felt they had given the game away rather than be outplayed after being four points up with only three ends to go. This wasn't the first game where Dave missed a last shot, but considering the magnitude of the game, it could have been devastating. But as history shows, the team rebounded with its fourth Brier win in four years to tie Regina's Ernie Richardson and his foursome. David Nedohin drew into the four foot on his last shot of the game to secure that fourth Brier.

Did Dave learn something from the loss of one year earlier? How many teams would get an opportunity for redemption at a Brier so quickly or even at all? The Brier history books are filled with players and teams who came so close, never to return again. If nothing else, Dave came back with more maturity, resolve, and determination than ever. Hard times sometimes teach new lessons, sometimes they reinforce old lessons, sometimes they make seasoned veterans like Dave Nedohin and Team Ferbey even more determined, and sometimes it's a bit of all of the above.

Adversity, or tests, happen to all curlers and curling teams. Adversity can come in as slumps, losing streaks, facing superior opponents, learning to come back when your team is behind, devastating losses, or work or family crises. Adversity can be one of life's greatest teachers. We don't have to always wait for negative adversity to strike before learning something significant, but for some strange reason, adversity seems to accelerate the process quicker than our successes do.

Teachers know that learning occurs best when the student is in a humble or coachable state of mind. Adversity tends to get our attention like few other circumstances. This is not to say one cannot learn through seasons of success, because it may teach lessons such as understanding and experiencing the process that leads to success. But, the key is to be in a coachable or teachable frame of mind.

One of my best and worst curling seasons happened back in my final year of high school in my hometown of Langenburg, Saskatchewan. Curling was probably at its peak back in the 1970s for my hometown. We had eighteen high school teams in our league and two nights of men's curling with twenty-four teams in a town of only 1,350. My dad was one of the more savvy players, having appeared in the South Saskatchewan Playdowns and was on teams that won bonspiels all over Saskatchewan, Manitoba, and North Dakota. He still curls masters and has skipped teams to four provincials.

My dad knew I had a love for the game and that if I was to improve, I couldn't simply curl at the high school level and expect quick improvement. When I hit grade ten, he made sure I curled with the men (often times with him) in the men's league to accelerate the learning process. He knew my game needed testing . . . a little adversity. In grade twelve, I thought I had the smarts to skip and win at the men's level. But just in case the winning didn't happen, I had a back-up plan.

I could play on two teams because the curling was staggered over two nights with early and late draws. I got to play on a second team as a third with a pretty good local skip named Cliff Ruduski. What a year! My high school team I skipped in the men's league finished twenty-third out of twenty-four teams, and my other team with Ruduski won the club championship.

At 7:00 P.M. my high school team would often get kicked all over the ice by the teams in the men's league, and at 9:00 P.M. my real team would be competing and winning the majority of our games in that same league. I always learned a lot in the men's leagues as a junior but learned even more about competing when I thought I was good enough to skip at that level with the losses piling up. But, I also learned how to win at that level by observing Mr. Ruduski's skipping style, which was to play to our team's strengths and take advantage of the other's weaknesses. He was very intentional in skipping this way and led a team to success that on paper should probably have only finished around the middle of the pack.

I remember my dad saying I could learn a few things by playing with him, and learn I did. The payoff, of course, was the club championship but also the high school championship, four bonspiel wins at the junior and men's level, and qualifying in four or five other spiels in the area. I curled 210 games that season as I had planned it so I had only two classes my final semester so I could get my honorary degree in curling. It truly was the best of curling years, but the worst in the win-loss column. Lots of losing and heartbreak, but enough success to keep me more than hooked.

Over the years playing, observing the game, and studying sports psychology, I have begun to view adversity as a friend and not to view it solely as a negative concept. Adversity can imply hard times, failure, and setbacks. But adversity is simply being tested in such a way that we mature and gain valuable experience for competing in tougher events and tougher opponents. The purpose of adversity when viewed as a friend or an ally is that we mature as curlers.

A team can enter every bonspiel under the sun knowing it is in over its head and never qualify in any of the spiels but approach these spiels with the intent of learning valuable lessons for the next season or future seasons. On the flip side, a team could go undefeated at a Brier or Scott and learn many lessons along the way, viewing the event itself as adversity—being tested by the best teams in Canada. It could be an end by end testing, with seeing challenges in the game scenarios such as being down and fighting back or sustaining the best team chemistry possible through learning to communicate and all be on the same page together, strategy wise. The bottom line with adversity is that if we can keep in mind that our goal is to gain experience, we mature as players when other tests or challenges occur.

Back in 1989, Joan McCusker and Marcia Gudereit teamed up with Joan's sister Cathy Trowell in Regina. Looking back fifteen years later, one would assume this team would have had even moderate success on the competitive women's circuit. But in 1989, Joan and Marcia had not yet been to a Provincials, let alone a Scott, Worlds, or Olympics. Cathy had not yet been part of a Canadian-mixed championship nor skip of a Saskatchewan women's Scott team.

They all felt that if they were to compete with the best in their sport they would have to play the best on a regular basis. So they set out to enter as many high-level bonspiels as they could, including Regina, Saskatoon, Kelowna, Winnipeg, and many points in between. Joan said in an interview for *Gold on Ice*, "We never won a dime, not a dime, but learned an incredible amount that still benefits us today."

One year later, Joan and Marcia joined Sandra Schmirler and Jan Betker to form arguably the greatest curling team of all time. Cathy Trowell, pregnant with her third child, took the year off from competitive curling, so Joan and Marcia needed a team. Perhaps Sandra and Jan noticed a maturity in these two up-and-comers from all the adversity they faced in the win-loss column in 1989. **Adversity builds character** or maturity, not perfection but experience, inner toughness, and confidence.

Claire Carver-Dias currently works for the Olympic program in Toronto, and is one of the Olympic program's most requested public speakers. In an interview specifically for *Between the Sheets,* Claire told us about the importance of remembering the lessons learned along the way, whether from success or failure.

Every person on my team kept a daily goal book. We would write down our goals for the day in the book, plus some steps on how we planned to achieve those goals (action plan). Every day we would record in our goal books our successes and how we would make improvements the following day. Those books were the greatest training tools I have ever used. Not only did they help us approach each training session with intense focus and drive, but they also acted as chronicles of our successes. It was a confidence builder just to think about how many seemingly insurmountable goals we had tackled and overcome that were recorded in those goal books. When a new goal seemed challenging, we could just look at those books and think, "I achieved tough goals before . . . what's so different about this one."

Recording experiences works for some people and doesn't work for others, but the point is to have some mechanism in place for yourself and/or your team to remember the lessons learned and previous obstacles overcome.

George H. W. Bush called these homegrown motivators. One form is oral history; another is having bull sessions when teams get together and brag on each other or remind each other of past victories. Bush would use phrases like "remember Iowa" when he was in situations where a comeback was needed.

During his first presidential run, he was losing by a significant margin in Iowa, but, with the help of his team, pulled out one of the more significant comebacks in political history.

The late George Plimpton, the zany and well-loved sports writer, lost a game of horseshoes to Bush after he heard Bush utter the phrase, "remember Iowa," under his breath. Many curlers in trying times will remind each other of previous games or bonspiel triumphs where they overcame the odds or learned a valuable lesson. I'm sure there are phrases said by curlers all over the world like "remember Yorkton," "remember Vernon," "remember Nagano," or "remember Duluth."

Will the 2005 Manitoba Brier reps say "remember the MCA?" Randy Dutiaume of the Valour Road Curling Club in Winnipeg was the favorite of the fans and many of the players at the Edmonton 2005 Brier. Randy came into the Brier as a virtual unknown to the rest of Canada. Like with the Stanley Cup-winning Tampa Bay Lightning of a few months earlier, the feeling from the experts was that his team caught lightning in a bottle. They claimed victory at the Manitoba provincials, beating out such world-class teams as Burtnyk, Boehmer,

Peters, Stoughton, Scales, Fry, and Lyburn. Picked to finish in the middle of the pack at best, Randy Dutiaume and his team of Dave Elias, Greg Melnichuk, and Shane Kilgallen, came one shot away from meeting Randy Ferbey in the final, finishing with a Brier bronze.

What is even more remarkable was the journey this team took to the Brier. Two months earlier, Dutiaume was essentially fired by two of his teammates just before playdowns. Thinking his season was over, Randy still wanted to enter the famous MCA Bonspiel with some players that could give them a shot at competing. The Manitoba Curling Association (MCA) bonspiel is one of the oldest in the world, and in most years, the largest, with anywhere from five hundred to one thousand teams. The winner receives one of the berths to the thirty-two team Manitoba provincials.

This was the last hope for Randy Dutiaume, with about one hundred other legitimate threats, including most of the aforementioned world-class teams, participating. Seventeen games later (16-1), Dutiaume won his berth out of the MCA. Few took his team seriously as they entered the traditionally tough thirty-two team provincials. Yet, the roll continued as they lost only one more game on their journey to the Brier.

All of a sudden Randy Dutiaume went from being questioned whether he was good enough to skip at this level to finishing a very strong third in all of Canada. How many Brier medallists have lost only six games their entire season together? At the Brier, he played like the seasoned curling veteran he really was, making clutch shot after clutch shot. In Manitoba he was a highly respected player who had been to a handful of provincials. Randy always felt he had a chance if he could find the right combination of players and click at the right time. Again, adversity builds character.

The forty-two-year-old Dutiaume had curled for over twenty years, and followed curling his entire life. Bob Picken, the Canadian Curling Hall of Fame veteran radio voice of CJOB and one of curling's top media people, said:

I remember Randy as a kid with his parents down at the Valour Road Club where I curled out of. He grew up around the game yet never took it seriously as a player until his early twenties. Really, his late twenties as he was on Canada's national fastball team on a few occasions. He also played semi-pro fastball in New Zealand. He has played at a high level of sports for a long time.

Randy Dutiaume is an athlete who learned lessons in other sports that he could apply on the ice. Handling pressure at the national level really wasn't totally new territory for him. Playing in front of large crowds and hoards of media attention wasn't entirely new, either. Playing fastball, which is notorious for low scoring, close games, prepared him well for the tension of playdown and Brier curling where each and every shot could conceivably determine the outcome.

Adversity builds character is a reminder that everything in life can make us better people or mature us as curlers if we heed the lessons. One of Canadian sports lore's most documented stories of adversity and greatness comes from the 1983 Stanley Cup finals between the New York Islanders (aka the Prairie Islanders, as over half the team was from Western Canada) and the upstart Edmonton Oilers.

The Islanders were on the verge of winning their fourth straight Stanley Cup versus a sexy full-throttle team on the verge of greatness. Surely, offensive explosions—the likes of which the NHL had never seen—could overcome one of the most disciplined defensive units in NHL history. The Islanders were getting "sports old," banged up and long in the tooth. The Oilers were averaging almost six goals a game, unheard of at the NHL level. However, when all was said and done, the Islanders won their fourth straight Cup in four straight games.

The young Oiler players were dumbfounded but quick learners. In the many versions of this story, it is told that Wayne Gretzky, Kevin Lowe, Andy Moog, and Mark Messier all left the arena together. They dreaded walking by the Islanders' dressing room. What they expected to see was a great celebration of champagne and screaming. They saw the celebration but didn't see many of the veteran players like Bossy, Trottier, Smith, and Gillies.

Instead, as they walked down the corridor they walked past the Islanders' training room and saw the warriors they thought they'd see celebrating with ice packs, stitches, massage therapists, and doctors. The message was loud and clear. These young Oilers hardly had any bruises, let alone stitches or black eyes, since they hadn't fallen down in front of pucks, gone into the corners consistently, back checked, or generally sacrificed their bodies for Lord Stanley's Cup.

Over the next seven seasons, these Oilers played with a passion rarely seen. They learned the value of defense, sacrifice, falling down in front of pucks, and playing with many bumps and bruises, and most important, the total commitment it takes to be a champion. The result was five Stanley Cups in seven seasons and some of the most exciting hockey every witnessed. These four players have all made reference to June 1983 in that arena on Long Island, New York, as the turning point in what it takes to win and win consistently. The Oilers did a lot of growing up that day in New York.

With her share of curling successes and failures, Cheryl realizes that the path to success is not a smooth one. Even for the best, that path usually involves three or four steps forward and two or three steps back. I like how she says:

> No amount of losses will ever make me quit this game. I get up, dust myself off, learn from the loss, and move on. I love this game too much. The day I quit will be the day I lose my love for the sport . . . or they put me six feet under. I'm not sure which it will be.

The key is remaining teachable and coachable because these lessons of adversity can always be used and transferred to other parts of our lives.

Success means different things to different people. Whitey Herzog went to baseball's World Series as a manager with both St. Louis and Kansas City. In the world of competitive pro sports, the primary goal is always a championship. In Herzog's way of thinking, however, the greatest coaches or players are the ones who have a way of putting their teams in a position for the post-season on a consistent basis, giving themselves the opportunity for a championship. His teams usually made the post-season and earned themselves a nice paycheck bonus. Success for Herzog was developing consistency in performance at the highest levels.

Mike Krzyzewski, or Coach K, is the coach of the Duke Blue Devils basketball program. He currently has the best winning percentage (.790) of any active coach who qualifies for the NCAA Division I men's basketball tournament. He has coached for twenty-nine seasons—twenty-five at Duke. He has guided his teams to twenty NCAA tournaments and has won three. Success for almost all university coaches is simply to be invited to the tournament. But he says, "Sixty-five teams start out, and sixty-four of them leave with a losing taste in their mouths. I've been at Duke for twenty-five years and have left the tournament with a sour taste in my mouth seventeen out of twenty times, or 85 percent of the time we have closed our season off with a loss, and we're one of the more successful programs."

Krzyzewski is the first to admit that success is not just about winning. Graduating most of his students, winning the Atlantic Coast Conference (ACC) countless times, and watching an overachieving team make the Final Four when it had no business advancing that far can all constitute degrees of success. For Coach K, his greatest satisfaction is players who mature and grow in character under his tutelage and seek to make a difference with their lives.

Success is a relative term. Building character or maturity is ongoing and lays the foundation for creating curling champions. This is not to say we learn to settle when we obviously underachieve, but we pay attention to the lessons curling can give in all its ways of challenging us.

Adversity builds character! The key to all this can be found in *The Drowning Pool*, a 1975 film that starred Paul Newman and his wife, Joanne Woodward. Woodward played Iris Devereaux, a Louisiana beauty who describes Newman's Lew Harper and his character. It seems like no matter what obstacles or adversities come along, Lew Harper hangs in there. Devereaux says, "You have no talent for surrender!"

Sounds like some curlers we know.

Chapter Fourteen

Playing in the Now

"There's really no magic to it. Work hard. Work out. Don't allow any complacency because that will kill you. I have learned you prepare the best you can and you'll win your fair share. There's no magic to it!"

—Kevin Martin

"You play out of your mind when you're out of your mind!"

—Cheryl "Yogi Berra" Bernard

Yogi Berra, the great catcher and hitter of New York Yankee fame, is well known for his pithy sayings and clever remarks. If he were born north of the forty-ninth, he probably would have been the consummate curling psychologist because of his perceptions into the mental game. At times, Yogi could come across like the bumbling television character, Columbo. But once you got to know him, he was well respected for his insights into the mental game of baseball.

I have thought for years that baseball and curling are the kissing cousins of the athletic world. Pitching and hitting are those isolated aspects of a team sport that are quite similar in mental make-up to throwing a curling rock. Catching a ball game is very similar to skipping a game in setting the strategy and tempo. Standing in a batter's box about to face a ninety-five mph split-finger fastball can be similar to sitting in the hack about to get your mind around a hack weight tap back through a port trying to wick off a rock and roll your shooter into scoring position.

From playing the game and writing about curling, I often find myself thinking of Yogi, Greg Maddux, Sparky Anderson, or even Crash Davis of the film *Bull Durham* when curlers start talking about the mental game and playing in the now. For players like Sandra Schmirler, Jan Betker, Peja Lindholm, Randy Ferbey, and especially Cheryl, the mental game tends to be one of the biggest areas of conversation.

Learning to play in the now is the ultimate quest for a baseball player or curler. And as the great Yogi likes to say, **"Ninety percent of the game is half mental."** Maybe Yogi wouldn't get his honorary doctorate in math, but he should have one in sports psychology.

Berra was trying to say that successful hitting happens when the mind is not cumbered with negative thoughts, looking too far ahead, or focusing on past failures. Berra admits to saying that the best hitters empty their minds and stop thinking, but he has clarified this comment recently. Yogi says that he didn't mean you shut your brain off entirely. Instead, you must learn to control what you are thinking and limit your thoughts in the batter's box to one or two beneficial thoughts, which will keep you in the present. Sounds like he has spent a little time in a hack over the years.

Bill Tschirhart of the National Training Center says the sports psychology books he recommends for his high-performance curlers to get "into the now" are tennis and golf books. Cheryl and I concur, and have both read masses of them. Books by or about Brad Gilbert, Chris Everett, Bob Rotella, Jack Nicklaus, Sam Snead, Harvey Penick, and Ben Hogan are great resources to study and would make great additions to every curler's library. But, I have often thought baseball was a slightly more realistic relative to curling because curling, like baseball, is so individual yet team oriented.

Even as a kid playing Little League, I would often think of the almost uncanny similarities of the two sports. Being from Saskatchewan and growing up in the glory days of George Reed and Ron Lancaster, football was my first love, followed by the exploits of Gordie Howe and the Red Wings. But, when it came to the mental aspect of sports, my head would always go back to baseball or curling to help my play calling or my feeble attempts of being a left winger for the minor hockey Warriors. I noticed that I maintained a respectable batting average when I didn't worry about past failures or get ahead of myself. If I could keep my head in the now and stop thinking of things that would distract me while in the batter's box, I could more than hold my own.

Sandra Schmirler had some very interesting insights into playing in the moment. She loved to talk about getting in the zone or that ideal place where your confidence is through the roof and you feel you can make any shot or call the perfect game. She said, "You can be successful without being in the zone. But, oh, if you are in the zone, you really do feel invincible. The normal adversities of the game are mere distractions." For Schmirler, this was the ultimate rush in curling.

Bill Russell played for the Boston Celtics in their glory years of the 1950s and '60s and owns eleven NBA championship rings—more than any player in history. ESPN and *Sports Illustrated* both named Russell the greatest defensive player ever. Russell said one of his all-time favorite moments happened in a regular season game. He said:

> *I remember one time in a game when I could do no wrong and everyone else on the court—on both teams—was playing equally as well as I was. This went on for five, maybe six, uninterrupted minutes before the referee finally blew his whistle and called a foul on the other team. I was furious! My teammates looked at me as if I was nuts. But all I could think of was that this beautiful plateau of accomplishment, flight at another almost perfect level, had been interrupted. I had almost forgotten that the whistle meant a couple of extra points for the Boston Celtics.*

It was like everyone on both teams hit the zone at the same time, and the beautiful essence of sports was completely tapped into. He experienced just the pure joy and love of the game. But, there is a subtle nuance here, one that Cheryl talks about. Being in the zone and being in the now are not the same thing, although they could be. Being in the zone is where confidence and ability overflow at a high level. Being in the now is focusing on the basics, which give you a chance to be successful. Being in the zone and being in the now at the same time is when pure artistic and technical merit points are perfect. You can be successful without ever achieving the zone, but you cannot be successful if you do not learn to play in the now consistently.

Bill Russell understood this well. He explains:

> *Success is a result of consistent practice of winning skills and actions. There is nothing miraculous about the process. There is no luck involved. Amateurs hope, professionals work.*

From a mental perspective, learning to play in the now is akin to being physically ready to play after all your pre-game stretching and warm-ups. The mind must also be in shape going into a game and obviously have mechanisms or triggers in place during the game to help keep in the now. This is all easy to say, but it is much more difficult to practice.

Trying to stay in the now and maintain a positive mind-set can be a constant battle. *What the Bleep Do We Know?* is an artsy alternative docu-film which came out in late 2004 that did much better than the writers of the film ever dreamed. In one part of the film, Dr. Miceal Ledwith, president of Maynooth College in Ireland, is interviewed about this dilemma of trying to live in the present and how much of a chore it is for all of us to maintain a positive mind-set. His insight seemed to come straight from the eighth end of a ten end curling game where a team has blown a two-point cushion "with hammer" and now finds itself down by a couple of points.

Dr. Ledwith says, "It's a wonderful idea, positive thinking, but what it usually means is that I have a little smear of positive thinking covering a whole lot of mass of negative thinking. So, thinking positive is not really positive, it's just disguising negative thinking that we have." So the big question for curlers, or athletes period, is why do we tend to spend 80 to 90 percent of our energy on the physical part of our game when we acknowledge that our game is 80 to 90 percent mental or emotional?

Coach and mentor Lindsay Sparkes encourages her players to get their minds to what she refers to as *the ideal performance state* because the game starts well before the first rock is thrown.

This was a critical concept for Team Schmirler. While stretching before a game, each team member reminded herself of the task at hand. As Joan McCusker puts it, "I remind myself of my potential. I leave my concerns at home. I don't feel good because I played well—I play well because I feel good. I choose to execute because I know I am capable. I don't allow any emotional baggage to control my performance."

There are not many curling books on the market, let alone curling books that deal with the mental game of curling. The few we do have at our disposal, whether written by Ken Watson, Eddie Lukowich, Paul Savage, or even the *Curling for Dummies* book, reiterate that successful curling is 80 to 90 percent a cerebral challenge. Many curling games are decided while stretching or having a contemplative coffee or fruit juice long before the coin toss has happened.

Curling doesn't use the Elias Sports Bureau that tracks statistics for Major League Baseball and many other sports. But one of the ESB's more unique findings for MLB is that almost a third of the runs scored in a baseball game occur in the first inning. Is curling any different in that many games are decided in the first end or two?

My dad has curled for over fifty years and has earned four zone crests plus a crate full of bonspiel trophies in Saskatchewan. He has constantly reminded me over the years that far too many games are won (or lost) in the first end. There are two main culprits for this. One is not having a good grasp of reading the ice right off the bat, and the other is that far too many players aren't mentally ready in the first end.

Playing in the now is not taking the basics or fundamentals for granted. It is respecting the basics that help you execute at both the individual and team dynamic level. Cheryl has a routine that gets her to focus on the basics of her delivery. Before every delivery, she says to herself "lift-back-foot-weight," which helps her focus only on her delivery and not the potential outcome of the shot or the magnitude of the game. This is a trigger Cheryl uses to keep her in the now.

There are as many triggers as there are temperaments. Heather Rankin, one of the WCT's top players, hums a tune before she throws. Arnold Palmer, the sixty-two-time PGA winner, also uses a little song in his head to keep his tempo the same for his pre-shot routine and striking of the ball. The song or the positive thoughts create a habit to follow the fundamentals.

Teams have fundamentals which create an environment for staying in the now. Cathy King, the six-time Scott participant and 1997 Scott champion from Edmonton says, "We have a rule that if you are not skipping you can vent between the hog lines and mainly to yourself. But, once you cross over the hog line to throw your next shot, you must be in pre-shot routine mindset. Otherwise you are going to end up missing the next shot, too." This reinforces to the player and team that the bad shot is over and it is time to get ready for the next shot of the game.

Being in the now has everything to do with living in the present. Cathy King goes on to say:

Close games are usually not a problem to stay focused in. It's the other extremes. If you are down, you can't get too far ahead of yourself so patience is really what you need along with a few misses. When you are

up by a few points, pretend that the game is closer than it is so you don't
get distracted and feel that you have already won.

Nine-time NBA champion coach Phil Jackson has said that the majority of his emphasis in coaching is to get his team to live in the present. He would always get his teams to pretend or he set other goals to keep his players interested when playoff spots were already clinched or games got out of hand.

When players are mentally locked into the past or future, they forget or become sloppy about the fundamentals they must perform in the present, which can easily come back to haunt a player at a critical time. This concept was not that hard to teach Michael Jordan. When he arrived in Chicago, Jordan was one of the few athletes who instinctively and consistently practiced this concept. Human nature is to either live in the past or to dream about the future, but the high achiever is one who lives for the present, respects the past, and has goals for the future.

Peja Lindholm understands the importance of curling's most basic fundamental skill to master when he says, "I will never ever throw a rock without a purpose, whether it is in practice or a game. If my mind is not in a good place before I throw, I will either pause in the hack or stand up for a few seconds, and, when my mind is back to the place it needs to be, I will then throw." It often seems that if a basic fundamental that makes someone successful is violated a person will start to digress.

Stuart R. Levine is the author of the 2004 book *The Six Fundamentals of Success* and illustrates that in anything in life there are generally four to eight fundamental principles to master to be successful. Levine says, "Living these rules or fundamentals will require discipline . . . and the biggest reason people struggle with success is they understand the basic concepts but don't follow-through consistently." The *Harvard Business Review* published a fascinating book around this very concept called *The Knowing-Doing Gap*. One of the premises of this book is that fundamentals are easy to understand but hard to do consistently because of the discipline involved.

Marv Levy may have best summed up the importance of focusing on the basics in his weekly column for NFL.com in January of 2005. He wrote:

It doesn't matter whether you employ the West Coast offense, the single-
wing, the no huddle, the Arctic Circle offense, or the hoochie coochie

because in order to win a football game, all you really have to do is run, throw, block, tackle, catch, and kick better than your opponent.

Curling is much the same but with only two basic technical fundamentals to master.

Over coffee one morning and going through research for *Between the Sheets*, Cheryl sounded like the femme version of Mr. Levy when she blurted out, "You know what it all it boils down to?" I thought she had stumbled onto the secret to life, so I grabbed my pen and notepad.

Hit the broom, and at least miss it on the right side, have a consistent release, throw the right weight, and, if your team does this better than the other team, you should win almost all the time. Really it isn't more complicated than that. If it wasn't for our mind getting in the way and cluttering up the process, it would be easy.

As a marriage and addictions counselor, I find that there are four fundamental keys to a fulfilling marriage called the **4 Cs of Love**: commitment, communication, compromise, and common values. Practicing these 4 Cs of Love will help a couple live in the now and keep their relationship healthy.

Throughout my twenty-three years of counseling, I can safely say that in 97 percent of the cases where a relationship is in trouble, one of the 4 Cs of Love is being neglected or misunderstood. In my own marriage of twenty-three years, I see the correlation between contentment and practicing the Cs of Love consistently. My affection for Carla grows, and I'd like to think vice versa. Neglect of the Cs of Love, even for a short period of time, and I'd almost bet that she begins to wonder if a trade-in may be appropriate. Overall, it's a reminder to both of us that we need to be practicing one or more of the Cs of Love—even after twenty-three years of marriage.

Under each fundamental—whether in a relationship or curling— there can be dozens or more nuances involved. There have been tens of thousands of books written on mastering the art of communication, and plenty of books, essays, and articles written on the art of throwing a curling rock. It's easy to identify the hows in each case, but hard to master exactly what to do.

I remember reading an article on the Iceman, Al Hackner, who owns one of the smoothest deliveries in the history of our game. Yet, he said that it takes him four to six weeks every curling season to feel comfortable with his delivery and release and constant practice throughout the season to maintain his delivery. If he doesn't, he feels he isn't much better than the average club curler. Fundamentals—the basics, essentials—are never completely mastered, but they must be worked on and honed throughout one's career just like a relationship in marriage. Let healthy compromise go, and twenty to thirty years of good marriage can slowly filter away.

To stay competitive, you can't live off past glories or fantasize about how it may all come together. If the mastering of the fundamentals is given only a half-hearted effort behind the scenes and if you are not using mechanisms during the game to stay focused on the basics, you cannot be successful. Focusing on the basics is what keeps us in the now. And how we get there is a matter of temperament.

"We are what we repeatedly do. Excellence, then, is not an act, but a habit."

—Aristotle

"Learn from the past. Prepare for the future. Perform in the present."

—Team Bernard's motto
from their 2004–2005 curling season Web site

Chapter Fifteen

Fatal Distractions

"During the off-season our team makes a contract with our wives or significant others so that we will all understand our plan for the upcoming curling season. Our families are so supportive and understanding anyway, and this helps us all minimize any potential distractions at home where we need the most support."

—Peja Lindholm

"You know what I think was one of the main reasons why we won this bonspiel?"

This was one of those rhetorical questions thrown in my direction in Kitchener, Ontario, at the 2001 Canadian Clergy Curling Championships (aka the Friars Briar) by Andy Jones, the one non-clergy player we could have on our team.

Jones continued on, "Because we made friends with the venue."

I asked him what he meant.

"Didn't you read your own book, *Gold on Ice*? Isn't that one of the things Team Schmirler talked about? How they'd like to get to a venue early to get comfortable with its surroundings. You know, get a feeling for the building and the atmosphere, throw as many rocks as possible, and try to make the venue or club like home field advantage. Get to know the ice technician, talk to some of the locals, and gain whatever advantage one can."

Jones was onto something. He really captured an important subtlety in giving your team a possible edge in winning. Our team had flown in from Calgary a day before this event began, so we took advantage of the extra time and went down to the original Kitchener-Waterloo Granite Curling/KWGC Club. The KWGC was a really cool, old building that had been around since the turn of the century. (Much to my chagrin they have recently rebuilt.) The building, to me, was like the Taylor Field or Maple Leaf Gardens of curling.

We arranged with the ice technician/manager for practice, and he set us up in what we called the dungeon for our team dressing room. This was a little bat-cave-like room just off the main dressing room where all the other teams congregated together. It was old and dingy, and we loved it. It created an atmosphere for downloading after games and for having our own place to stretch, talk, and joke around before the games.

Being in this room seemed to create an atmosphere of "spartanism" where we were instinctively reminded of the basics and what it takes to win. The room reminded me of the old hockey arena dressing rooms on the prairies. For some reason, the manager took a liking to us. He gave us little tips about the ice and treated us royally. Before the event even began, we all felt like the club was our home club. We came out of the shoot quite quickly and set ourselves up with huge momentum heading into the playoff round.

High-performance coaches of most sports talk a lot about distractions. Marv Levy says distractions can be different from team to team, although there are similar ones for every team. Family issues, romantic interests, businesses, time zones, playing conditions, illness or injuries, or, in the bigger events, trying to find tickets for friends and family are the most common. Levy says you can never eliminate all distractions, but you can learn to minimize them or prioritize them and find a balance. The key is to include the distractions you are aware of as part of your team's overall philosophy or game plan.

Larry Bird, the Hall of Fame NBA star and former coach of the Indiana Pacers, was convinced that close to 90 percent of distractions, came from the significant relationships in our lives. His players said that if they had an extreme off-game or a string of below par games, Bird would call them into his office for a chat. The first thing he'd ask is how things were going in their relationships. Bird said that in nine out of ten cases the problem wasn't the physical skills of the player but unresolved issues with these significant relationships.

He said it could be a spouse, girlfriend, business associate, child, or even parent. His solution was for these players to go home or wherever to straighten out the unresolved conflict, then get their heads back in the game. He would rather someone miss practice and go home and work on the relationship if that is what it took to get their game back. Deal with the distraction.

On the flip side, in the film *Slap Shot* and the best-seller *The Art of War*, distractions can be used to your benefit versus your opponent. But, before I go on, just a friendly reminder that curling is a sport of integrity with the self-governing rules that have existed for generations. The example I am about to use is strictly for a parable-like effect. In one of the scenes from *Slap Shot*, Paul Newman's character distracts the best player on another team by making rude comments about the player's estranged wife. Of course, the player he is trying to throw off is totally distracted, freaks out, and goes into a frenzy that earns him a game misconduct.

In *The Art of War*, it is suggested that you use the wiles of the opposite sex on your opponent as a last resort opposite an overpowering enemy. For what it's worth, this idea works in advertising far too often.

I have seen this tactic used accidentally on one occasion in a curling game. We have a family friend who modeled for a number of years and had a couple of Top 40 hits. Needless to say, "she is lovely in form and features and very fair to look upon" as the writers of the Bible would put it. She came to watch one of my curling games one night versus a skip who was fully aware of this woman's beauty and celebrity.

This team and ours tend to have close battles. On this night he made his first two shots, then asked me if the woman behind the glass was actually who he thought she was. When I said yes, he never made another shot, and we walked off in four quick ends. A win is a win!

How many times has your curling team allowed less than ideal ice conditions to throw you off and cost you a game versus an inferior opponent? This is when a distraction could be used to your benefit. Ernie Radbourne was the ice technician in the town where I grew up. He was considered one of the best in the area because of the horrible location of the Langenburg, Saskatchewan Curling Club.

My hometown is smack in the middle of the prairies, yet they built the rink over swampland. The ice we had was more than adequate, but on some days, the difference in draw shots from the home end to the far end could be as much as two seconds. Ernie learned his trade in

Regina at one of the best clubs in that city. He would remind us that the teams in Regina that tended to win the most city championships were those teams that played at clubs with less than perfect ice conditions. Or they were teams that curled at two or more different clubs to learn to deal with various ice conditions. He admitted that everyone loves ideal conditions, but the great teams and players learned to embrace the variances in ice.

Now, the early draws of the Halifax Brier in 1996 demonstrate an exception to this rule of bad ice. There are less than ideal conditions and then there is ice that can't be managed by either team, so the game becomes a crapshoot. Maybe two-time Brier winner from Alberta, Hec Gervais, put it best by describing that ice is more than just being the great equalizer. When a reporter at a Brier many years ago suggested that the ice conditions were the same for everyone, Gervais said, "I could give Jack Nicklaus a good game in a foot of snow."

At major events for curlers, distractions multiply rather quickly. A high-performance curler could easily go from a super-league or recreational mixed game one night to throwing at a national or world championship the next week. Great mental adjustments are required when a curler goes from crowds of two or three curious onlookers who just needed a place to sip their cups of coffee to sold-out arenas of ten to fifteen thousand people jamming the stands and nearly a million people tuning in over television. The biggest distraction the week before may have been remembering to plug in the block heater on your spouse's car. Seven days later you could be dealing with everything from media requests to sleep deprivation.

In talking with Brier and Scott reps, from Brad Gushue of Newfoundland to Michelle Englot from Saskatchewan, they all say their first national event is a lot like having your first child. Essentially, you learn as you go, mistakes and all. You may have received advice from some experts, but you have to experience the event yourself to really learn from it.

Cheryl has studied and thought about the issue of distractions a lot in context of major events. She sought advice from others who had competed at similar events before her first Scott and says, "It's not that all the advice didn't help and that you don't know better, but it is so easy for anyone to get caught up in all the hoopla and attention. All of a sudden, things you say can be picked up by a reporter and be in every newspaper in Canada and other interested curling countries."

Cheryl has found the major distractions for herself and her team-mates at major events involve sleep, crowds, media, keeping the team on the same page, length of the event, and the number of games. She feels the key is having a coach or team manager take care of the various outside distractions. Cheryl's coach is Calgary's Dennis Balderston, who has been to national juniors, the Brier, and seniors as a player, and knows firsthand how outside distractions can affect a team's performance.

Cheryl says Dennis is almost like the "team bouncer" or "front man." If someone wants to contact the team for any reason, they must go through him first. Marie-France Larouche and her Quebec team have a coach, psychologist, and full-time team manager. Manager Chantal Poulin takes care of all the outside requests and demands put on this very popular team. She may not be the bouncer type, but she is like a healthy mother hen.

Cheryl says that getting the proper rest is critical at a major event. By nature she is not a napper, but she finds herself constantly taking naps at these events. The emotional and mental energy of usually two games a day, where very few losses can be absorbed, can drain the strongest of souls. Physically the body needs time to reenergize. As Vince Lombardi preached during his heyday with the Green Bay Packers, a tired body creates a tired mind and a tired mind becomes sloppy and makes mistakes it may not normally make.

Cheryl also pointed out a subtlety that many curlers tend to forget at major events: they are often required to be at certain social functions even if only for a quick appearance. Selling the sport is a part of curling. The players-fans-media relationship has always been a major factor in the growing attendance at venues and constantly increasing television exposure, which can translate into sponsorship and even Olympic dollars. Being somewhat rested can help one socialize that much easier. Dennis helps screen phone calls and funnels calls after a set time in the evening. Some teams are even going the extra two kilometers by creating self-imposed curfews.

Learning to curl in front of large crowds can take some getting used to. The successful curler has learned how to embrace the crowd rather than being intimidated by it. Guy Hemmings of Quebec is the classic case of someone who has embraced and worked the crowd to his benefit. He talks with fans, waves at them, and gets them to feel they are part of his game. Guy is possibly the most popular player to hit the pebbled surface since the days of Mr. Paul Gowsell. And he must be doing something right because he becomes a crowd favorite whenever he curls.

He has curled at the WCT event in Yorkton, Saskatchewan, a number of times, and there is a definite rush of traffic at the turnstiles whenever his teams are playing. Guy has embraced the fans, thoroughly enjoys the atmosphere, and understands how fans can energize his team and keep the adrenaline flowing in a positive direction.

Rick Folk says another distraction can be the home team factor, or the crowd in general, cheering against your team. This would only serve to get Rick fired up. He said, "When the crowd is against us, I always feel it is our job to send the crowd home disappointed." The satisfaction of beating a hometown favorite can be one of the greatest feelings for an athlete. High-performance athletes have a tremendous amount of healthy inner pride and often perform at their peak when there is an "us versus them" kind of scenario taking place. Proving people wrong in a healthy way is one of the best antidotes for allowing bitterness or resentment to sneak in and rob a person of his or her full potential.

Sandra Schmirler had a little saying, "Kill them with kindness and on the scoreboard." Schmirler knew that this attitude keeps your focus on the task at hand and prevents getting even in destructive ways or in ways that can cost your team from playing up to their potential.

Athletes like Rick and Sandra enjoy proving to the skeptic or the antagonist that they are the best or among the best. There are certain athletes that you do not want to rile up. Maybe it's a Saskatchewan thing because Gordie Howe, Sandra, and Rick all grew up in the same home province. Mr. Hockey would always play at his best when he was riled up and felt like he was an underdog. The last thing an opposing team wanted to do with number 9 was get him angry or challenge his ability as a player.

Cheryl tells of someone who suggested to her team before their first Scott not to ignore the crowd but to look at a few people directly, find people they knew, and make them their friends. By taking the time to practice this, the crowd, regardless of the size, seems much more human and caring. A huge crowd can be intimidating, and one can feel like every eyeball in the venue is picking apart your every flaw. Picking out a few people makes the event seem more personal and can help you feel the emotional support is there, and the intimidation factor can be eliminated.

Cheryl said her dad, Bernie, brought that level of comfort for her team at the 1996 Scott when her team finished second in Canada. Her dad would stand up all by himself as the team was marched out on the ice and start to do the wave. The team saw it as comic relief, and it really helped them to calm down.

At first, Cheryl was a little embarrassed for her dad, thinking it looked a little undignified and that people might get some funny thoughts about her hero. But, her teammates said he sure didn't look bothered by it. The fans around him were smiling, and it helped calm the team's nerves. Cheryl said that by the end of the Scott, the first thing she would do after walking on the ice was to find her dad.

The media can be one of the biggest distractions or one of the curler's biggest allies at a major event. The key, according to Cheryl, is for the team to go in with a clear plan. She takes a cautious yet friendly approach. Being at so many of these events over the years has taught her that there is a sliding scale of transparency, depending upon who is interviewing her team. Some media folk will never violate the off-the-record comments where others may accidentally slip up. For a few, leaking stories is their hidden agenda.

Cheryl says one of the guidelines for her team with the media is to never allow them to mess up the routine of the team, and most of the media respect this request. She has seen it happen otherwise with a number of curlers from different teams who are asked to do interviews right away when the team is either in practice mode or having a team meeting. All of a sudden the focus can change just enough from preparing to compete to getting caught up in the atmosphere in such a way that the primary objective of playing becomes skewed.

The team is the priority! In order for a team to function at its fullest, it must be constantly working on the chemistry and be on the same page with its goals and objectives. Phil Jackson emphasizes keeping the team or family first regardless. He feels that his primary function over the years was creating a team or family atmosphere. He was more than okay with the Xs and Os and making adjustments during the actual games, but, in the many books and articles on his coaching style, he would constantly go back to his primary role of keeping his teams on the same page or gunning towards the same mission.

Cheryl says the team must become one: one in purpose, general overall goals, and philosophical direction. This must be guarded with vigilance. It must be a nucleus that no potential distraction from the outside should be allowed to penetrate, even when the distraction is someone or something you love to death.

Karen Ruus has curled with Cheryl for thirteen years and tells the story of her husband, Allan, making a last-minute trip from Calgary to Thunder Bay to watch the team play in the Scott semi and final. For our American friends, this would be like trying to get a last-minute flight from Spokane, Washington, to Chicago but finding out that all connector flights through Minneapolis were booked. Allan was home looking after their three children and worked it out to be there for Karen for the playoff run in Thunder Bay. He got a last-minute flight to Winnipeg but couldn't get a connection to Thunder Bay, so he hopped a Greyhound bus and took the ten to twelve hour ride to make it in time for the two playoff games. Needless to say, he arrived in Thunder Bay quite exhausted but excited to cheer on his favorite curler, thinking he was a shoo-in for the husband-of-the-year award.

A very sweet gesture, as Karen would concur. Yet, for those final few days in Thunder Bay, he only sat down and talked with Karen once or twice. At first, this caused a little marital friction from Allan's perspective. Karen felt like Allan was an outsider coming in and interrupting the routine that the team had developed. She felt guilty for feeling that way, yet this was the reality from the team dynamic.

Having these conflicting emotions surrounding loved ones is not uncommon for many curlers or athletes in general. Generally, male competitors don't mind hanging out and spending time with their wives or significant others. But, for the women, there can often be that feeling that if their husbands are around they need to pay some serious attention to them. Are we really as evolved as we like to think we are with the differences in the genders, or are there valid differences in our **general make-up** that must be acknowledged or addressed in healthy ways?

Team Schmirler would have their whole family entourage at as many events as they could, but they would only have one evening a week for supper with their husbands in the middle of a major event. They would acknowledge them during the week, but it was understood that the team and the game was the priority.

Casey Stengel, successful manager of the New York Yankees during the 1950s, felt that many men needed their wives around before a big game and that for many men the romantic involvement with their wives was a good stress reliever for his team. His concern wasn't the married players having an enjoyable night with their wives but the single guys who were out the night before a game looking for a date and using up all their energy in the pursuit of a romantic encounter.

Generally speaking, women tend to deal with stress when it is a distraction from an emotional foundation first while men tend to deal with stress from a physical foundation. Team Schmirler would often joke, but with a hint of truth, that they never felt they were ready to compete until each person had either a good cry just before the event or some other emotional release.

Randy Ferbey has said that before a big event, a good baseball movie or some inspirational film gets his mind in a good place to go and compete. This is like having a good pep talk from the head coach before a big game. Emotions are involved, but there is a physical component of going out and following it up with action on the ice.

The final distraction Cheryl touched on at a major event is the weeklong or more pressure of competing at such a high intensity level. A team must learn to pace itself. The focus must be on getting the proper rest, eating well, keeping an even keel with the wins and the losses, and being concerned only over those things your team can control.

Mark Dacey won his first Brier with Nova Scotia in 2004 in that dramatic comeback win versus the three-time defending champions Team Ferbey and his Alberta rink. Team Dacey went on to Sweden to the Worlds a few weeks later and was upset by the Germans in the semis after going through the round-robin almost without a challenge. Mark said, "I wonder if we peaked too soon during the week and because we were never seriously challenged, started to tail off a bit. In hindsight, maybe the Germans upsetting us wasn't as huge an upset as some people think. We were coasting along while they were battling for their playoff lives and gaining confidence with each victory." Keeping things in perspective is the key to pacing yourself and can sometimes be a full-time undertaking.

On the women's side in 2004, Dacey's fellow clubmates from the Mayflower Curling Club in Halifax went on to win their second World title after a slow start to the event. A very young and inexperienced Italian team upset Colleen Jones on the first day causing some Canadian fans back home to panic. As the week wore on, Jones and her team kept getting better and better and by the time they hit the playoffs, they were almost unstoppable.

Many of Jones' comments during the week were of the "why panic" nature. They were coming off their fourth straight Scott win, which meant they were at their fourth straight Worlds, a first for any Canadian team. Jones knew that if her team played consistently and they never panicked, the playoffs could be a very real possibility unless something quite strange happened.

She viewed the week-long event from the perspective that it was a week-long event and not just a weekend bonspiel. This didn't guarantee her second World title, but it did put her team in a playoff position to at least have a chance. Mark Dacey, in hindsight, wondered if his team's quick, dominant start worked against them as the week wore on. Not that they wouldn't have tried their best to win all their games, but from a mental place maybe they could have had a wider perspective.

Hall of Famer Don Shula holds the record for the most wins ever for a NFL coach. He was once asked how he could coach at such a high level for all those years. He said the secret, if there is one, was some advice he received from a fellow coach early on in his career. This wise coach told Shula to only concern himself with those things that he could control and refuse to lose sleep over things he couldn't control, such as the weather, schedules, injuries, or comments in the press. Shula planned for everything that he could have some control over; he also included a plan to deal with outside distractions.

He had a reputation of never being fazed or affected by whatever was thrown his team's way. People forget that during the Dolphins' famous undefeated season in 1972, they won almost all their games with their second string quarterback; Bob Griese had gone down early in the season with an injury and never returned until the playoffs. Shula viewed distractions—however big or small—as part of the winning process: they were something to manage or possibly eliminate but were, nevertheless, a fact of life.

In interviewing close to one hundred national or world curling participants, we've heard one comment or thought consistently in dealing effectively with all the possible distractions. The trigger point is to remember not to allow anything to disrupt the nucleus of a team. Keeping the team focused on the mission, which of course is giving your team the best possible opportunity to win, must be guarded as closely as possible. Whatever it takes!

> "You had to give it to him; he had a plan. And it started to make sense, in a Tyler sort of way. No fear. No distractions. The ability to let that which does not matter truly slide."
>
> —The narrator in *Fight Club*

Chapter Sixteen

Trust Issues

"Remember your training and trust your instincts."
—Rip Torn as Patches O'Houlihan,
Coach in the film *Dodgeball*

he most successful coaches I have researched and studied over the years would all concur with Patches. Phil Jackson was meticulous when it came to preparation with his coaching staff and players, but during games, his instincts were what set him apart. Bill Belichick, the latest NFL coaching genius with the New England Patriots, is well-known for his leave-no-stone-unturned preparation; yet like Jackson, he trusts his instincts in the middle of the fray.

Scotty Bowman, the NHL's winningest coach of all-time, said in a January 25, 2005, interview with *Toronto Sun* reporter Steve Simmons:

I've always believed that if you're going to do something different, be the first to do it. You have to go in with a plan and have an alternative plan, and another one just in case. And then you have to let your instincts tell you what is right.

Jazz musicians are the kings and queens of improvisation or trusting their instincts. What is the secret to their skill? Jazz musicians practice the basic fundamentals of the songs they choose to play as much or more than any other genre. A Jazz musician will tell you that the more you practice and master the basics, the easier it becomes to improvise when performing because the mind is free from the clutter of trying to play perfectly or trying to remember the exact notes. This works in all musical genres for the accomplished musician.

Dr. James Dobson of Colorado Springs once told a story on one of his "Focus on the Family" radio broadcasts of having a hotel room in Washington, D.C., next to one of the world's greatest cellists. His first thought was about what a glamorous life this man must be living—travelling the world and performing in front of thousands of people—and how maybe he would benefit from a free concert by listening to this man practice through the walls of his hotel room.

By the end of his trip, Dr. Dobson said he discovered the secret to this master musician's glamorous life. He said that almost every time he went back to his hotel room he heard not the melodious songs he expected but scales and runs and more scales and runs. These are the basic fundamentals musicians need to constantly hone in order to play their musical scores at their peak and to be able to improvise during the concert.

Ray Turnbull is a former Brier champion and one of Canada's favorite television curling analysts. Ray has commented for years that the one attribute he so admires about Eddie "the Wrench" Werenich and Kevin Martin are their abilities to sense when to take chances, play a shot or play an end on the unconventional side, or switch styles in the middle of a curling game. Martin and "the Wrench" are the consummate curlers who seem to get away with their gambles or risks as well as any of the great players in history.

Werenich and Martin have studied curling, analyzed the game, and practiced as much, if not more, than most of their peers. Whether they were aware of it or not, Martin and Werenich were polishing curling fundamentals on a constant basis, which allows them to free up their thinking to sense the game at a much deeper level. When the game is on, they aren't just reading ice, playing the percentages, or making sure their deliveries are where they are supposed to be. They are free to concentrate on the flow and tempo of the game, observe their players and the opposition, and adjust their games to take advantage of or exploit opponents' weaknesses. The game is not just throwing rocks and hoping to outplay the opposition. To players like Martin and "the Wrench," it is being able to focus on the many nuances of the game and find that slight edge that makes all the difference.

Trust is a huge aspect of curling. Trust not only leads us to a deeper level of the game by developing our instincts, but it is the basis for becoming better individual players. It helps form unbreakable team chemistry. A skip must trust the ice and how it reacts even when conventional wisdom or past history says otherwise.

Players must learn to trust their skips at the far end when delivery hitches are noticed and can be corrected. Players getting ready to deliver their rocks must trust their fellow players in the timing of the rocks. Teammates need to trust their skips and their strategy calls for the overall game plan. All curlers must learn to trust that their practice sessions have prepared them for games or events, and learn to trust coaches, team psychologists, or other wise counselors. Curlers must trust the skip puts the broom and how much weight to throw. We must also trust that what a teammate said in the heat of the moment is not to be taken personally and trust that the encouraging words of a teammate are sincere. And this is only a short list of what curlers need to learn to trust.

Cheryl tells of Jody McNabb, her second, learning a lesson in trust that we all have to learn and relearn. The team was in a spiel, and Jody was "wristing" her release at the last moment of delivery, causing most of her stones to be narrow on the broom. Knowing she was narrow on almost all her shots, Jody started to realign herself in the hack and was starting to lose her proper alignment, only making things worse. She kept consulting Cheryl who, of course, could see what the problem was, since Cheryl was standing at the far end holding the broom.

Cheryl said:

The problem wasn't her alignment, initially, because she was coming out straight on the broom, but putting the turn on the rock too late at release was causing her to dump it. Instead of her wrist being straight at release like a handshake, she had overturned it too much. She needed to get back to putting the turn on about a foot or two before release where her wrist would be straight at the release point.

Jody had a hard time believing me because she felt her alignment was off. She gave me one of those "I'd like to believe you" looks and slid away looking skeptical but willing to try and keep her wrist straight when releasing her stones. Jody took my advice, realigned herself like she normally did, and, even though she now felt like she wasn't exactly square to the broom, started hitting the broom almost every time the rest of the spiel. She stopped playing with the rock at release and was bang on because there was nothing wrong with her alignment. So, after making her next few shots, everything felt right for Jody.

When looking into the roots of the word, trust, or faith, the theological world isn't a bad place to start. Trust doesn't mean or imply that we believe without questioning. Traditional theology actually frowns on what is called blind faith. That's not only bad theology but bad advice. For trust to be beneficial, it must have a two-fold element: the first element of trust is to be persuaded or convinced that something is true or correct more than being persuaded or convinced that something is not true or correct. The second element of trust is that you are persuaded or convinced enough to commit yourself to what you believe in or trust.

This does not have to be perfect faith or trust, which as a preacher I know doesn't exist on this side of heaven. Many times the best faith or trust we can muster is a mustard seed faith, which means we are persuaded just enough that something is valid or true and then we choose to act on it. This is similar to Jody McNabb and her "throwing narrow" struggles. Jody was convinced enough to take Cheryl's advice even though Cheryl could tell there was an element of doubt in Jody's demeanor. McNabb's trust level may have only been at a 55 percent persuasion level, but she committed herself 100 percent to take Cheryl's advice and things worked out even better than she imagined. I would venture to say that if Jody's persuasion level with Cheryl's observations was at 49 percent or less, she would have kept trying to realign herself to the point of total disaster for that particular game and possibly the entire bonspiel.

In some theological texts, theologians actually put a number or equation on mustard seed faith or trust. One of these theologians was a Reverend Scholz from Germany in the 1800s. Most of my relatives are curlers, farmers, or potash miners, and not theologians, so probably there is no relation. The number Reverend Scholz used is 50.45 percent, rounding it off to 51 percent faith. In other words, people believe more than they disbelieve, and they act upon that 50.45 percent. When push comes to shove, what do we really believe or lean towards even in the midst of our doubt?

George Verwer, a best-selling author says, "Great faith is not made in the absence of doubt but as we battle through." The more we act on something that is true or valid, the greater the first part of trust's definition will grow. For faith or trust to be an ally, we must base it on something or someone. We need reasonable evidence, even though the evidence may not be absolute. Cheryl could have been wrong with her advice to Jody but because of her reputation, skill level, and experience, Jody had a confident starting point to put her trust in Cheryl's observations.

In basic Curling 101, a skip calls for line and weight. For a team to be successful, it must trust that the skip is putting the broom in the right location and calling for the appropriate weight. It is easy to say we trust our skips, but the proof is in the pudding when we attempt to throw the appropriate weight where the skip puts his broom. If we choose to miss the broom on purpose and/or throw a different weight than what is called for, we really do not trust our skip even though we may say we do. Trust is when we are persuaded our skip is making the right call and we commit ourselves to following through with his or her instructions. Persuaded enough and committed fully to follow; that is trust.

Richie Hall is the assistant head coach and defensive coordinator of the Saskatchewan Roughriders. He has played and coached in Canada for over twenty years. He currently holds the distinction as the only assistant coach with the same team in the CFL to be hired on by each of the four new head coaches over the last dozen years. Many in the CFL inner circles of power consider him one of the best teachers and coaches on either side of the border. Richie was born in Texas and finished high school and college in Colorado—not exactly curling hot beds—yet he watches his fair share of curling. He loved the exploits of the Sandra Schmirler team and was admittedly thrilled when he had opportunities to meet each team member.

We were talking one day and philosophizing about life and sports when he told me one of the primary teaching lessons he tries to constantly get through to his players. He wants cerebral players who react to what they see on the field and not to what they assume will happen. Richie says, "That takes trust because we teach tendencies and study the opposing team's tendencies. However, tendencies will change especially at the pro level because pro football is all about adjustments even if they are slight and most of them are slight. We teach players the fundamentals over and over and drill into them the opposition's tendencies, but we also try and teach them to react to what is happening on the field first whether the tendency is occurring or not. So often a player will come back to the sidelines after a blown play and the first words he'll say to me is, 'I thought (blank) was going to happen.'" Richie's response is, "What did you see? And why didn't you react to what you saw? Trust your eyes. I don't care what you thought, I care about what you saw unfolding."

As Richie went on to explain this concept of trust he said:

The coaching staff emphasizes the basics and the tendencies but not at the expense of throwing away a player's instincts. We emphasize them almost to the point of exhaustion so that players will be freed up to follow their instincts.

Even though one of my first criteria for bringing a player on to the team is how smart they are, I want them to get to the point where they aren't so much thinking as reacting. I tell them all the time I don't want you to think but to react accordingly to what you see. It's all about trusting your preparation.

So often we think that trusting has to do with something invisible and more often than not it does. But sometimes trusting has to do with what we can see and observe right in front of us.

Richie understood the concept within the perimeters of curling. He understands that ice is not always predictable or the same for a skip to figure out. Learning to trust the ice and how it is reacting is crucial for success. Believing the ice is reacting the same as in the past can be helpful if the ice is reacting in that way, but ice can change and a team must adjust accordingly. A skip, especially, must trust what he or she is observing. This also applies to scouting your opposition. Each team has tendencies but every now and then they may throw a wrench at you because of familiarity, confidence levels, or ice conditions. Learning to trust what you see is vital.

Cheryl qualified for the 2004 Alberta provincials at the Huntington Hills Curling Club in Calgary. The team clinched its berth in the B-Final. Huntington is famous (or infamous) in Calgary for its one- to two-second difference playing from one end of the sheet to the other. Cheryl had to draw the button to win the final or be dropped down to the C-Event or last chance. She hadn't thrown a draw since the sixth end, almost one hour earlier. When she went to throw her final stone, she asked Karen and Jody what the times had been running. Karen said, "It's about a half-second slower coming home than it was earlier in the game." This threw

Cheryl off. During the game, drawing to the home end was a full second slower than going the other way and now it was a second and a half slower or about six feet slower on the draw. Trust!

She said:

It was maybe looking a little slower but that much? And I thought to myself, Are they getting the correct times on the rocks? *But I had no margin for error in throwing my final stone, it had to be on the button. Karen and Jody are seldom wrong in timing rocks so I just said to myself,* Throw it as if the ice is a half second slower. *I trusted my sweepers and their ability to time rocks. I just got it in my head to throw accordingly, because if you throw with doubt in your mind you'll miss 90 percent of your shots regardless of whether the broom is in the right spot and the weight selection is correct. And what I've learned is that you'll probably make 80 percent or more of your shots or at least get close if you are slightly wrong but committed to executing what you desire to. I chose to believe Karen and Jody, and committed myself to throwing slightly more weight than I was earlier in the game. They swept it right to the pot, and we made provincials.*

Cheryl was persuaded that Jody and Karen were more right than their chances of being wrong and then paused long enough to commit herself to throwing at the broom and what she considered the right weight. Cheryl trusted her players, her preparation, her training, and her instincts.

"When you believe in a thing, believe in it all the way, implicitly and unquestionably."

—Walt Disney

Chapter Seventeen

Play to Strengths—
Minimize Weaknesses

"I know it's kind of cool and everything, and maybe when I'm done it'll be cool, but I don't want anything to get in the way of my preparation. I wanted to do what I could to get a win and keep us in the game and give us a chance to win, and not get wrapped up in everything."

—Greg Maddux,
Facing fellow three-hundred game winner Roger Clemens

reg Maddux is not the most over-powering pitcher in baseball history. He is not known for his strikeout totals yet will finish his career in the top twenty all-time. He is known for his location and control—in other words, he is known for getting the most out of his ability while minimizing his weaknesses.

Winning on raw talent and desire alone may work in the junior ranks to a point and, at the regional level for some, but it will usually be short lived. Even the greatest teams have acknowledged the importance of playing to a team's strengths and making an effort to minimize weaknesses.

Wayne Middaugh says, "Man, I have seen five, no, maybe ten teams in my life that have played an almost totally aggressive style with hardly any holding back. It's my favorite way to play, and it is the most entertaining way for the fans to watch. Werenich, the Howards, Ferbey, Morris, Martin, and our teams are committed to this style of play." Middaugh would be the first to admit that not every team can play this way and have the success these teams have experienced, but he would also point out that more teams could play this way and get away with it if they committed to playing full throttle. The teams Middaugh mentions seem to have all the pieces in place to get away with their high-octane entertaining style of play, but there are times even these high velocity teams will pull back on occasion and will find another way to win.

Playing to your strengths and learning to minimize your weaknesses is the key to finding alternative ways to win at a high level—or at any level. We see Tiger Woods, who would be a Team Middaugh or Team Ferbey kind of curler, often admitting he wins PGA tournaments with his "B-Game" at times. The Edmonton Oilers and their high-octane offense of the 1980s had to learn to play with adjustments before finally winning their handful of Stanley Cups. The New Jersey Devils have made a habit of winning this way, although we would be the first to admit their style of play resembles the pre-FGZ in curling-speak.

The most dominant football team of the NFL in the 1970s was the record-setting Pittsburgh Steelers with their four Super Bowls in six seasons. If not for key injuries to their nucleus, it could have been six for six. The most exciting team of their era and possibly any era was the San Diego Chargers and their aerial circus. But only one team is remembered for its greatness. The Steelers' philosophy was to play to their strengths and minimize their weaknesses. If their brand of football happened to be entertaining, it was a bonus because they could be high octane at times. Winning was the prime directive!

We will go out on a very short limb and say one of the most over-achieving teams in the first half of this new millennium is the men's curling team from New Zealand. They have appeared in four World Championships and improved on their record every time out. They come out of the ever-improving Pacific Rim region, which also includes Australia, Japan, South Korea, China, and Taiwan. Up until 2005, this region only got one rep at the Worlds. They now get to send two countries to the expanded World Championships.

Sean Becker is the skip and, along with fifth player, Warren Dobson, are the only native Kiwis on the team. The third man is Hans Frauenlob from southern Ontario, second man, Dan Mustapic from Thunder Bay, Ontario, and lead man, Lorne De Pape originally from Manitoba. Hans, Dan, and Lorne were all very good club players from Canada who at times had success on various teams during provincial playdowns. But none had ever been household curling names. New Zealand has an outdoor curling history in the southern part of the country but only opened their first full-fledged curling rink in 2005. This team qualified for the 2006 Olympics in Italy (meaning they had to place high enough in at least three World Championships to get enough Olympic standard points) and is expert at finding ways to compete with the world's best and often beat the best. No one takes this scrappy team lightly. How do they do it? Studying Team New Zealand is the basis for this chapter on playing to strengths and minimizing weaknesses.

Lorne De Pape is the senior member of the team. He will be one of the oldest Olympians in Italy at forty-nine years old. I have interviewed Lorne and his teammates on a few occasions, and he was gracious enough to share his thoughts with us on what Team New Zealand does to find ways to win. He also says they have not perfected the following points but that they are a work in progress.

Set Team and Personal Goals

We have learned to be clear and agree on goals, whether they are short term or long term. Recently, we set goals to try and win the Pacific Championship, which in turn would give us the opportunity to qualify for the Olympics. Even more important is the discussion about what will be required to reach these goals.

Personal goals, especially for games, are an area we have started to work on more intentionally. Each of us tries to outshoot the opposing player we are facing at our individual positions. Little things like reminding ourselves to shout "weight" gives sweepers a weight indication as the rock comes out of our hands [e.g., "I'm a little light."].

Analyze Strengths and Areas for Improvement

This is a key for our team. We won't play as many games together as other teams, or get as much ice time for practice [weakness]. So what do we do to offset that? We focus on off-ice advantages that we might have over other teams. We use our curling experience [strength] to focus on strategy, to develop good game plans, and good end plans. There is no ice required for this of course.

We use the gym to increase fitness as much as possible. Gym training is helpful for improving balance and having the necessary energy for the longer, more intense tournaments. Again no ice is required.

When we do train together, it is quite intensive and well-planned. We go to the National Training Center in Calgary a lot to prepare for major events (as much as two or three times a year sometimes). For us, this may be better prep than just trying to get in more games although we have many exhibition games and enter the odd bonspiel when we are in Canada, but the focus is not on wins and losses but on improving our team.

(Note: this team wins more than their fair share of games when in Canada and qualifies in most bonspiels they enter.)

We have learned to turn negatives into positives. The best example I can think of is we train very hard for those two or three weeks prior to an event and never suffer burnout from a six to eight month season.

Another strength we have is that all four [five] players are playing the position that matches their strengths and the position that helps the team the most. Each player is committed to being the best at that position, even though we have all pretty much played each position on a curling team in the past.

When practicing, we have analyzed what personal skills and techniques we need to each improve upon, and we commit ourselves to working on those areas.

Develop Strong Action Plans

We plan ahead what needs to be done to achieve the short and long term goals. Planning in curling is essential and for our team makes up for a lot of shortcomings (again no ice required). Prior to major events our training camps in Calgary are well planned out. Time management is maximized.

We also have a game plan for games and even a plan for each end. We strongly emphasize playing to our team's strengths and to trying to take the opponent out of their comfort zone.

Use Top-Notch Coaching

Working with people like Bill Tschirhart in Calgary for the last four years has contributed a lot to our success—both on and off the ice. Bill has helped with our technique, weight, and delivery consistency through the use of video analysis, speed traps, observing us, etc. More importantly has been his off-ice coaching, working on strategy, shot selection, game and end plans, mental preparation, and our on-ice communication.

Bill has encouraged us to use our team's experience to be more patient than our opponents, waiting for the right time to get aggressive, and to capitalize on our chances. We've shown that we can come back from deficits; Bill has encouraged us to stay focused and grind it out if we have to.

Bill has also worked with us on an area he is big on emphasizing—team dynamics. We have tapped into other resources in this area as well to work on our inter-personal communication, which has helped a lot to develop the chemistry that is essential for a team to maximize its full potential, to "deliver more than the sum of its parts," as Bill likes to say. We might not outshoot too many teams, but hopefully our team play will win some games for us.

Make Practices Meaningful

It is so important to challenge ourselves in the areas we may be struggling or are weak. With such limited time together on the ice as a team, when we do get together we make our practice time count. When practicing, we try to use specific drills to work on certain things, and, when playing practice games, we also have goals and plans.

Develop Team Communication

This, of course, can mean many things. Over the course of time I believe our team has developed pretty good on-ice communication, especially with our sweeping and calling line and letting each other know the weight, so that we can maximize our sweeping abilities. We're one of the older teams competing at Pacifics and Worlds, but knowing when to sweep and when not to sweep is as important as brute strength.

Office team communication is critically important, an area that we've consciously worked on a lot, to make sure that every one is in the loop so to speak with plans, ideas, etc. Since we live scattered all over New Zealand and don't see each other for months at times, our communication is very important. Then, when we do get back together again, we're quickly back in synch again, pulling together as a team. We also make an effort to be open and honest with each other, and offer critiques in a positive fashion.

Learning to Play Smarter Not Harder

We've learned to use strategy, game plans, and shot selection to offset lack of ice time and games. As mentioned already, ice time together as a team is our most limited resource compared to other teams around the world. So we try to offset that by playing smarter rather than playing harder. All of our team could be termed students of the game and contribute to strategy both pre-game and during the games, as appropriate. We analyze the detailed shooting stats provided at Worlds to see what can be learned, or if there is any edge that we might be able to gain in upcoming games.

Debriefing

We have post-game and post-event debriefing meetings. This is an area that we are still developing and something we plan to do more of in the future. We've used post-game debriefs, even if it's just for ten to fifteen minutes over a beer, to sum up what we did well and what we could improve upon for our next game. This is especially useful in a bonspiel or major tournament. After major events, we try to do a full written (e-mail) debrief, to sum up both what the team did well and what we could improve upon, as well as what we individually did well and could improve upon.

> "We are just a team of wily old veterans and we just grind it out, we play the fourth line checkers for the whole game! We just wear down the opposition and end up with cheap goal."
>
> —Lorne De Pape,
> Using a hockey metaphor and his Canadian roots
> to explain his New Zealand team's curling philosophy

Chapter Eighteen

Hollywood 101

"To beat Barry Bonds, you've got to be a good liar to yourself. And an idiot to believe in your own lies."

—Eric Gagne,
2003 Cy Young Winner

A t the 1996 Scott Tournament of Hearts there was a late round-robin clash of the two teams tied for first place between the eventual winner Ontario's Marilyn Bodogh and Saskatchewan's Sherry Middaugh (now of Ontario). Middaugh, who has been to five Scotts and three Olympic trials, says:

That was one of the key games of my life I'll never forget. It was my first Scott and probably the biggest game up to that point in my career. Marilyn is such a fierce competitor, was a former World Champ, and her team was on a huge roll. We won the game, and it laid the foundation for me that we could beat any team in the world—and when it counted. I knew inside we could do it and we had beaten almost all the big names up to that stage, but this was the Scott.

I have used that game so many times since in my career, especially when I am feeling negative or when I know we are not on top of our games. So sometimes I will pretend the other skip is Marilyn and envision Marilyn's head on the other skip. It reminds me that we have had huge success in the past and can do it again. It's so important to remember the wins and the big shots when you are struggling. This will more often than not help me to get back and focus on what we need to do to win and not to be intimidated or overwhelmed.

Sometimes we need to learn to be actors out on the ice. I have learned we can manipulate our minds and bodies so well that if we do it enough our instincts can take over and we can begin to believe we are champions and create the aura of being a champion. Pretending helps me to remember of what I am capable. So often we can project to the other team negative body language, and the good teams will clue into that so quickly and it will help them to pour the pressure on to try and finish us off quickly. And if we are projecting that to our teammates, it can be infectious if we aren't careful. This game is hard enough without us giving the opponent an advantage we can control with our minds.

When I am feeling dejected on the inside or sense that one of my team-mates is, I want us to fake it. Just start to walk the walk and be an actor out there.

Paul Newman, one of the top actors of all time, is among a group of actors who embrace the philosophy called method acting. This means actors pretend to be the character whom they will be portraying. Claudia Church, actress, Top Forty *Billboard* country singer, and top fashion model has studied acting extensively and comments on the effort and focus method actors put into their craft. She says:

Some people think it's the only way to go, but it is very exhausting. Daniel Day-Lewis is into method acting. When he shot the film Gangs of New York, *a friend of mine was in the film and when she went over to talk with him he was so into character that he treated her like his character would—not nice at all. Remember he played the butcher. Some actors stay in character the entire time they work on a film totally pretending to be the character 24/7.*

Newman found that when he consciously pretended to be the character he was acting, he also started to take on many of the characteristics of that person whether he wanted to or not. But the advantage that

Newman saw from this style of acting was that he overcame so many of his own insecurities or flaws by bringing the good qualities of the parts he was playing into his personal life. In addition, I believe it was Newman who also said, "Unless you are a totally dysfunctional human being, you should be able to toss aside the negative qualities you had to portray for a short while." Pretending or acting can help our minds focus in a positive direction, and if we do it enough, more often than not we become like what we are trying to emulate.

Observing little children even for short moments reminds us of the constant pretending and acting they do. This is not a developmental psychology book by any means, but we all know children often grow mentally and socially by pretending to be like their heroes.

My all-time favorite sports story on pretending was a peewee hockey dad from Cochrane, Alberta, whose son was tearing up the local league. The dad kept wondering what got into his son and his almost overnight transformation. One night after another outstanding performance, the dad asked his son, "What are you thinking about when you step on the ice?" The son simply said, "I'm Wayne Gretzky!" The dad prodded a little more, and his son said, "Well, when I have the puck I try to pass like Gretzky, and, when I have a chance to score, I feel like I am unbeatable."

Heather Rankin, one of the WCT's top money earners over the years and Scott participant, as a teenager growing up in Nova Scotia often pretended to be Colleen Jones. Wade Johnston, a two-time Alberta Junior champion and Brier rep with Ken Hunka in 1999, didn't dream of Stanley Cups and Grey Cups growing up in Edgerton, Alberta, but of playing in a Brier. His dad, Doug, said:

> As long as I can remember, Wade dreamed of the Brier. He loved other sports, but it always came back to curling and the Brier. Most Canadian kids pretend they are playing for the Stanley Cup or Grey Cup but not Wade.

(Doug told me this story back in 1988 when we were doing battle on the ice against each other at a cashspiel. I had my veteran rink, and Doug had Wade and two other teenagers. Let's just say there is a reason Wade has played in the Brier and I have not.)

Pretending or acting usually has its roots in practicing. Almost all the curlers interviewed for *Between the Sheets* talk about simulation. Whether they use the actual phrase or not, the concept is the same.

Georgina Wheatcroft, Olympic medallist and former World Champion, first started working with sports psychologist Dr. David Cox in Vancouver when she was on the "Super Team" skipped by Kelley Law. Georgina says:

> David would get us to simulate our practices all the time. He introduced us to a phrase I have adopted, called deliberate practice. We would constantly simulate game scenarios and situations. We would make up scores, what end we were in, do we have hammer, do we not have hammer, go over situations where we struggled or got beat in recently, whatever. We played in a regular club league with our team and sometimes found ourselves way up in a game or, at least, in control but realized maybe we haven't stolen a point for awhile, so we would pretend we needed to steal a point whether we really needed to or not and play that end accordingly.

> I believe in quality practice, and simulation is probably the best way to prepare as a team. A team has to learn to get its blood pressure up in practice to be ready for high-pressure tournaments. Preparation is the key, and I firmly believe the best-prepared teams win. We even practice our pre-shot routines in practice as much as we can. Every time you reinforce something important in practice or simulation the easier it does become when the real situation calls for it. And, as teammates, we can remind each other that we have been through various situations before because we did it in practice.

> I honestly believe that Colleen Jones reinvented herself by developing her pre-shot routine. Her mental discipline is so strong that she will allow nothing to distract her, nothing. I like when she starts her pre-shot routine over if she feels she has to. This is something I am trying to be so consistent at—when that red light goes on inside of me, reminding me that I am not ready to throw, to stop, get back, and go through my pre-shot routine. If you focus on things like this in practice, it becomes a part of who you are in games.

St. Bernard, a French priest from a few centuries ago, said, "We become like what we allow our minds to dwell upon."

C. S. Lewis, the brilliant author of *The Chronicles of Narnia* plus his classic best-selling theological book for lay people, *Mere Christianity*, strongly believed that any kind of lifestyle change happened first in pretending.

One of his most famous chapters of *Mere Christianity* is titled "Let's Pretend." In this chapter, Lewis says:

I dare say this idea of a divine make-believe sounds rather strange at first. But, is it so strange really? Is it not how the higher thing always raises the lower? A mother teaches her baby to talk by talking to it as if it understood long before it really does. We treat our dogs as if they were almost human: that is why they really become almost human in the end.

If we want to live a certain way or create a positive change in our lives, it all begins by pretending we can do it and living accordingly. Alcoholics Anonymous is known for their pithy mottos, and one of their most used is "fake it until you make it." And, as one recovering alcoholic with a very quick wit once told me:

If you fail, just keep trying to fake it until you make it. Eventually it might just stick, but don't give up because it sometimes starts with baby steps. Even in your failures, remember the progress and small victories. All of us alcoholics were bad actors in the first place anyways, and the more you act or learn to fake it until you make it, the better you become, or that's the theory anyways.

Don Bartlett is one of the most colorful players in the curling world and can never say enough good things about his coach, Jules Owchar, whom he inherited when he joined with Kevin Martin a number of years ago. Don feels that Jules is maybe the most underrated curling coach in the world—period. Kevin Martin has been coached by Jules Owchar for well over twenty years, going back to his junior days as a Canadian champ, and Bartlett has been Kevin Martin's lead forever in terms of curling years. Don said this is what he often thinks about in a pressure situation:

I think of Jules and what he told us to do in practice and believe in what he has to say. So I just throw my rocks, believe in what Jules has emphasized, and believe in myself that I can make my shots. You have to have some confidence built up in yourself before you become successful.

Don follows the script of his trusty coach and finds that if he focuses on what Jules has emphasized and taught in practice, it serves him well in games.

Even in Hollywood, actors are often influenced by the roles they play or the costumes they wear. Canadian-born Keanu Reeves and Oscar-winning Halle Berry are two of the most accomplished actors in Hollywood. Reeves played the lead role of Neo in *The Matrix* film trilogy. He stated that he felt filled with confidence and the ability to make quick correct decisions when he put on Neo's black jacket. He believes that has also filtered down into his personal life.

Halle Berry played Catwoman while going through her painful divorce that was splashed all over the tabloids. She believed part of her rebounding and getting on with her life was her role of Catwoman and friendship with Sharon Stone (who played her archenemy in the film). In an interview for *Big Picture News*, Berry said:

> *Putting on that catsuit everyday was empowering and liberating, and it really helped me make some life-changing decisions. I felt a real sense of myself. People would say to me, "Where did you get that walk from?" It's hard not to walk with confidence when you have that suit on.*

Learning to pretend, faking it until you make it, or simulation exercises can often be the difference in overcoming our fears, insecurities, or lack of experience before taking that next step in winning. Cheryl was highlighted with the quote of the month in the November 2004 issue of *Sweep!* magazine. She talked about representing Canada at the Karuizawa International Bonspiel at the site of the 1998 Winter Olympics in Japan:

> *I couldn't believe the feeling that came over me when I put on the Team Canada jacket and walked out on the ice, especially the first time. I felt like I could do anything.*

> *Representing your country, upholding its place of being the favorite in curling, and winning the honor to wear it. I really felt like I could curl well and would do well. I had no idea it would affect me as it did. Not that I felt invincible, but I honestly felt like I could make any shot and face whatever situations that would be thrown our way.*

For the record, Cheryl and her teammates went on to win the spiel despite many former or current national champions representing the top nations from around the curling world. The Karuizawa International

Bonspiel is the most prestigious spiel in all of Asia and was created as a legacy from the 1998 Olympics.

"Whenever you feel dejected on the inside—fake it. The pretending starts in practice. Put yourself in the environment you are about to face, and try to imagine what distractions there will be. When you go to a major event, there will be distractions. Simulate the upcoming games in practice. The more you have learned to fake it, the easier it becomes to perform when you have to. The pressure won't overwhelm you, and it's easier to focus on just executing."

—Sherry Middaugh

SECTION THREE

The Technical Game

Chapter Nineteen

Curlingmetrics

"When the orthodox doesn't work—try the unorthodox."

—W. P. Wrigley,
Founder of Wrigley chewing gum and
namesake of Wrigley Field in Chicago

Scouts in every major sport have always conducted a certain debate when evaluating potential talent. Do they focus primarily on an athlete's physical or traditional skills in sport, or should they give equal weight or more emphasis on an athlete's overall performance in spite of possibly grading low in some of the traditional tools? Is the scouted athlete someone who produces greater results in spite of grading low on traditional scales versus other athletes who grade high on all the tools but don't produce the consistent results? Does the scout recommend to his team the athlete who meets the physical or traditional tools criteria, relying on his potential and the possibility of developing? Or does he look for the athlete who may grade lower than the team desires on the criteria scale but has that knack for outperforming and producing winning results? Ideally, there should be a healthy balance of the two.

For instance, should a quarterback need to be at least 6'2" tall with above average arm strength and throw over the top rather than side-arm like a shortstop? If this was the only criteria, you wouldn't recognize many of the greats in either the CFL or NFL Halls of Fame. Joe Montana, John Elway, Fran Tarkenton, Ron Lancaster, Tom Wilkinson, or Doug Flutie wouldn't be there, for example. Yet "textbook" quarterbacks who the scouts salivate over (like Reggie Slack, Joe "747" Adams, Ryan Leaf, Jeff George, and Todd Marinovich) have filled the scrap heap of pro football and left their adoring fans with disappointment after disappointment.

Similarly, you want to build a curling team with players who can sweep like Huffin' and Puffin' (Pfiefer and Rocque), Storey and Sparks, or Gudereit and McCusker; throw the high, hard one like Walchuk or either of the Howard brothers; or look like Olympians such as Gustafson, Gushue, Flemming, or Law. Whether potential teammates have these qualifications or not, the primary issue may be moxie or SQ (sports quotient/sports smarts) combined with a minimum acceptable level of the technical.

Maybe, the only six-time Brier champ, Randy Ferbey, captured the main criteria curling talent scouts need to search for when he said in an *Edmonton Sun* interview during the 2005 Brier, "You can usually test the mettle of a champion-caliber curler by how well they throw in ends eight, nine and ten. It's easier to make shots earlier on in a game when the pressure doesn't seem as intense, but how do players perform when every shot seems so critical at the end of a big game?" It is important to have all the physical or technical tools, as well as the necessary intangibles like determination, passion, and the ability to embrace pressure.

Consider the following curling world champions and heroes, such as Hec Gervais, who looked more like an offensive lineman who gave his rocks a little push on delivery; Eddie "The Wrench" Werenich, who was singled out by the Canadian Olympic Committee to lose a pound or two back in 1987; fortyish Randy Ferbey, who has developed physically more into a slow-pitch body than his former baseball body; and Kelley Law who causes some to first think *Vogue* versus Olympic medallist. Would anal or narrow-minded curling scouts just looking for the physical/technical tools and trying to discover the next big thing have even considered these world champions at first glance?

Is there a way to discover players for your team aiming to be champions? No system is foolproof, but there may be statistics out there that could help the evaluation process.

Yes, realistic high averages are needed, but, as most high-performance curlers know, averages can be a little misleading at times. Degree of difficulty is never taken into account. Club ice is different than babied arena ice where the best ice technicians in the world ply their trade. We get to practice for ten to fifteen minutes before major events, which helps the averages. But, at the same time, a curler consistently below the low seventies won't cut it at the highest levels.

As Joan McCusker, curler and analyst, said on a CBC telecast during the 2005 Brier, "I dare any curler to have higher averages on normal curling club ice than on arena ice prepared for a major event. The arena ice is so good, and we get the practice time to get a handle on it." Statistics can be an evaluator, but we have to make it a worthy evaluator.

There are statistics for general fun and amusement, and there are statistics that can be quite relevant if studied properly. A stopwatch is a statistical measuring device which very few high-performance teams would be without. Yet many high-performance curlers, such as two-time World champion Rick Folk of Kelowna, balances technology and intuition. Although his teammates use stop watches, Folk does not, but he does consult them on occasion. Yet, for himself, he wants to have a sense or feel for when he goes to deliver his stones. Technology or statistics are tools that aid a more holistic or well-rounded game.

Curlingmetrics, or the study of relevant statistical analysis in curling, is a tool to discover and evaluate players. In addition, it reveals the strengths and weaknesses of a player and team in order to more intentionally work on those areas for improvement. First, a quick background on curlingmetrics.

A Brief History

Sabermetrics is one of the newer buzz words in baseball. The term hit its height in 2003 and 2004 when it was used in Michael Lewis's best-seller *Moneyball*. Sabermetrics is the study and analysis of relevant baseball statistics, or, as the founder Bill James says, "The search for objective knowledge about baseball *that helps evaluate talent.*" Sabermetrics stats are the key stats for the fad and foundation for Rotisserie (fantasy) baseball, which has turned into a respected part of the business on most fronts. ESPN and its baseball Web site have recorded sabermetric stats since the mid-nineties. The centerpiece of *Moneyball* centered on sabermetrics and the Oakland A's General Manager Billy Beane's application of its core principles. Beane has often been quoted, yet seldom published, in major articles saying that sabermetrics is only one part of many dynamics in putting together a competitive baseball team. Logic and stats must be counterbalanced with experienced, intuitive coaches and players.

(Note: Sabermetrics, the original word, was an acronym for the Society for American Baseball Research, and in the sports world has come to mean the use of relevant statistics as an aid in discovering and evaluating talent.)

The premise of sabermetrics is the use of statistical analysis to build better teams, but at its core, the focus is really on only a handful of relevant stats. Major League Baseball managers and coaches like Billy Beane want to know two essential truths. Number one is how runs are scored. The key stat here is the OPS: a player's on-base percentage and slugging percentage. Number two is how runs are prevented. The key stats here are ones that involve the ability to prevent walks and extra base hits.

Many within pro sports are taking notice of overtly sabermetric teams because of the uncanny success of small market teams like the As and recent turn arounds by the Dodgers, Padres, Indians, Blue Jays, and, of course, the Red Sox and their recent World Series victory. For a number of years, the Yankees have been an unofficial sabermetric team with their on-field philosophy.

As new and funky as sabermetrics sounds, the concept has been around for years. Branch Rickey, the general manager of the Brooklyn Dodgers in the 1940s and '50s, was the first to hire a full-time team statistician to track unofficial—yet relevant—stats on his players throughout the elaborate Dodger farm system.

The Tampa Bay Buccaneers of the NFL built their successful run of the late–1990s and Super Bowl win in 2003 on sabermetric principles in relation to football with their general manager, Rich McKay. Clashing with newly hired Bucs head coach, Jon Gruden, McKay was let go in late 2004. He was hired immediately by the Atlanta Falcons, who almost overnight turned their franchise around while the Bucs have been out of the playoff picture ever since. Gruden has admitted that McKay brought in the core of their Super Bowl team, and that he (Gruden) had a different way of running a team but made more money than Rich McKay. So, because of philosophical differences, Gruden won out. Perhaps it is not coincidence that the Bucs star-studded team was dismantled and the Falcons, perennial also-rans, made a run for the Super Bowl.

Curlingmetrics

Where do we go with this tool towards creating championship curling teams? Cheryl and I concur that many successful teams use statistical principles either intentionally or intuitively. Applying saber-metric principles to curling produces what we call curlingmetrics. This science may simply help identify the key statistical areas that are relevant and may help teams identify strengths and weaknesses to be reinforced or worked on for improvement. We also believe this short list of curling stats will be honed in and added to over the years.

Using Percentages as an Aid to Focus on the Pro-side Versus the Amateur-side

The scoring system for curling and individual players is a standard one that has been developed over the years. Therefore, this is where we will start our use of curlingmetrics by using the most known stat in curling and finding a very practical use for it.

A quick scoring review: Zero for a complete miss, four for a complete shot, one for at least doing something that could be used, two for a half shot, and three for a good shot but not quite complete or what was called for. It only stands to reason that the more zeros and ones a player throws, the lower the average and fewer the wins. The more threes and fours a team throws the greater chance of scoring and winning. A good player and team will major on pro-side shots versus amateur-side shots to minimize zeros. This phraseology of the pro side versus the amateur side was started in that curling classic published in 1981 simply titled, *The Curling Book*, by primary author Eddie Lukowich with help from Paul Gowsell and Rick Folk.

Learning to maximize threes and fours and minimizing zeros and ones can be a reminder to focus on pro-side shooting winning out over amateur-side shooting. I venture to say that over the years, page eighty-seven of *The Curling Book* has been photocopied or folded over more than any curling book page in history. Andy Jones is a curling coach of a bantam team in Calgary that has twice qualified for the Alberta southerns. He photocopied page eighty-seven for his team and continually reviews it with them before every event. During one bonspiel, an opposing player's dad asked what the photocopy was and wanted a copy for his team. What is ironic is that one of the players on that team was Paul Gowsell's son.

The following chart is from page eighty-seven co-mingled with *Between the Sheets* additions. We'll number the scenarios, give the shot and circumstance, and give the desired pro-side result versus the amateur result.

1. Take out on keen straight ice—a pro-shot does not miss wide and uses the sweeper. An amateur-shot throws it wide, into space. Nothing can help it curl.

2. Takeout on very swingy ice—a pro does not miss inside. Aims for outside 2/3 of the rock. An amateur throws inside and starts the rock curling.

3. Draw on keen ice—a pro throws to the front ring and uses the sweepers. An amateur aims for the tee line, is a little heavy; nothing can help now.

4. Draw on heavy ice (often the first end)—a pro throws correct weight with no sweep. An amateur doesn't believe how heavy it is and throws light and yells sweep, but it doesn't help.

5. Draw around a guard on swingy/curling ice—a pro does not get inside and throws to the sweepers. Sweepers, as always, keep it clean. An amateur throws inside and often too heavy and clips the guard.

6. Draw to a rock buried behind a guard—a pro makes shot or is just short for second shot and can now tap it up. An amateur makes shot or slides too far; all or nothing.

7. Hack weight around a guard to remove counter and rock is partly exposed—a pro makes shot or removes guard to open it up. An amateur makes shot or misses entirely, not even hitting the guard and still has the same problem left.

8. Splitting the house when you have hammer—a pro is in the house or just short of the house for tap up or split. An amateur is heavy and loses the opportunity for a side guard or split.

9. Splitting the house without hammer—a pro is not short of the rings. An amateur falls short, providing a side guard for the opposition.

10. Delicate hack weight shot—a pro throws slightly more than draw weight. An amateur tries to throw less than takeout weight, which is inaccurate.

11. Free Guard Zone control with lead stones—a pro makes sure it's in play but not in the house. An amateur either gets too heavy and slides into the house or too light and hogs.

12. Open hit to blank—a pro at least removes the stone to score one or makes shot. An amateur at least hits on nose to score one or misses entirely.

13. General rule on straight ice with little curl—a pro hits the broom, never throws wide, and is only two or three inches inside to allow for sweeping. (Note: the Lukowich Rule from his writings is that if you miss on the correct side of the broom by two or three inches, the sweepers should be able to compensate and you will make threes and fours on virtually every shot you throw if the weight is in the ball park.) Amateur will throw wide and will miss giving the rock no chance to come back.

14. General rule with swingy or curling ice—a pro never throws inside and only two to three inches wide if he doesn't hit the broom. An amateur throws inside and unless the sweepers are magicians or it picks, misses everything.

15. Hack weight shot—a pro throws to back rings and uses sweepers. An amateur throws to hack but probably throws bumper or more, not giving the rock a chance to curl.

16. Bumper weight shot—a pro throws to hack using sweepers and giving the rock a chance to curl. An amateur tends to throw more to the scoreboard not giving the rock a chance to curl or the sweepers to do their thing in keeping it straight or allowing it to curl or taking it the extra distance. In addition, for each heavier weight shot this progression plays out.

17. When in doubt on an open take out on virgin ice—a pro keeps weight up and takes little ice until he knows how it reacts. An amateur throws peel or quiet weight and watches the rock over curl and miss or fall back and miss.

18. Timing Rocks—a pro has at least two players timing every rock in the first few ends and keeping tabs throughout the game. An amateur may or may not use stopwatches but thinks early times will stay the same throughout, or doesn't check in consistently.

19. When the ice changes speeds—a pro believes timers and times and throws accordingly. An amateur believes past history of times and doesn't believe and adjust.

20. When lost and confused—a pro is open to consulting every teammate for tendencies in the ice or observations on delivery and release. An amateur relies on himself regardless and probably doesn't learn that pride comes before a fall and losses build up.

We like how Dallas Bittle's Curling Zone (www.curlingzone.com), the largest curling statistical analysis group in the world, views the use of percentages alone as an aid rather than using percentages in productive creative fashion to suit one's own skewed analysis. Bittle says, "We are among a group that believe the shooting percentage as a stat on its own is a 'naked stat' which often does not accurately reflect the situation of an end/game." The Curling Zone Web site has had as many as 250,000 hits in one season and is now used as a resource for both SportsNet and CBC during major curling events.

Efficiency with Hammer

Determining how often teams scored two or more points with the hammer or last rock advantage was a new stat thrown at the public during the 2004–2005 curling season on SportsNet during their coverage of WCT Grand Slam events. This stat, among other new relevant ones, was developed by Curling Zone. The four playoff teams were in the top third of the overall rankings.

The late "Badger Bob" Johnson—the cagey NCAA and NHL coach of the University of Wisconsin, Calgary Flames, and Pittsburgh Penguins—used to say, "You achieve what you emphasize." He felt that if a team was in the top third in relevant stats, the team would go deep into the playoffs. As noted earlier, he loved special teams and emphasized excellence in special team play. In hockey this, of course, was the power play and penalty killing. His teams were consistently in the top third in these two critical categories. He would also be the first to acknowledge that anomalies exist in every facet of life as well. But as a general rule . . .

Curling teams that score high with hammer efficiency have players who get their rocks not only in play but get them in the right positions to create big ends. In evaluating talent, does the player you are scouting get his rocks in play where the skip is calling consistently? He may play on a horrible team, but does this individual player do his part? Is this player aware of a good Plan Bs when he is throwing or sweeping?

Take One/Force Efficiency

Force efficiency is the team's ability to keep the other team to only one point when they have hammer. Again, the top playoff teams all scored high in the Badger Bob one-third ranking.

When teams get on rolls in a bonspiel or playdown event, they tend to keep big ends to a minimum when they do not have hammer. How can you scout a player for this skill? Game awareness may hold a clue, and this may be more of an evaluator for a skip and his game-calling ability. Does the skip tend to be aggressive regardless of how he understands the ice conditions, or does he play conservative (or at least semi-aggressive) until he has a grasp of the ice conditions? On the other hand, is the skip aware of how his teammates are throwing? Maybe his normally strong lead has some struggles with draw weight and he may have to curb the aggressive game without hammer until his lead is throwing more consistently.

Championship skips play to win rather than wanting to be correct—meaning they will forgo conventional wisdom at times to keep their teams in games rather than trying to look so smart and sexy in play calling. Jamie Bourassa and Myles Chapin, two of the world's top ice technicians, say it is quite funny to watch club curlers the week or two after watching a Scott or Brier on television. They have both said:

> These normally smart and successful club skips play to their teams strengths and weaknesses all during the season, and then they see the best players in the world being so aggressive with their play calling that they seem to think this is what brings success. They want to look like a Brier or Scott player, and all it does is get them into trouble because they don't have the horses to execute these shots consistently or they forget the ice conditions are so different.

Ratio of Plus-Minus

A stat that doesn't seem to be currently in vogue is that of position-by-position competition. For example, over the course of a month, does your lead outplay the opposition's lead more often than not? This is determined if your scouted player has at least a 5 percent average or better than his fellow competitor, then he would be given the check or win versus that player. If the two players are within 5 percent of each other, it would be considered a tie.

This stat helps a scout or team evaluate how each player does versus other players in the same game scenarios. If a player consistently gets outplayed by others playing the same positions, it could be a sign that he is not ready for high performance curling, needs to work on certain aspects of his game, or maybe needs to consider a different position on the team. In an intangible way, this could reveal that a player is very competitive-oriented and aware of outplaying his opponent, or it could reveal the opposite and that the player may be intimidated or in over his head.

The old truism in curling is that if each player outplays his opponent, it's almost impossible to lose; but this is curling, of course, and strange and unusual things occur on the ice all the time. This may be a good time to remind ourselves that these statistical tools are general rules or guidelines in the evaluating/scouting process and that curling is the ultimate sport of anomalies.

Intangibles

Moxie, SQ, refuse to lose/determination, communication skills, the ability to encourage even in quiet ways, work ethic, and being a self starter are only a handful of important intangibles. How does one grade these? A couple of clues. Talk to hockey, football, baseball, or basketball scouts, and study NCAA coaches and their recruiting methods. Lee Heindel of Kamloops, British Columbia, has scouted for various Western Hockey League (WHL) teams and is a pretty decent curler in his own right. He has shown me scouting evaluation forms, and intangibles are a major part of the equation. Considered under this heading are school grades, family dynamics, work ethic, ability to play with others, and ethics/integrity. The scout is not looking for perfection by any means, but he wants a player who has high standards, tries hard, and copes well with stressful situations.

Heindel says:

As an example, a player we are looking at who is trying to improve on his grades while playing a sport he loves will almost always make the WHL over another kid of equal talent who is letting his grades slip or doesn't care. I couldn't believe how strong the correlation was. And this may be a player simply improving from a D to a C, but he is working his tail off to get that C. Also, we look at how the player performed in pressure situations or when he has been given more responsibility. We ask questions to see how has he rebounded from slumps or adversity on and off the ice.

There is no official statistical category to grade here, but the scout or NCAA recruiter/coach takes the time to interview key people in the player's life. This ranges from family, teachers, and boyfriends/girlfriends, to former coaches, players, big brothers/sisters, ministers, and to personal interviews.

Damage Control Regardless of Hammer or Not

Damage control is a little more subjective but could easily be used as an evaluator by a coach or seasoned scorekeeper. Teams that learn to control potential damage (damage control experts) have a knack for being in almost every game they play. Big ends can occur whether you have last rock advantage or not. Frank Macera, husband of Jan Betker, has hardly ever thrown a curling rock but has probably watched as much or more high level curling than any sports fan, and usually close up at the arena. Frank played on one of the Regina Ram National Junior Championship teams before meeting Jan. He said, "The one thing I noticed about Team Schmirler compared to other curling teams is their ability to limit big ends scored against them. They seem to have a sense of knowing when to take chances and when not to, and when to bail out when an end is going badly. I really believe this helps them win some games maybe they weren't supposed to."

This statistical tool is probably once again more of an aid in evaluating skips or thirds, and their ability to call games. High-performance curling is about winning! Are the good skips able to keep their teams in the vast majority of the games they play? Every team gets blown out or hammered over the course of a season (and usually a few times), but over the course of that season, is the team competing in most every game they play?

Stats from the Brier and Scott from over the years (going back to at least 1987) show that the champions give up very few big ends (threes or higher) over the course of the events. Scouting players isn't just about high percentages on the stat sheet, but it is also about evaluating the players who call the game. Does the skip have the sense or is he at least improving his intuition in knowing when to bail, when to stay aggressive, or when to become aggressive? Ray Turnbull of TSN has said for years, "Watching the likes of Kevin Martin and Randy Ferbey is so much fun because they seem to have this sense of when to go for it and when to bail, and they are so seldom wrong."

Steal Efficiency

The Pittsburgh Steelers are traditionally one of the stingiest defenses in all of pro football. When they won their four titles in six years, the Steel

Curtain Defense was the foundation for their record-setting years. They had a pretty good and exciting offense to balance their team out, but their "D" set the tone and kept them in almost every ball game in that six years of dominance. If not for untimely injuries, they may have won six straight. Curlers who can steal as part of their game plan tend to be near the top of their leagues almost without fail. There is not a lot of curling in Pittsburgh, but teams that can steal are playing in the true spirit of the Pittsburgh Steelers.

This last of the big three new stats was introduced on CTV Sportsnet in 2005. This simply means how often a team steals points regardless of the number of points. The champion teams all rate high in this department, especially since the dawn of the FGZ. The key to stealing is the ability to make the delicate shot and to score at least a two to four consistently on the stat sheet with individual shots. When you discover a player (or team) that loves the challenge of stealing and executes the steal on a regular basis, you have probably discovered the complete package. You have found a player that can draw, make the delicate shot, and can hit with the best of them.

Curlingmetrics can be another tool in your arsenal in creating curling champions. Are you looking to develop a new team? Are you looking for that one missing piece? Are you content with your team but need a new tool to evaluate your progress to shine some light on your strengths and weaknesses? Curlingmetrics is here to evaluate, instruct, and keep you focused on the basics.

"Statistics are like bikinis; they show a lot, but not everything."

—Lou Piniella,

Major League Baseball Manager

Chapter Twenty

A Rock and a Broom

"This is a very simple game.
You throw the ball.
You catch the ball.
You hit the ball."

—Trey Wilson as Skip,
in the baseball film *Bull Durham*

One of my favorite curlers on the planet has never won more than a local bonspiel, yet he has curled in six provinces and in countless arenas across Canada. In his prime, he is what Major League Baseball would call a **tweener**. Probably not good enough for a sustained career in the big leagues but more than good enough for Triple A. In curling-speak, probably not quite good enough to play in a Brier but at the same time he would not have embarrassed himself one little iota, yet he is more than dominant at the club level. Canada, especially, is filled with hundreds of tweeners across its curling landscape. Players who, with a little more time to commit to their games, could have raised it that one level to compete with the best. But, other commitments like family, community, or day jobs took precedent.

Tweeners can play the game and compete because they have worked on their games enough to be competent shotmakers and effective sweepers. These are the kind of players you seldom, if ever, hear about but are often the players who lead good club teams that pull off these upsets of Brier contenders along the playdown trail. Every year you read about a former Brier or Scott team being eliminated in the Alberta playdowns in a small town like Hanna who got knocked off by a team of brothers skipped by a Ken Larence of the Huntington Hills Curling Club located just south of Balzac. Or you wondered what happened to the previous year's Saskatchewan Brier rep as they couldn't advance beyond their playdowns hosted in the metropolis of Langenburg. Or you wonder about what happened to that upstart team from Newfoundland whose last playdown game of the year was played in Goose Bay, Labrador.

Hanna, Langenburg, and Goose Bay are certainly not household city names that roll off the tongue in international curling cities like Oslo, Stockholm, Minneapolis, Sydney, Zurich, or Nagano. Goodness, curling fans in Vancouver, Toronto, or Montreal would be hard pressed to locate these towns even with the help of a geography teacher. Tweeners understand that you can do wonders when you learn how to deliver a curling rock with competence, learn to sweep effectively, and throw a little caution to the wind in facing the best your province has to offer.

The Reverend Arch McCurdy, a tweener, grew up in Ontario in a non-curling family. One of his first parishes was in Canora, Saskatchewan, in the heartland of curling. As Arch and his new bride, Phyllis, were settling into their new parsonage, they noticed this sleek-looking newfangled broom. Seemed a little unique-looking, but it seemed to get the job done. One of the members of the congregation noticed the McCurdys using this broom for the kitchen floor and quickly explained to them that it was a curling broom. Having never played the game and realizing that the hub of the community gathered around the hockey and curling rinks, they thought it would be a great idea to get to know their community and get a little exercise at the same time. Thus began a life-long obsession.

Both Arch and Phyllis were quite athletic and took to the game rather quickly, or let us say with a vengeance. He wanted to become one of the better players in the community, so he worked on the two skills that seemed to be valued the most—delivering a rock and sweeping. Arch concluded that to become proficient at this new sport, "You had to deliver a rock with the appropriate weight. You had to hit the skip's broom or at least miss it appropriately. You had to sweep the rocks."

But, as Arch would be the first to admit, "Yes, it's a simple game but one of the hardest games in the world to master, and you are constantly learning, learning, learning." Within a couple of years, the Rev. McCurdy became one of the town's best shotmakers, and he could sweep like a demon running away from Stephen Spielberg's Indiana Jones. Over the next thirty to forty years, the McCurdys, regardless of where they were pastoring, would arrive in a new community and first scout out the location of the curling rink.

How did Arch and his wife become so proficient at this new sport in which they fell in love? They worked and worked at the two primary skills necessary to be a competent curler: throwing a forty-two-pound piece of granite down a pebbled piece of ice at colored rings that looked like a giant archer's target and learning to sweep with power and quickness in front of the path of these rocks that rotated with such grace and beauty.

Bill Tschirhart wrote two articles for the NTC called "Straight, Simple and Silent" and "Brushing 101" that he has graciously let us use for this chapter. His articles have to do with delivering a rock, hitting the broom, and brushing. We'll let Bill's expertise take over for describing this simple-to-play yet complex game to master.

#1 You Had to Deliver a Rock with the Appropriate Weight

In Bill's article on delivering a curling stone, he writes of the three Ss—straight, simple, and silent. Straight and simple will cover our first point of delivering a rock with the appropriate weight. This really deals with the set up and delivery, up until the moment of preparing for the release of the curling stone.

From a technical point of view, it is obvious that virtually all the best players of our game have three aspects of the delivery, which are identical. I am amazed at how *straight* elite curlers can slide. There is nary a hint of drift in their slides. How do they do that? The key is the position and the movement of the sliding foot.

In the stance or hack position, balance—the real key to sliding straight—is achieved by placing one foot under the one shoulder and the other foot under the other shoulder. The *hack foot*—yes, that's the one actually in the hack—will have the toe on the bottom of the hack and the ball on the sloped portion. The *sliding foot*—the slippery one—

is flat on the ice with the heel of the sliding foot opposite the toe of the hack foot. Why? Balance!

But, the key to all of this is what coaches who have taken N.C.C.P. technical course from me know as *the silly little place*. The space is the distance between the hack foot and the sliding foot while in the hack position. But, most curler's don't do that. Most curlers have the sliding foot on the ice overlapping or directly in front of the hack foot. They say it gives them better balance in the hack—the jury is out on that by the way. Good idea except for one small item, the sliding foot has to *move!* If your sliding foot is in front of the hack foot, you will have to move it around the hack foot in a pattern we call a C curve. Think about this. You want to slide forward in a straight line, and the only thing that connects you to the ice you move in a curved path. Hmmmm! Bottom line, move the sliding foot as you will, but move it straight.

As the stone moves forward, the sliding foot moves behind the stone. And that's the other key. Some players don't have their sliding foot directly behind the stone for a very good reason. It has to do with eye dominance. If you are right-handed *and* right-eye dominant, it is unlikely that you will want to have the stone in the middle of your body. If you did, you wouldn't be seeing the target with your dominant eye, which is your right eye. You probably will shoot off your right shoulder. There was a time when, as an instructor, I might try to *correct* this fault, but I know better now.

Before we leave this topic, let's discuss line of delivery. The athletes with whom I work with all slide straight. You must do that if you have any hopes of playing this game at an elite level. A certified instructor can teach anybody to do that. It's strictly mechanics. But what's the sense of sliding straight if you slide straight off line most of the time? There is another ingredient, which you must do each and every time you execute a shot. You must establish the line of delivery. I enjoy asking players what body part they use to line up in the hack. I get quite a variety of responses from hack foot, to hack knee, to hack thigh, to shoulders to . . . I rarely get the best answer. It's *hips.* You see, the lower extremities can move around the whole body actually changing directions. Shoulders can't turn much without affecting the entire body. But, move your hips, and you move everything. Hips are the most reliable body part for alignment. As a result, I encourage curlers to stand slightly behind the hack, set the hips square to the intended line of delivery, get into the hack, then use some of the secondary body parts such as those listed above. If you can slide straight, it's over! Concentrate on the correct weight for the shot!

When I teach Level One technical courses, I use a red center line ribbon to demonstrate the various lines of delivery to a new curler. I place one end at the hack and roll out the ribbon to various places in the house at the other end of the sheet. Now, as a player, I can't help but visualize my red ribbon as I line up behind the hack and reach forward with my hack foot on line with my red ribbon—pay attention to this seemingly useless bit of trivia as it is foreshadowing. By doing this, you have established your line of delivery.

Where is the sliding foot during the slide? It should be directly below the base of the sternum—that long narrow cartilaginous portion of one's anatomy in the breast area that connects most of the pairs of ribs. That's the balance point for most people.

Simple refers to all the movements in the course of the delivery. Extraneous movements can only detract from the purpose of the delivery, which is to propel the stone with the proper velocity on the desired line. Only by examining one's delivery on videotape can one determine if all the movements are required. You don't need an instructor for this. Just ask yourself *why* each time you see a body part move. If you can't come up with a reason for it, then you might get some help. In most cases, you'll simply change or remove the movement. Extraneous movement is a dead giveaway that a curler either does not practice or does not have access to a delivery clinician. Keep it simple! All the best curlers do.

#2 You Had to Hit the Skip's Broom or at Least Miss it Appropriately

Silent, the last *S*, is probably the most important. It refers to the release. If you have a million-dollar delivery and a two-cent release, you have a two-cent delivery! It may seem strange that I would describe the release in terms of volume. I really don't mean silent as in the absence of sound but rather that it is so smooth it appears silent. We have all seen curlers whose release looks like an explosion with the hand literally flying off the handle—a noisy, inconsistent release to be sure.

A great release begins with the grip. The second finger pads are on the bottom of the handle. The side of the thumb is on the side of the handle. The wrist is high. The position promotes a smooth, silent delivery. In the hack, with this grip, the handle is set at either 9 or 10 o'clock—for a clockwise rotation—or a 2 or 3 o'clock—for a counter-clockwise rotation. As you slide toward the release point, rotate the stone, with a positive rotation from the initial position—2 or 10 o'clock—through to the 12 o'clock. Open your hand—it will now be in the *handshake* position—and leave it there until the stone comes into your field of vision. Don't look down at the stone as it is released. Remember *simple* and the why question? That's one of the biggies. Why would you take your eyes off the target to watch the stone leave your hand? Is someone going to come out onto the ice and steal it from your hand?

If all members of the team use this grip and release, the *look* is the same for all the players on the team. Life then becomes so much simpler for your skip. The whole team benefits.

By the way, when was the last time you checked the distance from the start of your rotation until the actual release? It should not exceed the length of a brush handle. Have someone stand along the sideline and drop one glove at the onset of rotation, and the other glove at the release point.

Another thing. As a team, does everyone release the stone at basically the same place? Take four cups and place the numerals one through four on the bottom of each cup. Place them at the release point of each player—the lead is one, the second is two, etc. Be sure to check a variety of weights when you do this. If you discover that release points are all over the map, make some changes. This is a team sport.

Oh, by the way, please don't stifle your follow through. Let your delivery come to its natural conclusion, all the while posing with that release hand. And when you do come to a stop, check to see if you're still on *my red ribbon*. You should be if you slid straight.

Here's a coaching hint. Try to impress upon your athletes that if they are to perfect a curling delivery, they must first understand it. Ask your athletes to describe their delivery in detail. You will be amazed how many struggle to do this. It's the *in detail* part that is the key. If one hitches his trousers or pulls on her panty hose, it should be in the description. If he hitches his panty hose, you might want a gender test. Once you understand the biomechanics of the delivery, it is easier to examine one's own and then change it.

In former World Champion Eddie Lukowich's must-read book for curlers, *Curling to Win*, he offers this little tidbit of advice on hitting the broom.

> *This may sound like kindergarten—throw the rock at the broom. However, very few curlers can do it. Most players have the rock follow a slightly different pattern. Left and right handers are direct opposites . . . a swing and delivery that are 90 percent on line will make many shots. Once you have achieved a much-improved delivery, you can concentrate on refining your game further.*

> *How should a stone react? If the player has a straight swing and the rock can be released* at the broom *without any steering, the rock will react. If it is two or three inches wide, and not swept, it will react and curl. If the release is narrow, the sweeping will hold it straight. A rock thrown* at the broom *can be swept effectively. You will know if you are throwing* at the broom *because your rock will react extremely well to the sweeping calls. It is an honest rock.*

#3 You Had to Sweep the Rocks

a) To Be Effective, You Must Brush Quickly, With As Much Downward Pressure As Possible

Now there's a revelation, but there's much more to that than first appears. Let's deal with the downward pressure part first.

When curlers switched from corn brooms, many decided that to maximize downward pressure it was necessary to grasp the handle of the brush as low as possible. It really did *look* as though the athlete was pressing down really hard as opposed to one who grasped the brush higher on the handle. In fact, just the opposite proved to be the case. You can easily test this out for yourself and your teammates.

Get an ordinary bathroom scale and assume that low-hand position. Press down with the brush on the scale and get a reading. Now, position your hands higher on the handle. Get the weight of your body on the balls of your feet and angle the brush as close to perpendicular as you can. Now press down and read the scale. I have an old corn broom that says you have increased the downward pressure substantially.

Although the evidence is in that this *high hands position* will indeed produce greater downward pressure, what's the sense assuming this position if the stroke rate is significantly reduced as an undesirable side affect? It's not! Therefore a compromise is in order between hand position, body position and handle angle, which will allow for the greatest amount of downward pressure and maximum stroke rate.

Let's talk hands. It is generally accepted that it is best if the palm of the upper hand faces *up* while the palm of the lower hand faces *down*. The handle of the brush is then secured between the upper arm of the higher arm and the rib cage. Remember, keep those hands as high on the handle as possible without sacrificing too much stroke speed.

b) Good Brushers Can Brush From Either Side of the Stone and Will Wear Grippers On Both Feet

Another change that brushing brought about is the relative positions of the two brushers. Let's return for a moment to those days of old when the brushers were, tah dah, *sweepers*. Both sweepers were usually, not always but usually, on the same side of the stone. This made sweeping in unison much easier and due to the nature of the action of the broom, two sweepers could literally be shoulder to shoulder without disturbing one another's footwork. This is *not* the case when two *brushers* brush. The footwork is entirely different.

I like to describe the footwork when brushing as a combination of basketball shuffle and cross-country skiing. Generally, the feet face toward the target of the stone—especially the front foot. And even though the brusher wears grippers on *both feet*, the feet can still *slide* enough to make the movements of the feet smooth. But, this cross-country ski action takes up a lot of space, certainly much more than the footwork of those two *sweepers*, so it would be awkward at best if two brushers were on the same side of the stone. It is difficult to describe in words the action of the feet. It really is trial and error. You adopt a method which allows you to maximize brushing effectively.

The gripper/gripper idea first started when brushers realized that to brush *on the opposite side of the stone*, it placed the *slider foot* as the rear or push foot. This was awkward and somewhat dangerous. So the answer was to place one's gripper over the slider while brushing on that *opposite side*. Little did we know that the other, very positive spin-offs would occur. They include: added safety, increased heart rate recovery due to the fact that the athlete must *walk* back to position rather than use the push/slide method, and greatly reduced stress on the knee of the slider leg. Who would have thought? It is now commonplace for curlers to go *gripper/gripper* for all the skills of the game except executing the actual delivery of the stone.

Grippers are not expensive. Get new ones each year. They dry out quickly and shed easily. *They are the primary cause of picked stones!*

c) Use a Brush That Is Suitable for the Environment

Most elite curlers agree that under frosty conditions, a hair type of brushing device might have an advantage over a synthetic device. Ice technicians tell us that from a pebble-wear perspective, the synthetic brush head *appears* to actually wear down the pebble to a greater degree than a hair device. The type of device selected is very much a compromise between the needs and wishes of the team and the athlete. Don't select a brush that is too heavy or too long for example. Oh, by the way, no tests, which have been conducted, have proven that one type of generally accepted brushing device is more effective than any other! But, tests certainly have demonstrated that brushing is effective in helping the stone maintain its momentum!

Besides the actual *brushing surface* of the brush, the head of the brush tends to be manufactured in different lengths as well. Right now the most well-known brushing tandem are *Huff and Puff* (aka Marcel Rocque and Scott Pfeifer) the front end for the world champion Randy Ferbey team. They both use very long brush heads. I must admit I don't really understand why they use such a large brush head. The running surface is only half the diameter of the stone. It's rather small. Even a *small head* brush, placed at the correct angle will keep a running surface at all times—a key point for most excellent competitive brushers. It's a matter of personal preference. Some brush heads are *angled* to the handle of the brush so that the brush head moves across the path of the stone in such a way as to always be perpendicular to the path of the stone. That certainly promotes maintaining a portion of the brush head in front of the running surface of the stone.

The Author's Search for the Ideal Delivery

Here's my search for the right delivery . . . How I went from hacker to at least the tweener level. Of course, I am cocky enough to believe that if I could take a three-year sabbatical from my day job and devote myself to the degree I would really like to, I could advance to that next level. Whether that is true or not, we may never know. But this is a good story nonetheless!

After reading the two articles Bill Tschirhart donated to this chapter, I got quite excited. Bill crystallized his thoughts on the delivery and release in a way that I have come to firmly believe in since 1987. I kept thinking, "Bill, you speak the language I understand and articulate the delivery and release the way I understand them." I had started curling in 1974 and had an epiphany in January 1987.

Up until then, I just figured that my athletic talent was good enough to compete with any curler on the planet. I thought I didn't need to analyze my delivery and get all technical on myself. Then, I encountered the slump of slumps. I lost my in-turn and my teams went on a 2-8 tailspin after starting the season so well; the losses were mostly my fault because I was curling so dawg-gone horribly. I did what I usually did in a slump. I went to the rink by myself and practiced my brains out.

However, even in practice, I was missing with my in-turn like I hadn't missed since my junior high days. Finally, I humbled myself and got a friend to come out and analyze my delivery. He used a bunch of technical mumbo jumbo but basically said I was over-curling my wrist at release. That made sense. I decided then and there to at least get a delivery and release that I could be consistent with and analyze when the next slump came along. The teams I was on finished the year 26-3, winning three bonspiels. It was the first time ever I had skipped three teams in the same season to bonspiel wins.

This began a fifteen-year quest to study everything I could get my hands on regarding the delivery and release. (Actually, it's probably going to be a lifetime search to continually perfect and improve.) I read

Ken Watson's books, everything Eddie Lukowich published, found some stuff (by a fluke) by the USA Curling Association, the CCA materials, an old Scottish book on curling, and talked to my uncles, my dad, and other curlers I respected. I paid attention to Don Duguid on CBC and listened attentively to the advice of Ray Turnbull and Linda Moore on TSN. From all these masters of their craft, I learned the fundamentals were basically the same.

For the record, the teams I played on pre-1987 had a winning percentage of 49 percent. The teams I have been a part of post–1987 have a winning percentage of almost 69 percent! That is almost a full 20 percent improvement since getting serious about understanding my delivery. Granted it's a team game, so that goes into the equation, but I think my going from hacker to at least tweener helped boost the winning percentage somewhat.

"No, it's not just a rock. It's forty-two pounds of polished granite, beveled on the belly and a handle a human being can hold. And it may have no practical purpose in itself but it is a repository of human possibility and, if it's handled right, it will exact a kind of poetry.

I've drilled oil in ninety-three countries, five different continents, and *not once have I done anything to equal the grace of a well-thrown curling rock sliding down the ice. Not once!"*

—Paul Gross as Chris Cutter,
in the 2002 blockbuster film *Men with Brooms*

Chapter Twenty-one

Physical Fitness and Performance in Curling

by Bob Comartin

"When I do curling clinics for young people, I like to tell them a team needs to buy into all the right stuff in order to be successful. Things like chemistry, making goals and focusing on them, remembering it's only a game and not to beat themselves up too much after bad games, and the importance of working out. I've been working out with a trainer for a few years now. Oh yeah, and the last thing—go out, have fun, and kick butt!"

—Greg McAulay,
Skip of the 2000 Men's World
Curling Champions

This chapter was written by Bob Comartin, who is currently the senior sports and fitness leader with the city of Port Coquitlam, a suburb of Vancouver. Bob completed his bachelor of human kinetics in 1992 from the University of Windsor (Ontario). He worked as an athletic therapist and strength coach for the BC Lions (CFL) and has since worked in private practice in rehabilitation and sports conditioning. Bob is a certified strength and conditioning specialist, certified fitness consultant, registered kinesiologist, and has spent considerable time studying sports medicine. He's worked with curling Olympians and World Champions Kelley Law, Georgina Wheatcroft, and Diane Nelson.

Physical training is an important part of a curler's season preparation and lifelong physical health. The better the overall fitness of a curler, the better one will be able to handle the physical and mental stress of the game. An ideal delivery position should allow the curler to perform at the highest level while keeping in mind the longevity of playing in the sport. Training the long-term athlete is discussed in many settings and can lead to improved methods of coaching and training. The health of the curler should be of primary importance, and longevity in the sport should be emphasized.

I once heard Marcel Rocque ask this question at a high-performance camp, "What is the most important piece of equipment you bring to the rink?" I wanted to jump up and say "You" of course. However, that wasn't the answer, and it got me thinking how so much is done to improve sliders, brushes, and crutches without as much emphasis on improving the curler. Similarly in golf, so much time and money is spent improving shoes, clubs, balls, and accessories. It wasn't until Tiger Woods came along, and began incorporating sport science principles, that a golfer ever discussed exercise.

I'd like to thank Diane Nelson-Dezura for her patience in enduring many workouts while I attempt to understand and experiment with new ideas. My involvement in training curlers would not have happened without her dedication to best practices in sport science.

Physical Demand Assessment of the Sport of Curling

There are three identifiable physical components in a game that can be affected by training. Sweeping, delivery, and prolonged standing can fatigue or strain an athlete with poor posture, fitness, and performance parameters.

Because of the repetitive nature of sweeping, the potential for throwing rocks while cold, and placing the body in biomechanically weak positions, micro tears may become chronic injuries if not handled with proper warm-ups, cool downs, and overall training. The flexed torso, rounded shoulders, and extended/ulnar deviated wrist are no doubt responsible for sweeping injuries from overuse. During the delivery, the greater the forward knee flexion combined with rotational stress, the greater risk of knee injury. Also, in the delivery position, the player experiences great surface instability, creating an excessive load on hip stability.

A team's lead and second can expect to sweep six rocks each end, resulting in as much as sixty repetitions of up twenty seconds in a 10-end game. A team's third can expect to sweep four rocks each end resulting in a total of forty repetitions. Besides the anaerobic lactic nature of sweeping, speed or turnover is also of importance. Sprinters refer to the speed of their leg action as turnover rate. In a similar manner, curlers refer to it as sweep rate. Therefore, the condition of high-performance front end curlers should be similar to high-performance sprinters.

The delivery position requires bilateral hip flexibility, sliding leg hip stability, pelvic and lumbar stability, and hack-leg power.

Lastly, and somewhat overlooked, prolonged standing in a cold environment can influence circulation and muscle suppleness creating fatigue and stiffness. While sweepers maintain a degree of circulation, it is important that skips maintain some level of movement. Whether this movement is occasional sweeping, crouching, or other activity, increased circulation and flexibility preparation for their delivery can influence performance.

Some curlers and coaches think that I'm overanalyzing the curler and going overboard on my suggestions; however, it is only the unusual athlete who will do unusual things. Then, when they become successful, as with Tiger Woods, the whole world begins hiring conditioning coaches.

Overall Athlete Assessment
Before embarking on any testing or training program, it is best to get medical clearance. Understanding that there is some inherent risk with any testing or training program, the athlete is responsible to seek medical advice if he or she is unsure of his or her current condition.

Testing parameters can be split into three divisions: postural-related testing, fitness-related testing, and performance-related testing. Procedurally, postural parameters are tested at any point throughout one's season. Postural testing includes musculoskeletal alignment, joint specific flexibility, and muscular imbalances. Postural awareness can reduce the stress/strain of day-to-day living. This should be completed by experts experienced in this area such as physiotherapists, athletic therapists, or experienced kinesiologists.

A postural-related test will examine the curvatures of the spine; the alignment of the hips, knees, ankles, and feet; and the position of the scapulae, shoulders, and elbows, all in a standing position. Furthermore, tests of balance, squat mechanics, gait, full-body joint flexibility, and specific areas of strength will also be measured.

This is followed by fitness parameters, as they are the building blocks or stepping-stones of performance. A solid fitness base will enhance the performance measure. This procedure follows the guidelines of beginning with general training and moving towards sport-specific training. Fitness testing elements include an aerobic capacity test, a sit-and-reach test, the Appley scratch test, a push-ups test, a wall squat test, and grip strength.

Performance testing elements would include an anaerobic, lactic heart rate recovery test, sweep rate test, single-leg squat test, core plank test, and jump test. Both fitness and performance parameters should be provided by an accredited fitness appraiser, an exercise physiologist, a certified strength and conditioning specialist, or a kinesiologist.

Training the Curling Athlete

Now that we have some general understanding of the positions, bio-mechanics, and bioenergetics of curling, let me explain the components of exercise and how they relate to curling. Although individual testing and training is recommended, the program below can be viewed as an example of the types of training a curler can expect to be introduced to.

The Off-Season

The off-season is a great time to test fitness-related parameters, such as aerobic conditioning, flexibility, and strength. Once the test results are in, a training program can be created. Let me attempt to explain these in greater detail.

The following is a typical arrangement of off-season workouts through-out the week:

Day 1	Day 2	Day 3	Day 4	Day 5	Day 6	Day 7
Aerobic Activity	Strength	Aerobic Activity	Strength	Aerobic Activity	Strength	Day Off
Stretch	Stretch	Stretch	Stretch	Stretch	Stretch	

Aerobic Activity

Aerobic training can include any activity that allows the body to work in an oxidative state—using oxygen as fuel. The body will work in an oxidative state when the activity is moderate in intensity and lasts more than a few minutes.

Aerobic training is important in curling as it can improve a body's ability to withstand physical and mental stress. Due to its relationship with the metabolic process, it can also aid in the physical recovery process between games and days of high, physical exertion.

Aerobic capacity can be tested in many ways. In large groups or as a team, the Leger Shuttle Test allows the entire group or team to be tested at once. It has excellent reliability, and since athletes finish the test having completed a specific stage, it also helps them set tangible goals with their training.

There are three distinct levels of aerobic training: base training, threshold training, and speed training. Based on the results of the aerobic capacity test, athletes are placed in one of these categories or in between two categories and given an appropriate program. The ideal length of a pro-gram is approximately eight weeks as that allows significant time to make physiological changes. A retest will allow the athlete to notice improvements and reset goals to the next level. Programs can also range a great deal depending on the history and goals of the athlete.

My advice to athletes regarding aerobic activity is to engage in walking/running, as it can be done anywhere. For the most part, curlers are busy people. Whether active with family, work, or other activities, one can always put on a pair of shoes and run. When the weather turns worse, running can be done in pools or with snow-shoes. Options exist. Should a medical reason not allow you to run, any other form of cardiovascular activity will suffice.

A typical base training program is as follows:

Base Level Aerobic Endurance Workouts

Week 1	Week 2
Session 1: run 1 min.—walk 4 min.—x5	Session 1: run 1.5 min.—walk 3.5 min.—x6
Session 2: run 1 min.—walk 4 min.—x6	Session 2: run 2 min.—walk 3 min.—x5
Session 3: run 1.5 min.—walk 3.5 min.—x5	Session 3: run 2 min.—walk 3 min.—x6
Week 3	**Week 4**
Session 1: run 2.5 min.—walk 2.5 min.—x5	Session 1: run 3 min.—walk 2 min.—x6
Session 2: run 2.5 min.—walk 2.5 min.—x6	Session 2: run 3.5 min.—walk 1.5 min.—x5
Session 3: run 3 min.—walk 2 min.—x5	Session 3: run 3.5 min.—walk 1.5 min.—x6
Week 5	**Week 6**
Session 1: run 4 min.—walk 1 min.—x5	Session 1: run 5 min.—walk 1 min.—x6
Session 2: run 4 min.—walk 1 min.—x6	Session 2: run 6 min.—walk 1 min.—x5
Session 3: run 5 min.—walk 1 min.—x5	Session 3: run 6 min.—walk 1 min.—x5
Week 7	**Week 8**
Session 1: run 7 min.—walk 1 min.—x4	Session 1: run 8 min.—walk 1 min.—x4
Session 2: run 7 min.—walk 1 min.—x4	Session 2: run 10 min.—walk 1 min.—x3
Session 3: run 8 min.—walk 1 min.—x4	Session 3: 30 minutes

Retest aerobic capacity after week 8

A typical threshold training program is as follows:

Threshold Level Aerobic Endurance Workouts

Week 1	Week 2
Session 1: 20 minutes	Session 1: 25 minutes
Session 2: 20 minutes	Session 2: 25 minutes
Session 3: 25 minutes	Session 3: 30 minutes
75 percent intensity	75 percent intensity
Week 3	**Week 4**
Session 1: 30 minutes	Session 1: 35 minutes
Session 2: 30 minutes	Session 2: 35 minutes
Session 3: 35 minutes	Session 3: 25 minutes
75 percent intensity	75 percent intensity

Week 5	Week 6
Session 1: 30 minutes	Session 1: 35 minutes
Session 2: 30 minutes	Session 2: 40 minutes
Session 3: 35 minutes	Session 3: 40 minutes
First and last 10 minutes: 70 percent intensity	First and last 10 minutes: 70 percent intensity
Middle part: 85 percent intensity	Middle part: 85 percent intensity
Week 7	**Week 8**
Session 1: 40 minutes	Session 1: 45 minutes
Session 2: 45 minutes	Session 2: 35 minutes
Session 3: 45 minutes	Session 3: 30 minutes
First and last 10 minutes: 70 percent intensity	First and last 10 minutes: 70 percent intensity
Middle part: 85 percent intensity	Middle part: 85 percent intensity

Retest aerobic capacity after week 8

The following is a typical threshold/speed training program:

Threshold/Speed Level Aerobic Endurance Workouts

Week 1	Week 2
Session 1: 25 minutes	Session 1: 28 minutes
Session 2: 28 minutes	Session 2: 32 minutes
Session 3: 35 minutes	Session 3: 30 minutes
85 percent intensity	85 percent intensity
Week 3	**Week 4**
Session 1: 30 minutes	Session 1: 35 minutes
Session 2: 35 minutes	Session 2: 40 minutes
Session 3: 32 minutes	Session 3: 38 minutes
85 percent intensity	85 percent intensity

Week 5

Session 1: warm up—10 minutes slow
        increase pace—30 seconds
        decrease—1.5 minutes
        repeat 5x
        cool down—10 minutes slow pace

Session 2: 35 minutes—70 to 80 percent
Session 3: warm up—10 minutes slow
        increase pace—30 seconds
        decrease—1.5 minutes
        repeat 5x
        cool down—10 minutes slow pace

Week 6

Session 1: warm up—10 minutes slow
         hill repeats—15 seconds up
         45 seconds—relax down
           and recover—8x
         cool down—10 minutes slow pace

Session 2: 40 minutes
Session 3: warm up—10 minutes slow
         hill repeats—15 seconds up
         45 seconds—relax down and
           recover—10x
         cool down—10 minutes slow pace

Week 7

Session 1: warm up—10 minutes slow
         increase pace—1 minute
         decrease—2 minutes
         repeat 5x
         cool down—10 minutes slow pace

Session 2: 45 minutes
Session 3: warm up—10 minutes slow
         hill repeats—25 seconds up
         1 minute and 35 seconds—relax
         down and recover—6x
         cool down—10 minutes slow pace

Week 8

Session 1: 30 minutes
Session 2: 35 minutes

Session 3: 30 minutes
         70 to 80 percent
Retest aerobic capacity after week 8

Muscular Strength and Endurance

Muscular strength and endurance is the ability to produce maximal or submaximal force in a muscle, or set of muscles, repeatedly or over a given period of time.

During stone delivery, the muscles of the hips, pelvis, and core must contract at submaximal levels in order to maintain a controlled position through the release of the rock. Strength is a precursor to power, which is important for the hack leg as one "breaks through the pane of glass" as Bill Tschirhart calls it. With brushing, endurance is important as to allow the player to withstand fatigue from a solid core contraction while rapidly brushing.

Strength can be tested when performing a one-leg squat; endurance can be tested through pushups. Based on the testing results, programs can be developed on a level 1, 2, and 3 basis to set achievement goals and to motivate athletes.

The following program outlines 3 levels of general strength exercises:
Week 1–2: endurance   Week 3–4: hypertrophy/endurance
Week 5–6: hypertrophy   Week 7: strength   Week 8: recovery

	Level 1	Level 2	Level 3
E	Forward lunges	Added weight	Bar overhead
	Ball hamstring curls	Raise hips with ball pull	Single leg
X	Ball wall squats	Hold bottom position for 3–5 seconds and return	No ball—hold bottom position
	Push ups— male version —on incline	Male version	Feet on ball
E	Lat pulldowns	1/2 body weight	Chin ups
	Seated rows	Pull-ups in squat rack	Feet on ball
R	Lateral raises	On one leg	Start with arms raised, drop one and raise, alt.
C	Back extensions— on floor	45° bench	Ball or add arm raises
	Tricep pressdowns	Supinated grip	Increase weight
I	Bicep curls— dumbbells	On one leg	Start in mid–range of motion, drop one and raise + return to start position and alt.
	Crossbody lifts	Hands and knees	Ball—on floor
S	Wheelbarrow knee tucks	Single leg tuck	Nelson/Dezura twist
E	Double crunches	Medball in hands	Increase distance of hands and feet away from body

Flexibility

Flexibility is defined as having optimal range of motion (ROM) around a joint. It only takes one look at a delivery position to determine why this area is important in curling. Hack leg hip extension and slider leg hip FABER (Flexion/Abduction/External Rotation) are the sport-specific joint ROM necessary to play the game. It is noted that most over-use injuries do occur due to the strain created in the game and a lack of stretching that would allow a return to optimal ROM. Therefore, it is important to develop a stretching program that reduces the tension created on the ice. Complete at least one repetition of each stretching exercise. Time your stretches and hold them for thirty seconds. Repeat stretches if you lack full range of motion or if indicated by your sport science specialist.

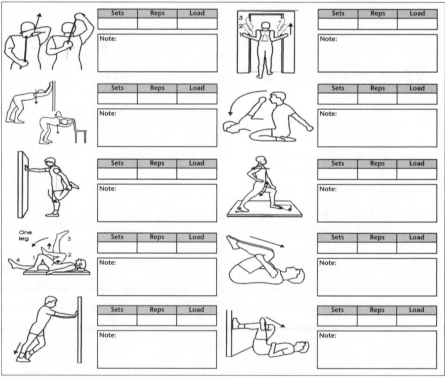

Illustrations used by permission of PHYSIGRAPHE (www.physigraphe.com).

The Preseason

In preseason, we move from fitness-related parameters to performance or sport-specific parameters. This is not to say that we eliminate fitness training entirely, but rather it will be reduced to allow for an emphasis on elements that are more curling specific. Sweepers will place training emphasis on the anaerobic lactic system, core strength, and upper-body speed and endurance. Skips can continue to focus on aerobic capacity during this period. All curlers should work on strength and flexibility as well as leg power.

The following is a typical arrangement of workouts throughout the week:

Day 1	Day 2	Day 3	Day 4	Day 5	Day 6	Day 7
Power/ Jump Program	Anaerobic Sweep Training	Power/ Jump Program		Anaerobic Sweep Training	Power/ Jump Program	Anaerobic Sweep Training
Sport Specific Strength	Cardio Recovery	Sport Specific Strength	Day Off	Cardio/ Recovery	Sport Specific Strength	
Stretch	Stretch	Stretch		Stretch	Stretch	Stretch

Sport-Specific Strength

Strength continues to be emphasized in-season; however, it is refined in more specific movements, such as stressing the body in delivery-specific positions and working on core strength in brushing-type positions. Here are some examples:

1. The curler gets into a delivery position, using a balance apparatus for the sliding foot; a trainer may lightly tap the inside or outside of the knee to stress the hip stabilizers.

2. Crossover step-ups allow the hip, knee, and ankle position to be stressed in a similar manner as in the delivery.

3. Core plank exercises and practicing breathing while in this position can greatly simulate a brushing position. I have seen many high-performance curlers hold their breath while sweeping (you know who you are), and this is a good way to practice. Many variations or activities can be combined with plank exercises to continue keeping these fresh and interesting.

These activities can be done almost anywhere. I'd like to thank Georgina Wheatcroft for being my test subject on several innovative ideas.

	Level 1	Level 2
E	a) Balance—single leg on floor, try eyes closed or standing on a balance apparatus (i.e., sit fit, rolled towel, balance rail, or BOSU ball	Single leg on floor or balance apparatus, place other foot on light weight plate and create small circles
X	b) Water bottle placements	Eyes closed or balancing on an object or place object further from your foot
E	Crossover step ups	Add weight
R	Supine hip external rotation press ball into wall	Press ball into wall with hip slightly externally rotated
	Inverted pull up	Place feet on ball
C	Dips on chair weight support on feet	Move feet to ball or single leg on ball or try suspended dips
	Shoulder external rotation tubing or cable	Side lying shoulder external rotation with weight
I	Lateral raises standing	In kneeling position
	Wrist pronation/supination —elbow bent	Elbow straight
S	Beetle on his/her back, knees bent	Knees partially bent
	Prone single-leg raises	On ball or bench double leg raises
E	Cable or tubing rotations	Add unstable surface
	Double crunches	Add med ball

a) balance for approximately 2 to 3 minutes

b) 1 set = placing to all three positions (outside foot, front of foot, inside foot)

*in order to minimize time spent in a gym, alternate between two opposing exercises (super setting) or two different muscle groups with minimal rest between sets. Rest 90 seconds between exercises.

Sets and repetitions outlined in weekly arrangements.

Power

Muscular power is the ability of the muscle to contract both forcefully and quickly, often referred to as explosive strength. Due to physiological make up, men tend to be generally stronger than women and have an easier ability to throw hit weight. One of the most common questions asked at camps by both athletes and coaches is, "What do we do to develop more power out of the hack?" The answer is somewhat complex, in that there is not one single activity.

An athlete should begin by developing leg and core strength, while maintaining flexibility. A significant strength base is required for jump/plyometric-type training. This type of training attempts to produce high intensity stress over a short amortization phase, which eventually leads to a muscle's ability to produce a greater amount of force out of the hack. I hope that didn't confuse the issue. This type of training can include vertical jumps, horizontal jumps, medicine ball training, depth jumps, or Olympic lifting.

The best way to begin training for power is to use explosive sport-specific actions. Therefore, the plyometric activity in this power program will be forward jumping. Begin with a ten- to fifteen-minute warm up by cycling or walking/jogging. Concentrate on each jump just like you would in your delivery.

Double Leg	
Week 1	**Week 2**
Max standing long jump—4 reps	Max standing long jump—5 reps
Rest 15–30 seconds between reps	Rest 15–30 seconds between reps
Walk 1 minute, repeat second set	Walk 1 minute, repeat second set
Week 3	**Week 4**
Max standing long jump—4 reps	Max standing long jump—5 reps
Rest 15–30 seconds between reps	Rest 15–30 seconds between reps
Walk 1 minute, repeat second set of 4 reps	Walk 1 minute, repeat second set
Walk 1 minute, repeat third set	Walk 1 minute, repeat third set

Single Delivery Leg Only	
Week 5	**Week 6**
Max jump off push leg, land on sliding foot and walk through—3 reps	Max jump off push leg, land on sliding foot—4 reps
Rest 15–30 seconds between reps	Rest 15–30 seconds between reps
Walk 1 minute, repeat second set	Walk 1 minute, repeat second set
Walk 1 minute, repeat third set	Walk 1 minute, repeat third set
Week 7	**Week 8**
Max jump off push leg, land on sliding foot—5 reps	Discontinue if you begin practicing on the ice
Rest 15–30 seconds between reps	If you are not on the ice, repeat week 6
Walk 1 minute, repeat second set	
Walk 1 minute, repeat third set	

Anaerobic Lactic System

Anaerobic lactic training is the muscle endurance activity that produces a waste product of lactic acid that can inhibit proper muscle or cell function. This training helps anyone who brushes rocks for approximately eight seconds or longer. This bioenergetics system can be trained by repeated bouts of high intensity activity while allowing optimal recovery between bouts. A sprint for ten to twenty seconds will induce lactic acid production by fast-twitch muscle fibers similar to sweeping for ten to twenty seconds. In actual fact, sweepers are sprinting with their shoulders in order to create an ideal level of friction.

Sweep Rate

Speed training is a newer form of training for brushers. The greatest comparison in training is to that of a sprinter. Just like sprinters have a higher degree of fast-twitch muscle fibers in their legs, sweepers may develop this in their upper body.

I've heard of curlers doing sweeping drills on linoleum or tile flooring. The downfall of this is the higher degree of resistance from these surfaces will require a sweeper to move slower than on the ice. This can train a sweeper to be slower. Sprinters use a method of speed training called over-speed training. It is common for them to use bungee cords to assist in being pulled forward, or run downhill to run faster than they would normally run. This is well studied in athletics. Neurologically, it induces a muscle to fire at a faster rate and, therefore, improves the consistency of fast-twitch muscle fibers.

It is possible and recommended to combine speed and anaerobic lactic training to improve sport specificity. The development of a gradually progressive program with proper rest intervals will allow for an improved anaerobic system.

The machine that I have been using over the past few years is developed by Fitter International out of Calgary, Alberta, and is called the Pro Fitter. Originally designed for knee rehabilitation for downhill skiers, I have found it to be an excellent training tool for sweep rate in curlers. This machine has bungee cords attached to the sliding mechanism, and, when one pushes the mechanism, it wants to pull you back. This allows the movement to be sped up and thus follows the principles of over-speed training. I've had to purchase a second unit since Diane Nelson-Dezura wore out my first one.

Sweep Rate and Anaerobic Workout
The first number is the sweeping simulation interval and the number in parentheses shows the rest interval.

Workout Time (rest)	
Week 1	**Week 2**
5 (15), 10 (30), 10 (30), 10—rest 1 min.	5 (15), 10 (30), 10 (30), 10—rest 1 min.
5 (15), 10 (30), 10 (30), 10—rest 1 min.	5 (15), 15 (45), 15 (45), 10—rest 1 min.
5 (15), 10 (30), 10 (30), 10—rest 1 min.	5 (15), 15 (45), 15 (45), 10—rest 1 min.
5 (15), 10 (30), 10 (30), 10	5 (15), 10 (30), 10 (30), 10
total time = 7 minutes and 20 seconds	total time = 11 minutes and 40 seconds
Week 3	**Week 4**
10 (30), 10 (30), 10 (30), 10—rest 1 min.	Repeat week 2
5 (15), 15 (45), 15 (45), 10—rest 1 min.	
5 (15), 20 (60), 20 (60), 10—rest 1 min.	
10 (30), 15 (45), 15 (45), 10	
total time = 13 minutes and 40 seconds	

Workout Time (rest)	
Week 5 10 (30), 10 (30), 15 (45), 10—rest 1 min. 10 (30), 20 (60), 15 (45), 10—rest 1 min. 10 (30), 25 (75), 15 (45), 10—rest 1 min. 10 (30), 15 (45), 15 (45), 10 total time = 15 minutes	**Week 6** 10 (30), 15 (45), 20 (60), 10—rest 1 min. 10 (30), 25 (75), 20 (60), 10—rest 1 min. 10 (30), 25 (75), 20 (60), 10—rest 1 min. 10 (30), 20 (60), 15 (45), 10 total time = 15 minutes and 45 seconds
Week 7 10 (30), 15 (45), 15 (45), 10—rest 1 min. 10 (30), 25 (75), 20 (60), 10—rest 1 min. 10 (30), 20 (60), 20 (60), 10—rest 1 min. 10 (30), 20 (60), 15 (45), 10 total time = 16 minutes and 20 seconds	**Week 8** Repeat week 6

The In-Season

In-season training depends on the number of times someone competes and practices. Teams should schedule their season in order to allow periods of opportunity to ramp or increase their overall conditioning. Postural training allows the body to maintain alignment, reduce overall strain, improve recovery, and give sufficient feedback on current condition. Although this outline may not suit everyone's needs, it provides guidelines under ideal settings. Postural training can be done leading up to the day before an event. Aerobic activity can be done up to four days prior to the event. Strength training can be done up to six days prior to the event. On all other days, the focus should be on recovery and regeneration principles.

The following schedules are typical training schedule scenarios based on beginning play on Thursdays (day 5) and dependent on the number of days to prepare for an event.

1 Week Scenario Prior to Competition

Day 1	Day 2	Day 3	Day 4	Day 5	Day 6	Day 7
Balance/ Core	Recovery	Recovery	Recovery	Play Recovery	Play Recovery	Play Recovery

• 2 sets of 10 on core strength

2 Week Scenario Prior to Competition

Day 1	Day 2	Day 3	Day 4	Day 5	Day 6	Day 7
Strength	Cardio	Recovery	Strength	Cardio	Recovery	Strength

Day 1	Day 2	Day 3	Day 4	Day 5	Day 6	Day 7
Cardio	Recovery	Recovery	Recovery	Play Recovery	Play Recovery	Play Recovery

- strength program: 3 sets of 10–12 reps
- cardio program: front end players choose scenario 2 and 3 aerobic endurance combined, 3rds choose scenario 1 and 4 combined, skips choose scenarios 2 and 4

3 Week Scenario Prior to Competition

Day 1	Day 2	Day 3	Day 4	Day 5	Day 6	Day 7
Recovery	Strength	Cardio	Recovery	Strength	Cardio	Recovery

Day 1	Day 2	Day 3	Day 4	Day 5	Day 6	Day 7
Strength	Cardio	Recovery	Strength	Cardio	Recovery	Strength

Day 1	Day 2	Day 3	Day 4	Day 5	Day 6	Day 7
Cardio	Recovery	Recovery	Recovery	Play Recovery	Play Recovery	Play Recovery

- week 1: 2 sets 12–15 reps on strength
- week 2: 3 sets of 6–8 reps on strength
- week 1 cardio: front end choose scenarios 1 and 2, back end choose scenario 4
- week 2 and 3 cardio: front end choose scenarios 2 and 3, 3rds choose scenarios 1 and 4, skips choose scenarios 2 and 4

These programs should be individually tailored to the athlete's current condition.

The following list outlines some general principles of recovery and regeneration:

1. Sleep seven to nine hours usually best
2. Active rest—especially on the road
   - light aerobic training
   - dynamic range-of-motion exercises

- stretching
- pool exercises
- games that are low intensity and fun team-building in nature

3. Nutrition—difficult to eat healthy on the road, planning is essential
   - avoid fad diets
   - learn the Canada Food Guide
   - eat to be healthy

4. Hydration—coaches can help remind athletes to continue to stay hydrated
   - for every glass of alcohol or caffeine, add two glasses of water

5. Warm/cool shower/bath after a full day of competition, when you feel you have overexerted yourself, can help stimulate removal of waste product
   - two minutes each, repeated 3–5x is sufficient

6. Ice injured areas
   - mild aches, 10–15 minutes, 1x immediately after competition
   - mild/moderate aches and pain, 10–15 min., 1x/hour for 3 hours
   - moderate/severe pain—ice as above and see a physician

7. Mental visualization and imagery—helps prepare for the next event, relax the mind, and reduce muscle tension

8. Massage and other therapy treatment if necessary

Sport Injuries

Overuse, stressful positioning, poor warm-up/cool-down, lack of using recovery principles, and lack of conditioning contribute to most common injuries in curling. These common injuries in curling consist of tennis elbow (curler's elbow), upper back/neck strain, low back pain, slider leg anterior hip pain, and slider leg knee pain. Upon initial analysis of the sport, low back and knee problems present as the obvious. After taking up the sport and conversing with hundreds of curlers, I am more aware of the stress and strain on these other areas.

Falls contribute to the majority of acute injuries. Concussions, neck pain, and low back, hip, knee, elbow, and wrist injuries have all been reported in the sport.

We are currently studying the specifics of overuse and acute injuries in an effort to better understand the needs within the physical development training programs.

Tips to the Curler

Planning and Organization

Organizing one's schedule! If you just don't seem to get to your training regularly, this one's for you. Sit down with your DayTimer, Palm Pilot, dry erase board, or something that helps organize your week. Take your training one week at a time, then plan one workout at a time. For me, this works best on Sunday, but anytime is a good time to begin. Once I've taken a look at my work and family responsibilities, I begin scheduling my training time. After reviewing my wife's schedule, I let her know when my training time is so that we can plan other things like house and yard work. Communication with the family is important so that everyone is on the same page.

Once I know what to expect in my week, I then create a meal plan based on where I'm going to be and what we have to do. From my meal plan, I then create a grocery list.

After planning comes preparation. Head to the grocery store for groceries, wash all workout clothes and get a bag ready, as well as preparing for family and work stuff.

Now all there is left to do is to be persistent with my plan. Remember, "There is no problem, condition, or situation that is any match for planning, preparation, and persistence."

Taking Care of Injuries

Our sport is repetitive in nature and long in duration. If certain areas of weakness have not been strengthened, then you may have experienced an overuse injury. Sports like running and swimming have their own set of repetitive injuries and their most common are labeled runner's knee and swimmer's shoulder. Perhaps there will soon be a label for curlers like curler's knee, curler's back, curler's hip, curler's elbow, or curler's shoulder.

If you have had one of these injuries and have been given advice from a sport science/medicine health care provider, then keep up the advice. If you think it will just go away on its own, good luck with that. Otherwise, if you need to see someone, check out your local sport medicine directory. An injury that is taken care of now may not bother you when it comes time for the provincials. An injury not taken care of may be your reason for not getting there. One of my favorite quotes is by Dr. J. Taunton, "On any given day, it is the healthiest athlete who has the best chance of winning." Give yourself the best chance of winning by following best practices for peak performance.

In-Season Training Compliance
As most of you have been traveling to cashspiels, playing, practicing, working, studying, and taking care of family matters, conditioning has taken a back burner. A break in your curling schedule is a great time to get back on the fitness wagon.

In-season training is something that should be carefully planned in order to maximize benefits and prevent over-training. If you look at the first page of the in-season program, there are outlines as to the types of training and how often to do it, leading up to your next event. The first measure is to look at the amount of time you have leading into your next event. In your planner/DayTimer, begin to count back and write in the type of training that should be done on each of the given days, up to the current day. Next, decide how this is going to happen within your work, school, practice, super league, and family life. If you cannot get to the gym for a workout, ask how you might be able to make some changes in order to workout at home. Dust off that old exercise bike or treadmill that you've piled clothes on for years and just do it.

The best teams in any sport are the organized, committed, planned, prepared, and trained (both in and out of their realm of play). Remember, "To fail to plan is to plan to fail."

Pregame Warm-ups
Warm-ups, prior to getting on the ice, can play an important role in preparation for the lead's delivery, the second and third sweeping, as well as the skip's mental alertness.

An off-ice warm-up allows for the transition of blood flow from the core to the extremities and the periphery. Once this occurs, dynamic range of motion activities allows for synovial fluid (joint lubricant) to surround the joint and prepare it for a greater increase in activity. A quick stretch (three- to five-second holds) to ensure full joint range of motion and you are ready for your on-ice warm-up.

A proper warm-up will ensure that you are physically prepared to play and that you reduced the risk of strain created from repetitive high intensity activity. The strain created from this activity due to poor preparation may not necessarily be felt after one or two games; however, by the end of a weekend, knee, hip, elbow, and shoulder pain are certainly caused by a gradual accumulation of strain combined with a lack of recovery activity or cool down.

Warm-up benefits:
1. Increases circulation
2. Increases oxygen delivery
3. Adequate range of motion to easily get into delivery position
4. Reduces leg stiffness with prolonged standing
5. Decreases risk of injury
6. Improved mental alertness
7. Improved overall metabolic function

Cool-down benefits:
1. Relaxation of tense muscles
2. Improved circulation to fatigued muscles
3. Maintains ideal range of motion
4. Reduce leg stiffness improving recovery
5. Centralizes mental focus to debrief
6. Improved overall metabolic function

Recovery activity may also include icing injuries, using warm/cool environments to facilitate removal of metabolic waste, extra stretching, other therapy, mental relaxation, hydration, and replenishing nutritional needs.

Flexibility and Stretching

Flexibility for curlers means more than just being able to get into a delivery position. Skips, have you ever had a sore back or legs from prolonged standing? Sweepers, have you ever had soreness in your forearms, mid-back, or inner thigh? Sometimes stretches can help alleviate soreness, if you know the right ones to do. After a game or on recovery days, a few minutes of low-intensity, continuous activity followed by static stretching can improve recovery dramatically.

Here's the low-down on relaxation stretching:

1. Complete a stretch once if there is no restriction and full range of motion (ROM) is achieved.
2. Complete a stretch two to three times if tension is felt at, or prior to, full ROM.
3. When a muscle is placed on stretch, the stretch reflex is activated. The reflex wants to contract the muscle to prevent from tearing. If the intensity of the stretch is low enough, the muscle will relax and allow for lengthening to occur. Therefore, the intensity of stretching should be low enough to allow for relaxation. The intensity of stretching should not cause facial grimacing.

Studies report that maximal stretching benefits occur when holding stretches between twenty to sixty seconds. I also recommend stretching in a relaxed environment. If an area is tight but not painful, placing heat on it or stretching in a hot tub can be beneficial (remember to hydrate).

The more that teams apply the science of sport, the more professional the sport appears.

Fighting the Indulgence Monster Over the Holidays
No matter how diligent we want to be in controlling nutritional intake over the holidays, we somehow manage to go from Dr. Jekyll to Mr. Hyde. Buffet dinners are also culprits in hypnotizing us into eating poorly.

Here is a list of ways or activities to help protect against this monster.

1. When it comes to choosing your food, remember you are a high-performance athlete and you choose to eat like one.

2. When you're looking at high fat desserts and other high fat food, tell yourself, "That is for other people."
3. Take walks regularly. Take the whole family for a walk. Be a leader.
4. Plan physical activity throughout your week(s); you'll feel better when it's over.
5. Plan team training sessions in the middle of the holidays to keep you accountable.
6. Buy your teammates personal training sessions and tell them their first appointment is later today.

Good luck, play well, and good curling!

It makes an enjoyable training or testing session when curlers are eager to learn and apply training principles. Of all the curling athletes I've ever worked with, Diane Nelson-Dezura deserves the "most dedicated" award. Very few, even in my years as trainer for the BC Lions, have demonstrated such focus and dedication. Her interest in training fostered my interest in curling to the point that I can now call myself a curler.

In summary, the preparation for Team Law heading into the 2002 Olympics made me, as a trainer, quite proud. I receive several raised eyebrows when I tell people that I train curlers. Their verbal response is usually "and I thought all you had to be good at is drinking beer . . ." But when I tell them Team Law's fitness scores beat theirs, a muffling whisper of embarrassment permeates the room. It is by training and acting like professionals that curlers can change the general public's perception of the sport and gain respect in the multi-sport games environment. Team Law gained much respect having put so much into best practices. After all, wouldn't you want to give your best effort if you had a chance to win an Olympic medal?

"In every situation, there is a possibility of improvement; in every life the hidden capacity for something better. True realism involves a dual vision, both sight and insight."

–Lester B. Pearson,
Former Prime Minister of Canada and Nobel Prize Winner

Chapter Twenty-two

Nutrition

by Billy Lee

"I wasn't feeling well in the first half. I felt down, man. I had three slices of pizza before the game, and the food took me down."

> —Leroy Loggins,
> after a sluggish performance in a
> playoff game in 1986 for the Brisbane Bullets
> of the Australian Pro Basketball League

Billy Lee of Calgary was gracious enough to take the time to write this chapter on nutrition. Billy has been involved in physical fitness his whole life. As a hockey player, he realized the value of consistent training and its positive impact in competitive sports. This is a lesson he took with him as he started to train others professionally. Billy created Summit Fitness Systems after graduating in 2002 from the University of Calgary with a degree in political science. Billy is currently Cheryl's personal trainer, and she has been impressed at the difference it has made in her stamina and overall fitness. Much of the reason for his rapid success is his mandate that every individual has different needs, slightly different as they may be. By addressing these differences, clients receive a more customized and efficient approach to the pursuit of their goals. He is certified through the Saskatchewan Parks & Recreation Association (SPRA) and the National Fitness Leadership Advisory Council (NFLAC), and has completed university courses in advanced strength training. If you wish to contact Billy he can be reached at summitfitness@canada.com.

The world of nutrition, especially as it applies to sports, is a very fluid and dynamic entity. There are as many different areas as there are individuals with different needs and goals. For that reason, it may be useful here to establish some parameters under which this chapter will operate.

First, all the information contained here is taken from medical journals and medical research studies, as I believe it is important to provide reputable sources for information. With that being said, any prescriptions mentioned here are best undertaken after consultation with a physician.

The first section of this chapter deals with nutrition from the angle of enhancing the cognitive ability of the competitor. The second deals with nutrition from a more traditional view, with regards to its effect on aesthetics or the overall look of one's body.

Although the biology of the body suggests the recommendations made here will yield similar results for everyone, much of the information given in this chapter pertains to competitive situations and competitive athletes. Regardless of the sport, competition between the elite of that sport is invariably close and dependent on a myriad of small and sometimes subtle factors. Take the example of elite sprinters. The difference between first and last in a heat is a difference of hundredths of seconds. This translates to an understanding that the difference between winning and losing pivots on very slight and fragile details.

The notion of the "devil in the details" is known by the elite of any sport where the outcome will not be decided by who has a better grasp of the fundamentals but who can exploit the details best to their advantage.

Although physical fitness is necessary, curling is not a sport like hockey or boxing where one's level of physical conditioning has a direct impact on the outcome of the game. Curling requires a level of fitness decent enough to not impede the competitor's game and to prevent injury. After that point, the level of physical fitness becomes moot.

As an example, let's say Lance Armstrong was a competitive curler. He is arguably the most fit athlete in the world today. If he were to curl against another player who had been curling for a number of years he might win, but that win would not have been decided by his physical conditioning.

With that being said, curling is a much more cerebral game than others and has a static quality that enhances its cognitive importance. In competitive situations, being successful in curling is more often a triumph of strategy than of physicality. Nutrition can contribute not just physically but cognitively to the successful outcome of a competition, specifically curling.

As any athlete can attest, one cannot be successful in competition without dealing with stress. This is not a profound statement, but few have stopped to examine what it means. What is stress? Is the stress physical or mental? What are the physiological manifestations of each, and how do they affect performance? Finally, how does one deal with these affects?

Stress, at least for the purposes of this chapter, is a medical term used to describe external stimulation, either physical or psychological, which causes a physiological response. This physiological response is the stimulation of the adrenal glands causing the release of the hormone cortisol. This results in a variety of undesirable symptoms including anxiety, irritability, and elevated heart rate to name a few.[1]

There are very few games as naturally strategic as curling. Good players learn to visualize moves and options far in advance of their occurrence. This necessitates clarity of mind and an ability to properly assess the situation and the best options. This is reminiscent of a game theorist's playground where all decisions must be weighed and designated value. The body's stress response, or cortisol release, needs to be dealt with in this atmosphere in order to assure that the employing of strategy (i.e., calling the best shots) and the deploying of that strategy (i.e., physically making the shot) are done without the deleterious effects of that stress.

There are probably very few who would disagree with the above proposal as well as with the clinical findings that stress impedes one's ability to make effective decisions and think clearly.[2] The logical next step is to find how one can remedy or at least mute this problem. The answer, nutritionally, is relatively easy and can be accomplished with very little intrusion into one's nutritional regime.

Vitamin C plays an important role in stress management, as it assists the adrenal glands in metabolizing or processing of cortisol. Now many may say they eat a lot of fruits and vegetables, so they are getting enough vitamin C. This may indeed be the case, but experience has shown that those same people are deficient in some of the most common vitamins. So, what will be suggested will be the recommended dosage for everyday maintenance and a higher dosage for competition days; it will be up to the individual to decide if they are getting the proper amount. For vitamin C, one should consider a daily intake of 500 mg for maintenance and 2000 mg for competition. Some foods high in vitamin C are parsley, strawberries, broccoli, oranges, and papaya.

B vitamins also play an important role in the body's stress management capability. Increased cortisol levels have been shown to rapidly deplete the body's B vitamins. These vitamins, specifically vitamin B5 (pantothenic acid), play an integral role in the support of the adrenal glands, especially in the onset of stress-based fatigue. This could be applied to a scenario where a competitor has a long, grueling match or possibly more than one match without a sufficient break. If these vitamins become depleted, it greatly increased the onset of mental fatigue.[3] Dosages for vitamin B5 are 500 mg for maintenance and 1500 mg during competition. Foods rich in vitamin B5 are sunflower seeds, mushrooms, cauliflower, and broccoli.

Despite being the busiest organ, the brain is the most undernourished in the body. Compared to its overall mass, which is just a fraction of total body mass, the brain requires over 20 percent of the body's calories.[4] This creates an environment where maximum cognitive efficiency is a difficult balance. Most people are aware that the brain functions on electric impulses. It can be easily seen that if a brain is not firing properly it cannot perform to its peak potential. This will often manifest in things like problems concentrating or the inability to hyper-focus.

There are many reasons for poor impulse stimulation, but a major one that can be corrected nutritionally is an abundance of free radicals. Free radicals are a by-product of metabolism of foods as well as various contaminants like smoke or pesticides.[5] Molecularly, a free radical is an unstable molecule as it is missing an electron. It takes electrons from other molecules, thereby exacerbating the overall instability of the brain's molecules and inhibiting impulse firing.

The antidote, for lack of a better term, is antioxidants. These are molecules that have an extra electron to repair unstable molecules and promote the impulse process.[6] Aside from these properties, antioxidants may have various cancer-fighting properties. Foods rich in antioxidants are berries, broccoli, tomatoes, garlic, and tea. The recommended dosage for these is unclear, as different individuals have different metabolisms and, consequently, different rates of free radicals. Suffice it to say, that given the volume of benefits of these types of foods, we should try to incorporate them into our nutritional regime as much as possible.

Another important aspect of cognitive efficiency is the neurotransmitter. For simplicity's sake, we'll say neurotransmitters are the language of the brain. Poor communication in the brain can lead to anxiety and panic attacks. To date, not all of the brain's neurotransmitters have been identified, but, of the ones that have the most importance for this discussion, are serotonin and epinephrine. If these neurotransmitters are in short supply, then communication in the brain cannot be at its peak. Serotonin can be found in the amino acid tryptophan. This amino acid is also a good natural sleeping aid. It can be found in foods like red meats, tuna, bananas, and nuts. Epinephrine can be found in the amino acid tyrosine, which can be found in foods like meats, dairy, and nuts.[7]

Another nutritional issue that can affect the brain's function is blood sugar levels. Most people have experienced this at some point in their life. As the body runs low on sugar, one may experience symptoms like light-headedness, irritability, or anxiety. It doesn't take much of a stretch to see that if one is in a competitive atmosphere, an episode of low blood sugar will have a detrimental effect on his or her performance.

Here may be a good place to digress for some foundational information. Blood sugar levels are primarily the work of carbohydrates. Whatever form they enter the body—whether it be as fruit or grain—they all, for the most part, get reduced to glucose. Subsequently glucose is the brain's main fuel source. The difference between carbohydrates lies in their absorption into the bloodstream. If they absorb quickly, they would fall on the high end of the glycemic index; if their absorption is slower, they would score lower.

Now, this topic alone has been the subject of many books, so it will be simplified here by saying that the best-case scenario from a blood-glucose perspective is to have a diet that has as its carbohydrate source low glycemic carbohydrates at regular intervals. This will ensure that one's blood sugar level will not get too high, where it has a tendency to fall quickly, nor too low thanks to the regular intervals. Some good sources of low glycemic carbs are whole grain foods, spinach, apples, oatmeal, sweet potatoes or yams, as well as almost all vegetables.

A safety net of sorts from the problem of low blood sugar is the amino acid glutamine. If a competitor has problems with hypoglycemia or is playing for an extended period of time, this amino acid can save them from experiencing some of the physiological pitfalls of a falling blood sugar level. It does this by providing an alternative source of fuel for the brain.[8] Recommended dosages for this vary greatly, but a dosage of seven grams daily seems to be more than enough for the above issue and is reported to be the optimal dosage for other hormone stabilization. This amino acid is best found as a food supplement either in powder or pill form.

So, for the competitor who is looking for an additional edge, one may consider a dietary program that has a healthy dose of the elements discussed here on a year-round basis, then increase those elements slightly approximately ten days prior to competition. During competition, one will want to have a very regimented regime that includes regular eating to ensure ease on the digestive system and mood regulation, as well as establishing regular sleeping patterns. If a snack is needed during competition, almonds or peanuts provide a good macronutrient profile in one food.

Most curlers have an off-season and like to relax their training as well as their eating habits. What is offered here can be called a preseason clean-up diet. The goal of this program is not cognitive, as was the previous prescription, but purely aesthetic.

It should be noted that this program is geared toward a specific group of people. It is not meant for weight loss purposes but for an active person who wants to tone his or her body along with a regular work-out program.

It is obvious this nutritional program is quite intensive and not for a beginner. Although this program offers a healthy macronutrient selection, its lack of variety makes it realistic for only a few weeks at a time. It must be noted that it is possible to have great variation to this program, but, for the purposes of this book, it will not be discussed here. (If there are any questions, please contact Billy Lee with the information provided.)

Meal 1	**Meal 4**
2/3 cup oatmeal	1–2 scoops protein powder
4–6 egg whites + 1 yolk, scrambled	1/2 cucumber with oil and vinegar
1 8 oz. glass water	1 8 oz. glass water
Meal 2	**Meal 5**
1 cup cottage cheese (preferably dry curd)	4–5 oz. chicken breast or 5–6 oz. fish
1 piece of domestic fruit (preferably apple)	Assorted green salad
1 8 oz. glass water	1 8 oz. glass water
Meal 3	**Meal 6—optional**
1/2 can–1 can tuna	1 cup cottage cheese or 1–2 scoops protein shake
Whole wheat pita	1 piece domestic fruit
Assorted vegetables	1 8 oz. glass water
1 8 oz. glass water	

* a fat supplement of some sort (1 tb. Udo's Choice is a good brand) should be included every day

Notes

1. Farid Wassef, RPh, CCN, "Stress Less: Live Longer and Healthier," *Alive: Canadian Journal of Health and Nutrition*, issue 271 (May 2005): 44.

2. Ibid.

3. Ibid.

4. Billie J. Sahley, PhD, CNC, "Amino Acid Brain Boosters," *Diplomate, American Academy of Pain Management*, (2004).

5. Betty Fielding, "The Body-Brain Connection," *Healthy and Natural Journal*, vol. 7, issue 33, (April 2000).

6. Ibid.

7. Sahley, "Amino Acid Brain Boosters."

8. Ibid.

Chapter Twenty-three

Seventh Heaven

"To create a romantic moment on the field takes hours and hours of practice and preparation behind the scenes."

—Jerry Rice
(the greatest football receiver
of all time, after Ray Elgaard of course)

January 30, 2005, may have been the most romantic/sensational seven minutes of curling I have ever seen. And that is not just my opinion because the buzz at the local curling clubs over the next few days was, "Did you see that seventh end between Martin and Ferbey?" The Canadian Open Grand Slam event televised by CTV Sportsnet from the MTS Center in Winnipeg featured the top two money winners and big event winners from the previous five years.

Edmonton's Randy Ferbey versus Edmonton's Kevin Martin in the thirty-thousand-dollar final. This was the WCT event that put Team Martin into the one-million-dollar category, making it the first curling team to surpass that amount in career earnings. These two were dubbed by *Sweep!* magazine as the da Vinci and Michelangelo of curling, in reference to two of the greatest artists in history who just happened to live in the same era and city of Tuscany, Italy, five hundred years earlier. Team Martin and Team Ferbey will go down as two of the greatest teams ever. And, similar to da Vinci and Michelangelo, there is a rivalry and respect for these two Edmonton teams who just may be the two best teams in the world at present.

Let me set the scene. Seventh end of the final and Ferbey is up 5–3 without hammer. The first seven minutes of this end was typical Martin-Ferbey trying to aggressively fill the house up with stones around as much junk as they could create. Don Walchuk, Martin's third, is about to deliver his first stone facing four Ferbey counters. The Melville, Saskatchewan-born and raised Walchuk throws his stone to come in off one of their own stones to hopefully make a double and lie shot. He throws it better than perfect and takes out all four of Ferbey's counters. A quad!

Now, Martin is lying one, two, and three, and Ferbey, who throws third stones, throws his rock and makes a triple to lie shot. A triple! The beginning of the final seven minutes of end number seven. After making his triple, Ferbey turns to Walchuk and jokes, "Mine was way more difficult a shot than yours."

Six stones to come, and Ferbey winds up lying shot behind cover sitting right on the button. Martin has second and third shot, but his only shot is to play an "in-off" or "wick" off a stone outside the rings sitting about an inch away from the boards. Romantic moment number three.

Martin throws a perfect shot and comes in off the stone sitting almost right on the boards and rolls across the house to remove Ferbey's rock sitting on the button to score three and take a 6–5 lead. The MTS erupts with a standing ovation, the third one in seven minutes of the final seven minutes of that phenomenal seventh end. Martin went on to win the game on a very close last rock miss by David Nedohin who himself had a very sensational, or romantic, game.

Canadian hockey fans born before 1980 all remember Moscow, September 28, 1972, where they were, and what they were doing. I was in ninth-grade French class in Langenburg, Saskatchewan, pleading with the very cute Mrs. Goddard from England to at least bring a radio into the classroom for the third period. "Mrs. Goddard, what if this was England and the World Cup final? We'll study extra hard." She bought the first part of the argument and rolled her eyes on the second. I should have been a lawyer. Saskatchewan gridiron fanatics all take a holiday on November 26, the date the Riders won both their Grey Cups in 1966 and 1989. Danes around the globe all remember the summer of 1992 and their only international soccer title at the Euro Cup. And our American friends recall with fondness the hockey miracle of the 1980 Olympics on home soil versus the former Soviet Union.

Curlers have their top shot recall moments from big games. But five stand out for most: The da Vinci-Michelangelo (Ferbey-Martin) clash in Manitoba at the Grand Slam of Curling Canadian Open. The 2005 Scott final in St. John's, Newfoundland, and Manitoba's Jennifer Jones's last shot long angle in-off in the tenth end to win over Jenn Hanna, the upstart from Ottawa. The tenth end slim double for two by Hackner and his Northern Ontario team versus Pat Ryan and his undefeated Alberta team to set up the steal in the extra end in the 1985 Brier final in Moncton, New Brunswick. Cheryl's in-off shot in the Scott 1–2 game versus Marilyn Bodogh's Ontario Foursome in 1996, which sent her team straight to the Canadian Final in Thunder Bay. And, the shot of shots at the 1997 Olympic trials, also in Brandon, Manitoba, by the late Sandra Schmirler versus Calgary's Shannon Kleibrink, also in the seventh end of the final, to determine Canada's team at the 1998 Nagano, Japan, Olympics. Schmirler's shot was almost identical to Martin's in Winnipeg eight years later. Seventh heaven!

These are the shots that keep the fans watching, create new fans, and inspire new players. Wayne Gretzky has said that one of the favorite things to watch on television for many NHLers, including himself, is curling. Skill performers appreciate and love to observe other skill performers.

I once went to a Nashville Predators game with Ron Block of Alison Krauss and Union Station, the bluegrass band that has won more Grammys than any other. I asked Ron if he liked hockey. He said, "Not really but I love to watch high-performance people perform in anything because it is so inspiring. I just appreciate talent that is developed using their skills. You are reminded of all the hard work and effort they must be putting in behind the scenes. It motivates me to keep working on my skills." Ron is a Californian who married into one of curling's first families, the Balderstons, of the Peace Curling Association (PCA), one of the three major curling associations in Alberta. His in-laws are Kurt and Marcy Balderston, the 1992 Canadian Mixed Champs. The greatest bluegrass band of all-time has been influenced by curling.

Sensational shots at dramatic times. The romance of sport as Jerry Rice put it. These are the moments we dream of not only observing but also achieving on the ice—to have the smarts to call the shot in a big game and to deliver. What is the secret? Kevin Martin has been known to throw as many as one hundred or more rocks a day. Hardly a day goes by in the curling season where Martin and his team are not throwing stones. His rival, Randy Ferbey, went from throwing third stones for Pat Ryan in the late 1980s to skipping his current team and having David Nedohin throwing the skip stones. Ferbey said, "Until Nedohin came along I have never met anyone else who throws as many practice rocks as him and Ryan. Watching these two only serves to motivate me to keep throwing rocks."

Al "the Iceman" Hackner is also a practice fiend. Cheryl throws and throws and throws some more. Sandra Schmirler could be found down at the Callie Curling Club in Regina almost every noon hour or somewhere in the day during curling season.

Practice Habits from the Best

Brad Gushue

My curling broom and bag are in my car at all times, and whenever I get a spare moment in the day, I'll stop in at the club. I'll throw everyday during the season and twice a day if I can. As a team, we try and practice at least twice a week together, and our coach is often there to help us out.

Dordi Nordby

I run the curling club in Oslo and try to throw a bit everyday. Of course, before major events, I try to practice even more. Our team tries to get together at least three or four days a week to practice together.

Peja Lindholm

I practice a lot alone and try to practice at least four or five times a week. But before big events, we all try and practice together as much as we can.

Kevin Martin

I remember Eddie Lukowich saying something like a very good competitive team will win 80 percent of its games over the course of a season and, if you can do that, you should be one of the few teams to make some money at the end of the season. That has always been our goal. There is no magic to it— you have to prepare the best you can. When I first got started at the men's level, we were playing teams like Lukowich and Folk and getting beat a lot. I was getting tired of losing to these teams because they were so much smarter than all of us young guys. So I started thinking that if I throw more rocks and practice more than anyone else, we would hit a breaking point and begin to win our fair share of games and we'd keep improving. I just wanted to get to the place of making one more shot than the best teams, and the only way I could do that was practice. I have always practiced a tonne. As a teenager back in Lougheed (Alberta), I practiced every day. I still throw rocks every day of the curling season and, of course, practice more intently before the big events. In my younger days, I threw at least one hundred rocks every day.

After every event, win or lose, when I get back to the Avonair in Edmonton, I meet with my coach Jules Owchar at 4:30 the next day. We throw rocks, have coffee, and Jules tweaks my delivery if it needs it, and we talk about curling. For twenty-one years we have done that and will keep on with this habit. Jules has such a good eye for the mechanics of the delivery it's unbelievable and, of course, he knows me so well that it's easy for him to spot anything.

I'm not superstitious and have never used a sports psychologist. (Although not against anyone who does—but how many curlers have had the same coach for twenty-one years and counting?) There is no magic to becoming a good curler because it comes down to a commitment to having work ethic. It's so easy to say but hard for most to practice. I believe in the mechanics of sports. You prepare as well as you can, and that's all you can do before a game or an event. Go down and watch a junior golf championship then follow the champion around for about four days, and I'll bet you he or she is the person practicing harder than anyone else. I'll bet you the champion is the person hitting a couple of buckets of balls or more every single day. But, in the big scheme of things, that player—whether it is golf, curling, or any sport—will have to work and practice four times as hard as he already is to make it to the elite level.

Russ Howard

Howard is well known as a player who throws every day and as much as possible with his team(s). Russ likes to mix his practices up with little games to make it fun. He was the inventor of the Free Guard Zone, which has now been adopted worldwide and has made the sport more fan-friendly than ever. He likes to create scenarios that come up in games and to experiment with angles, shots, and situations that may be rare. Howard wants to be prepared for every possible situation on the ice. He even practices throwing the stones with extra spin or rotation for those extremely rare situations that may pop up. His team, like many others, will study angles and how rocks may react after being hit in certain spots.

Bill Tschirhart

The head of the National Training Center gives a couple of great tidbits of advice.

A player or team must practice with a purpose. Throwing rocks just to throw rocks is not always beneficial, especially if a player has created some bad habits. All they are doing is reinforcing the bad habits and making them more ingrained. Also, teams need to practice their weak shots or shots that they have been recently struggling with. Not all players do this.

Michelle Englot

Michelle is a five-time Scott rep from Regina and has valued practice her entire career.

The main thing I practice is my draw weight. In many practices I never even throw hit weight. For me, everything begins with the touch. I feel that if I have my draw weight everything else will flow out of that.

Kurt Balderston

We practice a lot. Our ice tends to go in a little later than most because of harvest, so we often feel we are a month or so behind the other curlers. We have learned to practice out of necessity to be able to compete with the best teams in Alberta. The ice technicians in Sexsmith and Grande Prairie are great and always have ice ready for us to come in and practice. We may practice more than curl games at whatever level over the course of a season.

Paul Savage

Paul wrote a book called *Canadian Curling: Hack to House* back in 1983. He wrote a chapter specifically on practice and how his Brier teams approached practice. The two-time World Champion said, "Consistency is the key to being a successful team in any league or caliber of curling. Consistency is the direct result of practicing." He wrote about three variations of practicing: by yourself, with another person, and with the entire team. When practicing by himself, he would throw nothing but take-outs for the first thirty-two rocks. He would consciously try to hit the imaginary broom at the far end on each shot, and he would track his practices to keep it interesting by setting goals such as trying to put his last eight or sixteen rocks into the rings.

Practicing with one other person or the entire team, they would work on the basics starting with take-outs again and eventually finishing with a fun game of one-on-one or two-on-two with, perhaps, lunch on the line to make it interesting or fun. He interviewed Harvey Mazinke, Larry McGrath, and Jim Ursel about their practicing habits. Mazinke and McGrath practiced more than Ursel. Both emphasized that between games and practice they wouldn't go more than two days without throwing. Ursel practiced once a week, but, looking back on his career, he was playing almost every day of the season. Practices for all four of these players/teams would vary from thirty to ninety minutes, depending on how much previous curling was happening or if a big event was on the horizon.

Ernie Richardson

Ernie Richardson and Mark Mulvoy wrote a book on curling in 1973 titled *Curling: Techniques and Strategy*. It sold for $2.95, yet, the wisdom in this little book is priceless for the serious curler. The famous Richardsons of Regina were one of the first teams of their era to take practice seriously. On the importance of practice, Ernie wrote:

> We ate, slept and thought curling twenty-four hours day. We decided to get serious about the game, so we sacrificed our free time and took off from work to play in as many bonspiels as we could. Once we made the commitment to compete everywhere, we curled four and five hours a day. We'd practice at the rink on the way home from work, and we curled many a morning when we weren't working. It all paid off.

Debbie McCormick

The first woman to skip the USA to a World crown in 2003 says:

> *It is hard for us to practice as a team since we live in three different states. But, we all practice on a daily basis as much as we can. Other than bonspieling as many weekends as we can, I curl in two different leagues in the Madison, Wisconsin area, one a recreational league where I curl front end for my husband. Family politics! And I curl in an open competitive league in Madison.*

Marie-France Larouche

Quebec's most successful women's team works as hard as any team on the circuit. They try and play one hundred games a season, practice twice together as a team each week utilizing their coach and team psychologist, and they each find time to practice individually if they don't have a game or scheduled practice. The only day off from the rink during the season is Monday unless they are in a final on the WCT.

Garnet Campbell

He is the most decorated curler in Saskatchewan history, the first Brier winner from the wheat province, and a provincial champion in men's, mixed, seniors, and masters. In total, he has won over twenty-five provincial titles. My dad played in four Masters provincials against Campbell, making the final eight in the province. Campbell won all four events in which my dad was able to qualify. My dad asked Campbell how often he threw rocks. "I throw every day and have my entire career."

My dad said there is the difference. "I hardly ever have practiced, and you see the level of the top three or four teams and the bottom four teams at the provincial Masters (plus sixty category). We have never finished higher than fifth. The best work at it, even when they are retired." In defense of my dad, he curled to win, but his primary motivation was to have fun and compete without great aspirations of Brier glory.

Warren and Chris Hassall

Warren and Chris, from Chauvin, Alberta, were Alberta junior champions in 1992. Warren is also ranked in the top fifty consistently on the WCT. They were part of the first rural-based team in Alberta to win provincials. I observed these brothers for four years curling out of the same club. They lived about ten kilometers north of the town but were finally given keys to the curling club because it literally was their second home during curling season. They had the attitude of "W.I.T." (Whatever It Takes).

They learned how to make ice, scrap ice, pebble ice, and baby ice. They constantly practiced and perfected working on their deliveries. Similar to Russ Howard, they would set up scenarios to practice and worked on their weaknesses as much as possible. And when they were desperate, they would challenge me to a one-on-one game for fun. It was always embarrassing for them when on those rare occasions they lost to the preacher. They finally gave me a key to the rink as well.

Cheryl Bernard

Cheryl values practice and has thrown rocks on her own since she was a teenager. One of the unique habits she'll do after an event is go to the NTC and sit down with Bill Tschirhart and/or her coach, Dennis Balderston, and ask them to go over her delivery. They'll go out on the ice, and Bill or Dennis will observe Cheryl's delivery.

She says:

> It's so easy to get into little, bad habits even after you have curled well and if you don't correct them, they could easily come back and haunt you somewhere down the road. I may have started to adjust my release on certain sheets of ice because of how it's reacting, or I can get into release habits on the fly to adjust for my own quirks. I got this from reading about Tiger Woods and how after each tournament he sits down with his swing coach to reevaluate his swing for any hitches or to confirm what he is doing well. I find this has really helped my game. Bill or Dennis will usually have me go back to delivery basics in the beginning to reinforce good habits, and we go from there.

Some Closing Thoughts and Ideas About Practice

My favorite author is C. S. Lewis. In one of his books, he begins a chapter by saying, "If you skip this following chapter you will not offend me because I am just giving you one of my theories or ideas that may or may not have merit." This concluding section is one of those!

I practice at least once a week along with my two to four club or bonspiel games. I have done this for almost thirty-five years. Two major reasons: it's so darn therapeutic, and I'd like to think it keeps me reasonably sharp. But practice does make a difference. Three quick, personal examples:

#1 The Neilburg, Saskatchewan Men's C Final, 1991

Not your average mid-competition spiel. Neilburg is located almost right on the Alberta-Saskatchewan border, and their spiel tended to attract four or five zone winners from the region. We were about to meet one in the final.

We had just won our semi-final game on my final shot late Saturday night. This created a potential conflict with my Sunday day job as a pastor. Now, it's in my contract as a pastor that I get two Sundays a year for my sporting passion, but this was late in the year and my quota was used up. The team was willing to get a sub or go with three players. The opposition we were scheduled to meet in the final was more than sympathetic to our conflict and went to the draw master to request that we reschedule about an hour after the next day's church service.

What our opposition didn't know was that I felt I was shooting with smoke and mirrors for the last half of that semi-final. I needed practice, and I needed it bad. My out-turn hits were all inside the broom. The church where I was pastoring was sharing the parking lot with the local curling rink. Like Warren and Chris Hassall, I had been given a key to the rink to practice anytime I wanted.

I think God will forgive me for this, but I got up about an hour earlier than normal, not to get extra prayer time in but to go to the rink, clean the ice, pebble it, run the rocks, and work on my out-turn. I realized the errors of my ways and stopped rolling my wrist at release point. My faith was restored in my delivery. We had a pretty good church service, I rushed off to curl, and we finished off our very thoughtful opposition in six quick ends to win the event.

#2 My Toughest Pressure Shot Ever

My wife, Carla, will occasionally practice with me. To make it fun (for me), we'd finish with a mini-game with the winner claiming some prize. The bet one night was who would get to change our newborn daughter's diaper. We were tied after the mini-game, so we decided our extra end with the closet draw to the button. Carla threw and covered almost two-thirds of the button. Knowing the babysitter we had, I realized the diaper probably wasn't going to be an easy change. I threw and covered the entire one-foot. Carla considered getting a new model for a husband. She got home, and it was arguably the worst diaper mess in our daughter's history. I don't know if Carla would say that was my most romantic shot ever, but Jerry Rice would!

#3 1ce—A Game I Invented for Solitude Practice

In 1ce (that's "1-c-e," as in number one for solo), I create a best of five or seven scenario. After throwing some warm-up stones, I throw five or six rocks an end and use the CCA scoring system for points on each rock. Zero for a complete miss, one for getting it in play, two for a half shot, three for an almost called shot, and four for a called shot. Or, if I'm in a rush and my brain is not awake yet, I'll keep it simple. Zero for a miss, one for a half shot, and two for a called or almost called shot. Each end is slightly different. One end may be just drawing, another end all hits, or I'll create an end or two with situations I don't like or am struggling with.

To win an end, I must throw at least 70 to 75 percent. Usually the first two ends are 70 percent minimum to win and the rest 75 percent. To win the game, I must win the best of five or seven. As a reward I get to eat at my favorite fish restaurant, but if I lose, it's macaroni and cheese.

1ce has evolved over the years to where I keep track of my 1ce games and play a mini-Brier schedule (I'm still Saskatchewan). This usually involves anywhere from fifteen to twenty practice 1ce games a year, which keeps me committed to practicing. If I win my fantasy Brier, it's the Mongolian restaurant.

> "You can't get much done in life if you only work on the days you feel like it."
>
> —Jerry West,
> NBA Hall of Fame Great

Chapter Twenty-four

Ice

> "...knowing that the enemy can be attacked and knowing that our army [team] can effect the attack, but not knowing the terrain is not suitable for combat, is only half way to victory. Thus it is said if you know the enemy and know your troops and if you know the terrain, your victory will be complete."
>
> —Sun Tzu in *The Art of War*

To be consistently competitive in curling, we must learn to conquer or manage our three major opponents. The most obvious is our opposition. Next, a team must not beat themselves, which may be the toughest opponent of all. As former Pittsburgh Steelers coach Chuck Noll used to say, "Before you win a game, you have to not lose it." Third, we must know the terrain; in the curler's case, the ice.

Your team may have the better talent and be technically more sound than your opposition. But, if your opposition has a better grasp of the ice, your chances of winning decrease significantly. Learning to read ice is critical to curling prowess. Champions in any field of life seek to master all the resisting forces to potential success. Looking to gain even the slightest advantage is often the difference between winning and losing, especially at the highest levels. All competent curlers are continually learning and relearning to read sheets of ice.

Could a slight edge in understanding how ice is made give your team the upper hand versus an evenly matched or better opponent? We're not talking about getting your PhD in ice technology. However, acquiring a basic understanding of the art of ice making can filter into your game. Having even a cursory knowledge of ice making can help the serious player gain a better respect for the ice and cause you to concentrate more intently when reading a sheet of ice.

It's very similar to a football or baseball coach who befriends the groundskeeper. When a groundskeeper likes a certain coach, he is usually quite willing to let out a few little secrets or nuances of that particular ball park. Both Vince Lombardi and Mike Holmgren, Super-Bowl–winning coaches with the Green Bay Packers, considered the groundskeeper crucial to gaining an edge. The stories in Green Bay are that the groundskeeping crew often benefited—with gifts from gold watches to extravagant meals—for their work and relationships with these two great coaches.

In researching this chapter, Cheryl and I wanted to go to one of the best —if not the best—ice technician in the world. Living in Calgary we never had to look very far. One of the most respected ice technicians in Canada is Jamie Bourassa of the Calgary Curling Club. Jamie is a career ice technician who understands the game well. He represented Alberta as a skip at the 1989 Canadian Mixed in Brandon. Overall, he has won ten Districts/Zones crests, qualifying to play in the Alberta Southern playdowns at both the Junior's and Men's. Jamie has been involved with ice crews at a number of Briers, Scotts, Alberta Provincials (at most of the levels), the GM Goodwrench Skins game, numerous district playdowns, and four non-sanctioned national or world events including the World Police and Fire Games, the Elks, and two Canadian Clergy events.

Allen Cameron, the full-time curling reporter of the *Calgary Herald*, said:

> *Ask a competitive curler of either gender who has the best ice in southern Alberta, and you'll draw a blank stare. But it's unanimously conceded that Jamie Bourassa of the Calgary Curling Club is the region's best ice maker, one of the best in the country, in fact, and his ice stands up remarkably well considering the heavy usage at the downtown facility.*

After winning the GM Goodwrench Skins game on CTV Sportsnet in 1999, Kevin Martin said, "We've won two Provincials, one Brier and now the skins game on ice that Jamie and his crew were responsible for. I better stuff him in my curling bag and take him to all the events we're in."

Jamie is known for making very fast ice with "lots of curl": the type of conditions that are the ideal for showing the skills of the best teams in the world. Jamie says:

We all have different approaches to how we make ice. I'd never want to say my way is better than someone else's. I'm always trying to learn and study better ways to do it. There are so many factors involved in creating good ice and keeping it at a high level. There are certain basics to keep in mind, but like anything else the nuances behind the basics are often very subtle and can change from venue to venue, from one part of the world to the next. Goodness, Calgary is a dry climate, with our particular club built next to a major river. If you went to Halifax, you've got to consider the constant humidity and salt air.

The Basics of Making Curling Ice

Clean Floor
You want to neutralize the floor with a mild detergent and rinse it clean.

Ice Plant
The ice plant or plants must be large enough to hold the ice. All ice technicians should be able to troubleshoot the ice plant. Jamie and his crew are constantly checking the plant each day of the curling season and maintaining it during the off season.

Floor Temperature
The ice is recommended to be between twenty-two to twenty-four degrees Fahrenheit. According to Jamie, "Most of us use Fahrenheit over Celsius because it's an easier range than Celsius. With Celsius you have more degrees and range of numbers to worry about." This is also the stage when most ice technicians insert the hacks.

Seal Floor with Light Water Sprays
This creates a bond for the cement and the paint. If you don't seal the floor, the ice will crack or lift off the cement. The amount of light spray varies from building to building. Some buildings may take only five sprays, others as many as ten.

Light Floods

This is to build up the playing surface. Water tends to seek its own level. If there are high spots, they will dry quicker. Lower spots will remain wet and damp rather than freeze. The floor of the building will determine how many light floods are necessary. Once again, this can vary from as few as six to as many as a dozen or more.

Painting

If the hacks are not already inserted into the ice, this would now be the time. Spray on two or three coats of ice paint. The next step is to seal the paint with a light mist of water. Slowly build the surface with ten to fifteen sprays. This process generally takes about half a day. Once the paint is secure in the ice, most technicians will conclude the process with two more light sprays.

Measure and Paint Circles and Lines

According to Jamie, "The key here is being professional, patient, and a little on the perfectionist side."

Seal It In

A light mist of fifteen to twenty sprays will usually complete this part of the process, sealing in the final painting.

Final Floods

Four to seven light floods of the entire surface should do it. This whole process from start to finish—from cleaning the floor to the final floods—takes two or three days.

Continual Care

Jamie says, "Constant control and hard work! We keep records of scraping and pebbling patterns and how it affects the ice. We check the ice plant every two to four hours when the club is open for curling."

Crucial Factors In Maintaining Quality Ice Throughout The Season

Facility

Jamie explains that:

*Every building is different. How good the insulation is or isn't will deter-
mine if any air from the outside is creeping in or not. The heating system
of your building is critical because the temperature will vary around the
arena. These two factors alone will drastically affect the quality of ice.*

In some clubs, the ice can get slightly or even drastically slower in
later ends as the pebble may wear off the ice surface. And, in some
other instances when some games go on a little longer than others, this
leaves fewer people on the overall ice surface; so there can be less body
heat out on the ice, which can affect the overall temperature and the
ice conditions. This is another reason timing rocks should be a consistent habit through the game.

Air-Controlling Humidity

Controlling the humidity is much easier in drier climates such as the
prairies, than in maritime or coastal areas. If there is too much moisture in
the air and the air temperature is too cold, there will be a frost build-up
on the ice, as cold air can't hold moisture. Thus, the need for hair-based
brooms for the sweepers rather than cloth. The opposite is true if the air is
too warm. The ice will turn into a film of water and can even feel sweaty.
Jamie emphasizes that there are three ways to control humidity, especially
if the air is too cold. He says, "Try to heat the air, which will expand the
moisture, which in turn will hold the ice firmly. Secondly, dehumidify the
air, and the moisture should hold. And, finally, you could simply exchange
the cool air with warm air. This is why good insulation is so important. You
can discover the cracks quite easily if the ice has any low spots that need
to be taken care of."

Temperature

The ideal ice temperature along the boards should be twenty-three
to twenty-four degrees Fahrenheit. The temperature at eye-level should
be between thirty-eight to forty degrees Fahrenheit. If the ice surface
temperature goes above twenty-seven degrees Fahrenheit, the ice will
become greasy and the pebble will disappear quickly making the ice very
heavy to throw on. It will be keen or fast at first and then get heavier and
heavier as the game wears on, and much too swingy for a decent curl
for the rocks. If the ice surface is too cold (anything below twenty-one
Fahrenheit), it will eventually become too heavy as well for throwing the
stones. If one of your front end players seems bored or suffers from a

mild case of A.D.D. have them become responsible for checking the temperature gauge on the wall. This may pay off at a crucial time in the game if the ice conditions are about to change.

Floor

Ideally the floor should be level, which then makes it easier to maintain surface temperatures. In some arenas, there can be anywhere from one inch to three inches in variation or even more in extreme venues. Therefore, surface temperatures will often change dramatically. For the ice technician this means more maintenance to try and create good curling ice. Some curling clubs and their ice speed can vary from one to two seconds in keenness throwing from either end.

Getting to know an ice technician at a club you are unfamiliar with and talking about his craft will most likely win him over, and he just may let you in on the little secrets. This may give your team an edge early on, before other teams begin to figure out the ice's nuances. Huntington Hills Curling Club in Calgary is one such facility. And what can be a little weird is that on some nights all eight sheets have this one to two second difference, but on other nights (full moons nights, according to the ice technicians) it is only sheets one to five. Sheets six through eight are the same both ways.

Water Quality

The purer the water (jet ice) the better the ice and the longer it will be able to hold a pebble. Impure water (particles and stuff) will break down the quality and the consistency of ice. This is similar to a stone-filled field in farming. The stones may all appear to be picked in the spring, but in stony soil they always work their way to the surface over the course of the year. In curling, these impurities can happen over the course of a game. Thus, curlers need to constantly keep the path of a thrown rock clean in order to prevent those horrible mistimed picks.

Maintain Equipment

The scraper must be constantly maintained. If the blade has a nick or jagged-edge cutting surface, it will put runs, little hills, and valleys into the ice. This can cause a rock to sometimes go against its normal turn (fall in the ice), or to catch a little hill and overcurl. Jamie and his staff try and scrape after every three draws or twice a day at his club. This keeps the ice at an optimal level. Otherwise, the ice will become heavier and heavier, and there will be less of a curl as the draws go on. His ice crew also uses a burner, which helps keep the ice level down, and saves on unnecessary work.

Staff

Experience is coveted but not essential. It is hard to find and keep quality staff. Jamie says:

Finding a curler who wants to be an ice technician is helpful, but I'll take a non-curler who is teachable and works hard. Some of my best assistants over the years have been non-curlers. One of them was one of the better ice pebblers I have ever had because he was very even and consistent in spreading the pebble. I'd say he was better than me, and I'm supposed to have all the experience.

The Rocks

This may be the biggest factor of all. Jamie has some great advice about curling stones:

You need to check the sharpness of the stones along with the wear and the tear. We check the running edge of the rocks. You can usually tell if a rock needs some maintenance if it leaves a white spot on the ice or a running trail. Or it may be that the pebble is too hard and the rocks are snapping off or crushing the pebble.

I used to curl with the Reverend Sid Haugen who has won zones in both Alberta and Saskatchewan. He is known as the second-best clergy curler in Canada (a little known fact is that there are close to twenty clergy curling clubs across Canada). Sidney keeps a book on curling stones to see if they match or not. I don't know how many times our team would win the toss and choose the rocks over hammer and it would make the difference in winning or losing. Our teams never dropped out of A-Block at the club level, and we qualified in every bonspiel we have entered over the years.

Knowing your terrain or playing environment can give the little extra edge to the educated over the person who doesn't pay attention to these realities of the game. Glancing at the temperature gauge on the wall and knowing the quality of water at a certain club can prepare your team to anticipate slight changes ahead or to be extra diligent in cleaning the running path of the stones.

The Ice Technician on Bettering Your Game

We asked Jamie, "Does being a career ice technician help your curling game?"

Sure it does. I understand ice a bit better because of all my training and work, but I still need to execute and get in a number of quality games to stay sharp at the competitive levels. I would love to go more competitive, but my job is my number one priority. But there are some advantages that come with the job.

Jamie finds himself constantly studying whether or not rocks match up. Does each rock react and curl the same? Does each stone have the same speed going down the ice? He is also much more in tune with watching how each sheet of ice may be reacting during a game. Every sheet of ice has tendencies which may change from draw to draw, so he is always finding himself watching for these changes. He enjoys studying sheets to see how quickly he can pick up the sheets' tendencies and changes.

From an overall perspective, Jamie acknowledges that working at a curling club and being around passionate curlers has accelerated his knowledge of the game, has enhanced his skipping skills, and improved his shot making. Jamie would like to throw rocks every day but doesn't. When he does throw rocks, it is usually work-related, checking for runs, spots on the ice, overall keenness, and whether the rocks are reasonably matched. He is always watching the ice when games are on and talks to curlers after the games. The curlers are usually more than willing to give feedback.

He says he has his few select favorite players he likes to chat with, competent curlers who don't complain unless it's valid. Jamie says:

When one of my favorites says something different about the ice, I'm usually ready to fall on the floor. These are the players that know how to play to their team's strengths and use the ice to their advantage. This is usually the quiet one who takes responsibility for his own game and whether played well or not. When a person like this says something that is negative, my ears always perk up because they tend to be dead on. I want to listen because they are usually correct, and it's constructive, specific criticism. I'll listen and rarely take it personally from one of my informal bird dogs. You've always got to consider the source. Most ice technicians I talk with have a similar core of players they like to talk to over the course of a season.

Jamie purposely hangs around the curlers after each draw and encourages his staff to do the same. He also likes to hear the comments in the background. The competent player will often be on the mark without being aware he is sharing pertinent information. The comments he may overhear are either a validation of acceptable ice conditions or constructive criticisms of the ice reacting a little differently than expected. He sees it all as a part of continued ice maintenance.

Jamie is very open to this type of constructive criticism, but he has learned over the years to develop a little selective hearing with the myriad of comments thrown his way. Some players are consistent excuse-makers. It is never their fault for losing or having a bad game. The ice could be the best in the area, but it is still the ice's fault or the ice technician's fault for that blowout in the loss column.

Jamie laughs when talking about the differences in the genders and how they talk about the ice. "Men tend to complain more than the women; if or when women complain, it goes like a domino and can wind up somewhat out of proportion." This goes along with what many sports psychologists have known all along, that men tend to look for excuses and blame first before taking responsibility. Women tend to blame themselves first, even if it's not valid, and then look at other factors second. This is why a former University of Calgary soccer coach says he would much rather coach a women's team than a men's team.

So how can a curler deal with ice that doesn't suit his fancy? Here's some advice from Cheryl, Jamie, and his number-one assistant, Myles Chapin, an accomplished curler in his own right.

If the ice is curling too much/swingy ice?
Don't throw inside the broom. A couple inches wide will seldom hurt you.

If the ice is too straight?
Don't get wide. A couple inches inside the broom can make it look like you missed the broom by ten or twelve inches on some shots.

If the ice is real keen?
Don't kick out of the hack so fast or strong. For a draw to the house, think tight guard weight.

If the ice has tightened up or is slower than normal?
Adjust! Kick a little harder coming out of the hack. Don't try and push the rock harder, adjust with your kick.

If the ice is dirty?
Clean every rock your team throws. Remember the advice of Mickey Pendergast, one of Calgary's top curlers for the last twenty-some years: "The sweepers have brooms in their hands and go up and down the ice following every thrown stone. Even if the rock doesn't look like it needs sweeping, they may as well clean the path of the stone anyway because it will give them something to do and it's good exercise." Also, consider why the ice may be dirty. Is it old shoes? How old are the brooms being used? Are the ice technicians using cloth brooms or corn-based brooms to prepare the ice? How old are the grippers on the slider shoes?

If there is a fall in the ice?
As Jamie said, "Use it to your advantage, and I'll fix it later on."

If the ice is just right?
Buy the ice technicians a coffee or put them on your Christmas e-mail list.

The ice is probably taken for granted by most curlers. Yet, this is what the game is played on. Knowing your terrain, as Sun Tzu put it, is a crucial element in overall preparation. The great Finnish skip, Markku Uusipaavalniemi, is Finland's Mr. Curling. Because of his many top-ten finishes and medals at the World level, his country saw the value of building its first-ever curling club to be used just for curling and not a hockey, figure skating, ringette, and curling mix.

Markku, out of necessity, learned to make ice and study all the nuances associated with it. He feels that because of having to learn this skill, his curling prowess accelerated that much quicker than most. Markku has said that in Finland he has curled on everything from great ice to "is it even real curling ice?" Knowing the nuts and bolts of ice making has helped him and his teams understand how to adjust and adapt their game to all sorts of ice conditions.

Champions seek out every bit of knowledge they can gain to find an edge. As King Solomon taught almost forty-five hundred years ago, to seek knowledge above even riches is the difference between gaining knowledge and becoming a truly wise person. He emphasized that we must first seek to gain knowledge; for the beginning of wisdom is to acquire knowledge. But wisdom comes from taking that knowledge and applying it where necessary. The wise person or the champion seeks all the knowledge he can gain but with the intent purpose to put it into practice.

"But you gotta learn to survive on the ice."
—From the 1986 hockey film *Youngblood*

SECTION FOUR

The Motivational Game

Chapter Twenty-five

Dirty Talkin'

"Take note of this: everyone should be quick to listen, slow to speak, and slow to become angry . . ."

—James 1:19

hroughout *Between the Sheets* we have emphasized the importance of communication. So often to the casual fan and far too often to the actual competitor, the assumption made is that all a team needs to do to win is find talented players and watch them make all their shots. But, how often in curling rinks around the world do you hear the savvy players and observers saying, "You can throw together the four best players at our club but that certainly is no guarantee they will have success on the ice?"

Mike Babcock is the current coach of the Detroit Red Wings. During the 2002–2003 Stanley Cup playoffs, he led the Mighty Ducks of Anaheim to the seventh game of the finals versus the New Jersey Devils before they succumbed. Talk about smoke and mirrors! Babcock did something right. In an interview during their playoff run he said, "We don't coach hockey, we coach people." He went on to explain how chemistry combined with talent and desire can take a team a long ways and how the foundation for this is in healthy communication and connecting with each player individually.

Curling teams with sustained success at the national or world levels tend to keep their core together. Peja Lindholm and his team have been together since they were young teenagers. Ernie Richardson had the same core throughout their run in the '50s and '60s. Kevin Martin's greatest success was with his core of Walchuk and Bartlett. Carter Rycroft was the young blood they brought in after his junior career, and he could be a longtime fixture with the way their team is going. Randy Ferbey and his record-setting crew have stuck together, and the way they talk, they expect this to be a long-term endeavor. Al Hackner and Rick Lang made a few front end changes but tried to keep teams together as long as possible. The names Hackner and Lang seemed to go together like Maris and Mantle, or Gretzky and Kurri, or Lancaster and Reed.

On the women's side, Colleen Jones's string of Canadian and World titles has come when her team stayed together over the long haul. Sandra Schmirler was going on a decade with her Regina juggernaut and would have continued on together if not for her untimely death. Elisabet Gustafson provides another amazing story when you consider the various cities in Sweden in which her teammates lived and the sacrifices they made to stay together en route to their four world titles. These three teams represent over forty national and/or world appearances and over twenty-five major titles!

More successful ventures in life break up before their time because of communication issues than anything else. And in most cases, when the dust has settled, it has come down to misunderstandings. According to Youth With A Mission (YWAM), the largest mission organization in the world and one of the more genuinely successful, the number-one reason missionaries leave the mission field is not lack of financial support or lack of converts but broken relationships with fellow missionaries. Almost every business, motivational or leadership book has a chapter or two on the importance of communicating.

How can teams build good communication into their structure? Very seldom does it just happen like it did for the Bob "Pee Wee" Pickering Team from Saskatchewan in the '60s and '70s. This team won five Saskatchewan Purple Hearts in six years. The late Gary Ford told me a story of how they decided what positions each player would be for that team. All four players were skips in their hometowns of Avonlea and Milestone. Gary said:

We went down to play our first game and kind of looked at each other. We all instinctively knew each other's strengths and weaknesses from playing each other so often and growing up together, so I just went and kicked my rocks out to throw lead because I could draw and sweep. Garnet Campbell wound up throwing second stones, and Jack Keys became our third, and the way Bob was throwing it just made sense that he should skip. Garnet and Jack eventually switched positions, but it was understood.

Being a certified counselor in the areas of marriage, addictions, and spiritual issues, I have come to understand the importance of communication. Being a passionate curler and following the game since my earliest memories, I realize there is some functional middle ground between the classroom training and Gary Ford's rural Saskatchewan wisdom. Healthy communication seldom just happens or if it does, some common sense principles have kicked in somewhere along the way. Developing communication on a curling team must be intentional yet not forced.

Having mechanisms or tools in place that the team **agrees to and implements** can often be the first and best step towards preventing misunderstandings or taking things personal to an extreme. Successful teams make this a priority and understand very quickly that two keys to sustained success for a team is when teams learn to not beat themselves on the ice nor off the ice. When teams learn not to beat themselves off the ice with communication breakdowns and unresolved conflicts, then their chances of success become even greater. Cheryl and I came up with five tools which can be quite helpful in building this key dynamic.

Dirty Talkin'

I'm working on an inspirational self-help dream writing project with a co-writer named Claudia Church who lives in Nashville, Tennessee. As mentioned earlier, she was a model for seventeen years, and graced the cover of many top fashion magazines as well as acted in commercials, films, and television shows. She was on the very last episode of *Dallas*. She is a former Dr. Pepper girl and was the "wei" in one of the annual Budweiser bikini pictures. This multi-talented 3.9 GPA femme also had two *Billboard* Top-Forty country hits not too long ago. So you can imagine my surprise about a year into this project when she blurted out with her very charming, slow-talking southern accent, "I think we need to start talking dirty with each other." Now both of us are in long-term marriages that should go the distance, so I wondered what mischief she was up to.

Working together for two week stretches in between our regular day jobs can get a tad intense at times, and it's critical communication not get bogged down in the process. Claudia went on to explain that she had recently attended a screenwriters seminar. The leader of this one particular workshop was lecturing on how to work together in a team atmosphere. He explained that when it came to screenwriting, songwriting, or book collaborations, those committed to these kinds of projects have a very strong emotional, vested interest and can get hurt quite easily. I immediately thought of curling teams and my family life.

He said it is so easy to take comments made during the writing process personally. In Hollywood, screenwriters have a phrase for the brainstorming phase of the process that they call writing a dirty script. During the phase of writing the dirty script, they remind themselves that the writing is rough/dirty and that any thoughts or written words are not final copy. The goal is to write a dirty script to the point where the major thoughts, ideas, and concepts are included. Then, the final phase of the project is to clean up the dirty script for presentation in order to have a clean copy.

At any time during the process when anyone is reminded of the phrase, "This is only dirty," the team of writers understand that the person speaking or writing hasn't formulated their thoughts and have no intent of saying or writing something to hurt anyone who is part of the process.

The spinoff of dirty talking or writing is that the core ideas are presented and, oftentimes in the process, the thoughts presented are a trigger for another team member to articulate what is trying to be said and the project is enhanced. So, Claudia suggested that when we are getting too emotional about something, we should use the phrase, "dirty talkin'." This has diffused potential communication disasters with the two of us on many occasions and has caused our spouses to wonder when they have walked by as one of us has said, "It's time for a little dirty talkin'." We know we aren't getting personal and using the phrase usually makes us laugh and puts us into a more objective listening mode.

Stop-Start-Continue

Throughout the curling season, a team will engage in a variety of activities to improve its performance. Some will be on the "cold side of the glass," but most will be on the "warm side of the glass." In that environment, wise is the team that takes stock of where it's going, and how it's going to get there.

There are many ways to accomplish this task. **Stop-Start-Continue** *is one of them. This is one that we use with the teams at the National Training Center regularly. The process is simple.*

Each member of the team (and don't forget the coach is a member of the team) is provided with a sheet of paper with the words, **Stop-Start-Continue** *at the top forming three columns.*

The thoughts that the team members will provide on the sheet are recorded independently in an "individual brainstorming mode." Even if a point might be considered relatively insignificant, others may record it as well, and collectively it may appear very relevant.

Under the "stop" heading, list all the things the team or members of the team must cease doing. Items listed might be irrelevant, negative, redundant or distracting. Below the "start" heading, list those activities that the team needs to consider implementing that up to that point has been ignored for whatever reason. The last column is absolutely critical and an area that teams generally do not visit enough, if it all. Here is listed the factors that make a team successful. Those areas the team has identified that will move its yardstick down the field of performance.

When each team member has "done the homework," the sheets are brought together unsigned. If possible, enlist the assistance of an unbiased party whose role it will be to read aloud by column the items listed on the sheets without identifying the author.

When all the items are read, then it is the responsibility of the team to discuss the results and embark on a course of action. The plan will be a good one, as with this exercise, wheels will stop spinning, the air will be cleared, and confidence will be the distillate.

(This tool was presented to us by Bill Tschirhart of the National Training Center in Calgary and can be found on their excellent Web site at www.ntc.curling.ca.)

The 24–48 Hour Rule

The ancient Hebrews used to say, "Do not let the sun go down on your anger, and in your anger do not sin [*do something stupid*]." Alcoholics Anonymous (AA) is huge on emphasizing this communication tool. The intent here is that if a conflict arises in a situation with someone you are close to, be it a spouse, co-worker, or teammate, try and clear up the conflict before the end of the day (or two days at the most). Sometimes a personal venting stage or time away from the situation is helpful at first. This was one of the keys to Team Schmirler and their chemistry. In most cases, they would try and clear things up within that day or, if the situation called for it, maybe two days.

According to my wife, Carla, our twenty-three years of marriage has been better than expected and has stayed pretty fresh and romantic. So, it isn't just in my male imagination and tendency to think things are better than they actually are. We can scrap with the best of them, but we made a deal in our engagement that we would practice this twenty-four-hour rule, "Not to let the sun go down on our anger." Idealist young things that we were! But, we have practiced this rule over the years with David Nedohin-like consistency. Some nights we have been up 'til the wee early hours or have at least called a truce to sleep on the issue and clear it up in the morning. I think I drive my curling teams crazy at times when I start to get a little touchy-feely and all open-hearted with them, but I do it in a strong, manly kind of way.

There is much research on this subject of how unresolved conflict can hinder creativity and performance. How often games have been lost, not because of being outplayed, but because teammates were preoccupied with existing conflicts instead of focusing on strategy and technique while trying to curl. I once observed a very high level Brier team (no names here) before a game. The one player was having a very heated discussion with his wife who had come to support her man. He walked away in a huff. I thought to myself, *If he doesn't go and declare a truce with his wife, he'd be lucky to curl 50 percent.* I thought I was probably exaggerating the percentage, but I don't think he topped the 50 percent mark that night and, of course, his team was in trouble most of the game and lost. As we mentioned earlier in this book, Larry Bird as coach for the Indiana Pacers felt this issue of unresolved conflict was one of the biggest hindrances to a player's performing at peak levels, and it usually occurred with family members or teammates.

Major On Majors, Not Minor Issues

I have a funny feeling that the foundational principle to "Pee Wee" Pickering's success and their "understood communication" was that prairie-farmer thing of being men of few words when it came to matters of the heart and their emotions. They had conflicts, but in listening to Gary Ford, they all had the ability to see what was major and what was minor; over the course of a season or career not many things are considered really major.

One of the things I teach in relationship counseling is to ask two questions: "Is the issue causing dissension coming from a place where it is a conviction of the heart or simply a preference? And second, is the decision causing a potential conflict that is about to be made by the person you are disagreeing with, what is their heart intent?"

Here is a common curling scenario. Let's say this is a regular club curling night or super league, but it's the second draw and the ice has not been nipped after the pebble has gone on. The skip decides to hit on one of his last rocks rather than draw when everyone in the building knows Kevin Martin would draw because all he needs is to bite the eight-foot. The draw looks easy to the sweepers and the handful of diehards behind the glass. The skip hits for one and keeps the game close. After the game, the team wonders aloud why the skip did what he did earlier on. His or her explanation is that he never had a clue about draw weight with it being only the second end and that if he did come up short or goes through they would have given up a three-ender.

Now, is the skip right or wrong because he could have flashed the hit or hit and rolled out? This is a preference call. Some skips would try and make the draw by adjusting to the times the front end is calculating. On some nights the skip may have the confidence to try a cold draw early on, but on some nights he may simply not have a "sense or feel" in his thinking to try it.

I may have the most supportive second man on the planet by the name of Bob Boschee, a steady club player who has been around Calgary clubs forever. Sometimes he gives me that look of, "What in the heck are you doing?" But Bobby will then ask, "Why are you doing what you are about to do?" And 97.3 percent of the time he goes, "Oh that makes sense, I just wanted to know why. That's what you are comfortable with." And he's awfully polite the other 2.7 percent of the time because he knows my heart is in the right place—I want to win as much as he does. And because he's curled about a million years more than I have, I will always listen to his suggestions throughout the game. He's talked me out of more than one or two of my blind spots along the way.

Very seldom will a team hit an impasse with a conflict if this principle is followed. When the goals are clear and the thinking of the skip or another teammate is understood, teammates can usually live with the consequences. Cheryl says:

> On our teams, we have a rule that what is said on the ice stays on the ice. We try to create an atmosphere or understanding that everything we do on the ice is geared towards winning the game we are involved in. Sometimes things are said out of frustration or in the heat of the moment or a decision has to be made quickly that could be perceived as saying harsh words. We honestly try and not say things that could be taken personally, although at times it could come across that way, especially to an outsider. We talk about this at our meetings and always try to reassure each other that we are each other's biggest fans or supporters. We also remind ourselves that each of us is focusing on the same overall goals. We look at each other's hearts first before making a rash judgment or having a confrontation.

Sometimes there are genuine philosophical differences and the parting can be cordial, but this is usually extreme when people are being reasonable. Now, it's important to remember the advice of Dick Vermeil, who won the Super Bowl coaching the St. Louis Rams. Sometimes players need to be let go, but, it is hoped, only as a last resort. Vermeil wisely advises, "Finding good character players is vital, but getting rid of bad character players is even more vital."

Gender Difference

I always type the following with a little healthy fear and trepidation of being misunderstood. This is a general rule of psychology and the complimentary differences in the genders. And there are always exceptions to every rule. Men *tend* to be more goal-oriented in their approach to building team unity or chemistry. Women *tend* to be more social or relationship oriented. Men value relationships and women love to meet goals, but we tend to attack this thing from a different premise or starting point.

Mark Dacey may have expressed it the best from the male perspective. I asked him in a *Sweep!* magazine interview how his team communicates and builds their chemistry. He couldn't give me a clear-cut answer, but as he talked he mentioned how each of his teammates had the same level of commitment, goals, and desire to win a Brier and world championship. The way he expressed it was that having the same goals covered over a multitude of potential relationship issues that could go south. The bonding happened through aiming for the same goals.

Mark said, "I think men can win without being best friends or getting along all the time as long as the overall goal is kept in focus." General Dwight D. Eisenhower echoed those comments when he said during World War II, "Morale is the greatest single factor in successful wars." Eisenhower went on to explain that there are many ways to create morale, but one of the quickest ways is to have success in battle, no matter how big or small.

On the women's side of the ledger, Cheryl mentions how women need to be liked and accepted in order to play well. It's the security they seem to need, and being liked and playing well are obviously interconnected. But, she says some of the things that have caused conflict on her teams over the years are not always curling related (whereas for the men it usually is). Cheryl laughs and admits, "Women tend to use tissues a lot more than men when it comes to conflict."

Again, these are generalizations or tendencies to keep in mind. And in my thirty-four years of curling, I have never seen a man cry on the ice unless he lost a *huge* final of major proportions, but I have observed on more than a few occasions my favorite gender using the aforementioned Kleenex.

To win a curling game, the performance on the sheet of ice will tell the tale, but what goes on behind the scenes will definitely lay the foundation for the high-performance team to have any shot at big-time success.

> "The most important single ingredient in the formula of success is knowing how to get along with people."
> —Theodore Roosevelt

Chapter Twenty-six

That Winning Feeling

"Players are too worried about hitting the broom. We try and worry about making shots—period! Teams or players will say, 'but we threw it well and hit the broom.' There's more to it than that!"

—Randy Ferbey,
Six-time Brier Champ and Three-time World Champ

Cheryl kept saying over and over again, "You have to sit down and talk to my coach Dennis Balderston. He may be the most underrated coach out there and one of the best among many. I feel so fortunate to have been able to secure Dennis as our coach. He can be so unassuming when you first meet him, but when he starts to share his wisdom there are few who compare."

Dennis has been to The Show! He earned his Purple Heart curling with Calgary's Harold Breckenridge. Balderston has been to four Nationals in total. He skipped the Saskatchewan High School champs back in 1963 by beating Eddie Lukowich two straight in the best-of-three Saskatchewan final. He has since gone on to two National Seniors with Breckenridge in recent years. Actually, Balderston has made it to six Alberta final games to represent Alberta at the Senior Nationals and has had his heart broken four times.

He is probably the only player in the Calgary area who can say he has curled with every Brier skip to represent that city since the 1960s.

To begin with he played with one of the greatest of all-time in Ron Northcott. He has also curled with the colorful Paul Gowsell, Wayne Sokolowski, Harold Breckenridge, and Eddie Lukowich, his old rival from Saskatchewan. As Cheryl says, "There must be something about Dennis that all these great skips saw in him."

Dennis is a deep-thinking man who has observed so many of the greats over the years. He is also an athlete equal to his peers. He reminds me of Bill Russell and Lou Boudreau. Russell won more NBA titles than any player, ever, and won a couple more as a player-coach with the Boston Celtics. Boudreau was the playing manager of the Cleveland Indians the last time they won a World Series in 1948. He not only managed that team to its last World Championship but he was also the league MVP in 1948 as its shortstop, the last player ever to manage, play at the same time, and win a World Series. Balderston is curling's equivalent to Russell or Boudreau with the skills and wisdom—and humility—that cause one to pay attention. He has those green Saskatchewan roots that run deep.

Dennis has a way of summarizing and articulating the core recipe for what it takes to win in curling. He talks about seven ingredients that go into the process of winning to create what he calls, "That winning feeling."

Dennis is about to become eligible for Master's curling to go along with his annual pursuit of winning the right to represent Alberta at the Seniors. He says:

> *It's kind of come together for me mentally or emotionally in approaching curling and what it takes to win. Not that I ever stop learning but winning is a feeling which is hard to explain. It's an attitude that is there. It's that feeling of when you step out on the ice versus any team, you know deep down inside that you're going to win, or it's a settled belief that you know you can win regardless of the competition and it's there almost 100 percent of the time. It's not thinking you can win or hoping you can win, but knowing you can win.*

Basketball's John Wooden said that when he turned fifty-four years old, all his philosophies and thoughts and convictions about winning and success crystallized in his thinking. Did anything change in his core values and philosophies? No! He explained that everything he had come to believe about winning and success somehow at this magical age for him all came together. It was who he was, and he knew what it took to win. He kept learning and was maybe even more coachable himself because he was the most secure in life he had ever been.

Wooden and his UCLA teams went on to set a NCAA record for basketball that may never be duplicated: seven straight Final Four victories and a record-setting ten overall. Wooden seemed to be describing what Balderston was describing—a feeling that came from mastering certain basic, fundamental ingredients that must be in the recipe for winning. In studying Wooden's many books, the ingredients Wooden talks about are almost identical to Balderston's core.

To continue using the cooking analogy, the ingredients that Wooden and Balderston so firmly believe in were worked on and studied for most of their lives. And as they enter their fifties and sixties (and now nineties for Wooden), they are still committed to the sports they love; they haven't retired from the competitive aspects. In their intellect and soul, these values and convictions made logical sense long before it felt like that winning feeling.

However, like the best meals, even though the chef understands the right ingredients needed to create a delicacy, it takes time to prepare the ingredients, and it takes time to slowly cook the ingredients to create the perfect meal. When the meal is ready to eat and enjoy, the food literally becomes part of who we are—that winning feeling! That winning feeling becomes part of our whole being—physically, mentally, emotionally, and spiritually (the place of our deep-seated values). You don't just believe it, you don't just understand it, you don't just practice . . . it becomes part of your entire psyche. To really possess that winning feeling takes time and has to be continually worked on over the course of a long career devoted to what you love.

Here's what Dennis Balderston outlined as key to that winning feeling:

The Ingredients in the Recipe to Create That Winning Feeling

Is there a recipe for winning or being competitive? First of all, I think there is a big difference between winning and being competitive. There are a lot of competitive teams and a much smaller number of what I would call winning teams. It's much like the difference in a good restaurant and an excellent restaurant. Sometimes the food in a good restaurant is better than the food in an excellent restaurant; however, over the long haul, the food at the excellent restaurant is better. What is the main difference? In the restaurant business, it is the quality of food, the recipe, and the service. The same thing in curling—sometimes the competitive team will beat the winning team, but the winning team will always win a higher percentage of the games against the competitive team. As for the recipe for becoming a competitive team and sustaining that competitiveness, I believe the main ingredients are the following. As far as becoming a winning team, I believe the same ingredients are there, but the commitment level is much deeper.

1. Technical Ability
You must, as an individual, have a fairly high degree of technical ability in order to excel at the highest levels of the game. Therefore, you need four players with a high degree of technical ability. All the players at the highest levels have this ability. My job as a coach is to create practices that are useful and fun and to show them the door to winning in order to help them all understand what it takes. The best players all practice and are committed to practicing.

2. Strategy
A very healthy mental understanding of the game is a necessary ingredient. To be a competitive team all team members must have a high degree of understanding of the strategy of the game in order to play their individual position, whether it is lead, second, third, or skip. This understanding of the game should apply to understanding all positions and all aspects of the game. The better each player understands the game the more success the team will have.

3. A Minimal Level of Fitness
Fitness speaks for itself. Many people do not understand the physical and mental exhaustion that occurs when a team plays six to ten games over a three or four day period. You may start the competition at the same level as the other teams, but you certainly will not finish at the same level if your fitness is deficient.

4. A Very Good Skip
The team will not be able to compete at a high level unless it has a good skip, a very good skip. Technical ability and a mental understanding of the game will generally allow you to be a good player on the team, but it is not enough to be a good skip on the team. What makes a good

skip? That's another million-dollar question isn't it? In some respects, it is something you are born with—you either have it or you don't. Here is where intangibles come into play. A skip needs some, if not all, of the following: ability to read ice in terms of placing the broom for the shot called, a strategist; the ability—as they say in hockey—to read the ice from a strategy point of view, meaning to think three or four shots ahead, or three or four ends ahead; be able to throw shots under pressure; have the confidence that they can make the last shot to win a major game and, most important, make the big shot anytime during the game when it is needed; and a skip needs to be fearless in the sense that they feel that they can make any shot at any time.

5. Team Chemistry

Team chemistry is something that has to exist both when a team is winning and when a team is losing. Chemistry is one of the hardest things to create, and, in some cases, it just happens. Sometimes winning creates chemistry, but to be truly there, it must also survive losing. Team chemistry requires a team leader and a team member who is a catalyst—the leader may also be the catalyst. The catalyst may come in different forms for different teams. On some teams the catalyst may be someone who reprimands individuals who are not performing up to their abilities, or the catalyst may know how to push each team member's buttons to get him or her going. Usually this comes in the form of encouragement, but the bottom line is the team needs someone to hold the team accountable.

Two practical ideas that may work to create team chemistry, especially for a new team, as follows:

- In the off-season, get to know each other better personally. That can be accomplished in a number of ways, such as team meetings where everyone is assigned an agenda item and everyone is required to contribute their views on each agenda item. Getting together socially with your significant others to familiarize yourselves with teammates and their home lives. Activities such as bowling, golf, or some other game or sport can give insight into how your teammates react to pressure situations, which can be extremely helpful. I guess what I am trying to encourage here is to get to know your teammates as best as you can before the season begins.

• At preseason meetings there should be room on the agenda to discuss curling situations, and the team should express how they would react and how they would like their teammates to react. For example, if a teammate is having a bad game, what type of support and reaction would they like from the team? It will give the teammates a general idea of how to treat each other on the ice. When the situations begin to occur, you will find out what actually works—sometimes what people say or think in the meetings does not correspond to the real situation. This may result because people know what the answer should be in the meeting situation. However, when they are in an emotional crisis, things are often very different. You need to analyze it on an individual basis.

6. Mental Toughness

This is where I find coaching becomes difficult, as this gets into the area of intangibles. A certain amount of mental toughness is just part of your character, and a certain amount can be developed. I find that as a coach I can lead a player to the door, but it is up to the player to enter and develop his or her own mental toughness. Here are some quotes or concepts I use regarding mental toughness:

• Competitive curling is played mainly on a six-inch playing surface—the space between your ears.
• The mind is the cause of more missed shots than the body.
• The most important part of a player's body is above his or her shoulders.
• Under pressure you can perform 15 percent better or worse—dictated by your mind.

Dennis is a very honest and humble man, and I asked him if his experience participating in four national championships, fourteen provincials, and numerous bonspiel championships would be a minor or a major factor in coaching a team like Cheryl's?

7. Coaching

At one time I would have thought it was a minor factor, but now I know it is a major factor. So many intangibles are involved in competitive sports, not just in curling. I know from my experience that it is very helpful to learn the nuances from someone who has been through the battles.

I see the essential roles of a coach as being a teacher, a leader, an organizer, a counselor, a communicator, a strategist, a technical advisor, and assisting in the overall development of the team. What I mean by that last point is to help establish goals, planning the overall season, designing and conducting practices, developing team strategy, fault correction, and designing mental and physical plans.

That winning feeling can only become a reality when a team commits itself to the ingredients that can create success. Easy to teach, easy to pay lip service to, but the great teams commit themselves to continually devoting themselves to integrating and practicing whatever it takes to become a champion.

In one of the many books that explain and analyze *The Art of War*, that ancient Chinese military classic that has been used and studied by many great military leaders over the centuries, there is a story of Sun Tzu confronting King Wu who hired him as a consultant for the military. King Wu liked Sun Tzu and enjoyed his theories and philosophies but had a hard time implementing all of his strategies in order not to upset certain people he liked in his army and kingdom. Sun Tzu saw an army living below its potential, and out of frustration and personal integrity, confronted the king. King Wu relented and started to follow the words of Sun Tzu and developed an army under Sun Tzu's leadership that became invincible for its era. I am going to offer up a couple of translations given for what Sun Tzu said. Just as some athletes may not like to hear criticism from their coaches, King Wu didn't initially agree with Sun Tzu's words. But, in order to make changes necessary to improve, King Wu got on board.

> "King Wu—you love my words but cannot stomach to put them into practice!"

> "The King is only fond of words, and cannot translate them into deeds."
>
> —Sun Tzu

Chapter Twenty-seven

"He Who Walks with the Wise Becomes Wise"

"Do you think you can win on talent alone? You don't have enough talent to win on talent alone!"

—Kurt Russell as Herb Brooks,
in the 2004 film *Miracle,* addressing his
1980 USA Olympic hockey team

*H*aving a mechanism in place to evaluate yourself and your curling team is extremely helpful. Is there something out there in the sports universe that could help that isn't too complicated and can easily be easily accessed and made part of a team's DNA? We believe there is.

To find this mechanism or tool, we searched for someone who has a proven track record in the sports world and has the respect of coaches, regardless of their sport. Who other than John Wooden? We have referred to this famed basketball coach a few times in *Between the Sheets.* Many high-level coaches of various sports refer to Wooden as either one of their mentors or someone they would love to emulate in their own coaching.

Bill Belichick of the Super Bowl-winning New England Patriots is a student of Wooden, as was the late Herb Brooks who coached in the NCAA, NHL, and Olympic programs, as well as Pat Summit, the all-time winningest NCAA basketball coach of the University of Tennessee

Lady Vols, to name only a very few. These coaches, along with John Wooden, are considered some of the finest sports minds in our culture; we would do well to learn from them and to heed the advice of ancient King Solomon of Israel when he said, "He who walks with the wise becomes wise."

Stephen Covey, author of *The 7 Habits of Highly Effective People*, is one of the most respected authors and teachers on the subject of leadership in the world. Covey said the following in endorsing John Wooden's book *My Personal Best*: "Legends like Coach John Wooden don't just come out of nothing. If you want to learn how to win, to really consistently win in life, read this book." Covey bases his best-selling books on his study of leaders whom are successful and why they are successful. He would readily agree with ESPN's appraisal of naming Wooden the greatest coach of the twentieth century.

Coach Wooden believes there are three principles or tools that any player or coach of any sport could use to evaluate performance. Wooden said in *My Personal Best* that he was devoted to the following three principles of coaching:

1. Conditioning
Supreme physical condition accompanied by mental and moral conditioning is foremost. Performance diminishes immediately when conditioning is insufficient.

2. Fundamentals
Players must have the ability to properly execute the basics of the game instantaneously without having to stop and think. This concept is taught through endless repetition of details.

3. Team Spirit
Most important of all, each player must be willing and eager to sacrifice personal glory for the good of the group. "One for all and all for one" is a phrase that still sends a chill down my spine.

Wooden strongly believes that if a team is committed to these three principles, they will probably play at their personal best regardless of how the win/loss column looks. If a team or player is not performing up to their capabilities, then one or more of these three principles are most likely being violated or neglected. He would always use these three principles as his primary evaluating tool at the end of each season in preparing what to work on for the following season.

One of my best days ever as a curling writer occurred just before the 2002 Winter Olympics in Salt Lake City, Utah. Both the Swedish and Finnish men's teams came to Calgary a couple of weeks before the games began to practice and to live in the same time zone as Utah. I had back-to-back interviews with Swedish skip Peja Lindholm and Finnish skip Markku Uusipaavalniemi, or F-15 as he allows North Americans to refer to him. As they talked about their curling philosophies, I thought of John Wooden and the principles he emphasized as a coach being so similar to what both Lindholm and F-15 were striving to achieve. Wooden just had a way of articulating universal truisms that all successful teams strive for whether they could articulate their theory or not.

Olympic Curling Lessons Based on Wooden's Three Tools
Conditioning

"The legs feed the wolf," is a common saying in the sports world for coaches who emphasize conditioning.

Physical, mental, and moral conditioning, according to Wooden, is essential. We all know that if a player or team gets tired late in a game, one's mental sharpness is also affected in a negative fashion. The moral conditioning Wooden speaks of is basic life integrity, such as keeping promises, living by the code of the team philosophy, and being committed to the highest good of the team and striving to make it successful. Wooden sees these three elements of the physical, mental, and moral as inter-connected and affecting each other. If one of these elements is weak—even though the other two may be reasonably strong—overall performance will be affected.

Peja uses a Swedish concept on the importance of overall conditioning when he says, "It's got to get to the point where it's in your spine." Being in shape physically, mentally, and morally is simply a part of what the team is. His team is committed to staying in top physical shape, working on the mental game, and being committed to the overall goals of the team.

Peja says:

It's a matter of taking care of the behind the scenes work that benefits you on the ice. I like to run. Even when I don't feel like running I know the importance of it and how it keeps me in shape, so I run. These small yet significant details such as working out, striving to be technically sound, getting along with your teammates, making sure your goals are clear, keeping the peace at home, and remembering to keep things in perspective all help when the actual games begin. Being in overall shape helps you get to the point where you feel safe and secure in relation to your confidence, and this comes from right thinking and preparation.

One of our team mottos is to stick with the concept and change the details, meaning the process of getting to a competitive place doesn't ever change but peripheral matters may. The basic concept is being committed to being in physical, technical and mental shape. The details are items such as what hotel are we staying at, what airline are we using, or where will we eat, or being flexible with our schedules when normal life doesn't play out the way you want it to.

Fundamentals

Great athletes all have one commonality—they understand the importance of consistently working on the fundamentals of their craft, and they understand that working on the fundamentals must be a lifelong habit one must commit to. How important are the fundamentals?

Joe Gibbs, the three time Super Bowl-winning coach with the Washington Redskins says in his book, *Fourth and One*, "To win it all, a team has to be obsessive about the fundamentals, the little things."

Michael Jordan's first game back after his first retirement was brutal, by his own admission. The morning after that game, his coach Phil Jackson heard a bouncing basketball in the team's gym at a really early hour. He thought at first that maybe the custodians were having fun after doing their work from the early morning shift. It was Michael Jordan working on basic basketball fundamentals.

Michael Jordan wrote in *I Can't Accept Not Trying*:

Fundamentals were the most important part of my game. Everything I did, everything I achieved can be traced back to the way I approached the fundamentals and how I applied them to my ability. They are really the basic building blocks that make everything work. I don't care what you're doing or what you're trying to accomplish; you can't skip fundamentals. The minute you get away from fundamentals—whether it's proper technique, work ethic, or mental preparation—the bottom can fall out of your game, your schoolwork, you're job, whatever you're doing.

When you understand the building blocks, you begin to see how the entire operation works. And that allows you to operate more intelligently. You have to monitor your fundamentals constantly because the only thing that changes will be your attention to them. The fundamentals will never change.

George Karl, coach of the Denver Nuggets, was quoted as saying in a April 11, 2005, article in *Sports Illustrated* about star prodigy Carmelo Anthony, "For Carmelo to be a leader of this team, he's got to be committed in practice and committed to focusing on the fundamentals. Right now he is a great talent but not a full-fledged professional. How many twenty-year-olds are? But I'm going to stay on him."

Harvey Penick, the great golf coach from Austin, Texas, said he wrote down some basic fundamentals for being a golf instructor back in 1929 in a little red notebook where he recorded life lessons from his job as a golf instructor. In 1993, when he wrote *And If You Play Golf, You're My Friend*, he said, "Like golf instruction these principles are easy to learn, but useless unless they are put into action. And like golf instruction, these principles are easy to forget. I need to read them every few days."

He wrote this sixty-four years after first recording them. He went on to say in *Harvey Penick's Little Red Book*, "If you play poorly one game, forget it. If you play poorly the next time out, review your fundamentals. . . . If you play poorly for a third time in a row, go see your professional." Penick believed that if one's fundamentals were sound and if a player understood the fundamentals, then a talented player should be able to achieve a very high level of consistency.

To achieve at a world level, both the Swedish and Finnish teams treat curling as a full-time occupation, as much as reason or sponsorship allows. They work very hard at the technical part of the game, in mastering the fundamentals. Markku says, "The most difficult part of putting together a competitive world-caliber team was finding four people of equal commitment. Commitment to train, practice, and play as much as we can against the top teams."

From mid-September to early April, these teams are on the ice almost every day between practice and games. It is not uncommon for these two teams to practice six to seven times a week, especially if their game schedule is not busy. Coaching, studying videos, and reading are all part of the training. Both teams have contacts in Canada who send videos of the Brier and other bonspiels that television covers. Markku says, "I like to think of myself as a Canadian-style curler from watching video. We are one of the few Euro teams that see the value of developing the big weight hit to get us out of trouble. It's a great weapon not many Euro teams use, but, of course, if it isn't working for you, one must adjust and do what is working. But, we do practice this skill along with other aspects of our game as much as we can."

Peja is a practice fiend. He and his teammates are committed to working on the fundamentals like few others. Remember Peja's commitment to practice when he says, "I will never throw a rock in a game or practice if I am not focused."

Team Spirit

Joe Gibbs (who also admires and studies John Wooden) said there was a third thing to be obsessive about in sports: "You have to understand the obsession a coach has about team unity. Whatever else we brought into a game, whether it was personnel or strategy, overriding it all was team spirit, togetherness, an all-for-one-one-for-all mentality."

Markku's team has been together for almost thirteen full seasons, and Peja's team is going on twenty-five years. They both said it takes a high commitment, goal setting, and the willingness to work through inevitable team conflicts in order for a team to become successful. Markku believes it takes a minimum of three years to build a team that gets along consistently. They both used the marriage analogy, and Markku hinted, "that it may even be tougher than marriage, but the longer a team stays together the fewer major conflicts arise that could destroy a team."

Peja says:

A couple of ways to develop a cohesive team spirit is through common goals and clear communication. Good communication is the most important thing for team spirit. With communication, we had to learn to be so clear with each other. Our team won't let a disagreement go beyond a day or two at most. We respect each other and know the buttons we shouldn't push with each other. The overall goal of striving to win a championship is far more important than trying to win an ego-based argument.

I can be a goal-setting maniac. Even when I do the dishes at home, I set a goal of when to get them done. When we go to any event, we plan things down to the smallest detail. We plan our entire day, when we get up, the meals, the down times for visiting or movies, practice times, meetings, whatever. We found in the past when we didn't plan out our weeks, when surprises or changes in routine would occur, these distractions or even laziness from inactivity would affect on-ice performance. This helps us stay focused on our goals, and, if one keeps their eyes on the overall goals, things like conflicts get resolved quicker and we have good team chemistry. Again, stick with the concept and change the details. I find the more planned or prepared I am, the easier it is to be flexible with the details.

Final Thoughts on All Three Elements

Team spirit or morale is the strength or downfall of almost every high-performance curling team. How often have you seen a talented, technically sound team that is also in great physical shape underachieve because there was little, if any, team spirit? Cheryl is a firm believer that team spirit can never be underestimated. She says, "Devote the same kind of time to team spirit as you do to conditioning and fundamentals, don't just assume that it will be there, it takes work and a conscious decision to make it a priority. The kind of team spirit where the team has somehow developed—*an enjoyable I can't wait to hang out with the family kind of feeling and we'll stick together come hell or high water resolve and you know we'll be there for each other atmosphere.*"

Functional families and highly successful curling teams aren't perfect. They will have disagreements. The difference between a functional and dysfunctional team is the mindset. The mindset of functional teams is that they believe the best about each other and they are committed to making things work rather than living in a defensive and blame-shifting mindset as the bases for evaluating each other. And in most functional families, one or both of the parents brings this overruling mindset of believing the best about each other into the culture of that family.

Cheryl takes a very similar view to that of Joe Gibbs regarding team spirit and unity. The one team she skipped in her career that baffled her in terms of underachieving when expectations were so high and seemed genuinely realistic was her 2004–2005 team. They started out like a house on fire in October of 2004, and, when all the WCT bonspiels were finished for the year, they were the number one team on the WCT circuit in December 2004.

When the calendar year shifted to 2005, the team went into a bit of a tailspin. They qualified for the Alberta Southern playdowns to try for a berth to the Provincials. The team had its moments and reached the finals of the C-side in the triple knockout format before being eliminated. Their next big event was the Canada Cup in Kamloops, British Columbia, to try and earn one of the final berths to the Olympic trials in Halifax later that season. To make a long story short, the team went 0-5 and never really was a threat to make the four-team playoff. After the season, they chose to disband as a foursome.

Cheryl felt there was something missing on this team; even though from a conditioning and fundamentals perspective, they were as competitive as any team in the world. She genuinely liked each player on the team but felt there was a spark missing. She felt it wasn't any one player she could point to, including herself, but somehow the four of them as a unit weren't clicking from that critical team spirit perspective. They were saying the right things, doing the right things, but that aggressive *let's go out and seize the game by the throat* attitude needed to be champions was clearly lacking.

I'll let Cheryl further explain:

I think it's like a marriage. I think anyone has the potential to be in a great marriage, but you just can't be married to anyone. I firmly believe that all four of us could be on teams that could qualify for a Scott and have a realistic chance to win it all. But together, for some unseen reason, the four of us didn't click emotionally on that level teams need to click on. It's similar to what we wrote about earlier in the catalyst chapter in that we were lacking a catalyst. And what is so weird is that each of us could probably be catalysts in the right mix of players on different teams.

There were different theories being thrown out about our team by well-meaning people, including our own analysis. Some thought we were tired from going so hard in the WCT every weekend trying to earn an Olympic trials spot. I don't really buy that one because personally winning and getting so close to a goal energizes me. I think it energized the other players too. Another theory was that we grew complacent, which may have an element of truth to it. We started out so strong with significant success and then lost the edge we needed when we really needed it for the playdowns and Olympic trials.

Personally, I believe that when we started out as a team in September we all wanted to do so well that we were constantly proving to each other that we made a right decision in putting this mix together. I think that when the honeymoon period was over the high emotional motivation we had was gone because it was artificial or temporary at its roots. We never snipped at each other when the losing started, which can happen so easily, but we had no person or mechanism in place to keep the emotional energy at the level we had in the first three or four months of the season. Team spirit, morale, the enjoyment of playing together, just wasn't strong enough to take us to the next level.

Maybe the million-dollar question that we'll never know is—could we have developed enough team spirit over the course of time? Again maybe, but when I went and talked to Karen Ruus (our lead) at the end of the season, she asked me if we got back together again as a team, would I be excited? My answer immediately was, no! I knew right there that we had to change things up. I have been on other teams with less success initially but knew I wanted to keep things together because the intangible team spirit was already there or really close and you knew it.

"It has got to get to the point where it is in your spine."

—Peja Lindholm

Chapter Twenty-eight

"The Seven Cs"—
Solid Rock Truisms

Jimmy Dugan (the manager/coach): "Taking a little day trip?"

Dottie Hinson: "I'm driving home to Oregon."

Jimmy: "S——— Dottie, if you want to go home . . . great. I'm in no position to tell anyone how to live. But sneaking out like this, quitting, you'll regret for the rest of your life. Baseball is what gets inside you. It's what lights you up, you can't deny that."

Dottie: "It just got too hard."

Jimmy: "It's supposed to be hard. If it wasn't hard, everyone would do it. The hard . . . is what makes it great."

—From the 1992 baseball film,
A League of Their Own
(Note: Dottie returns to the team and helps her team almost
win the first AAGPBL World Series as a Rockford Peach.)

Dottie's character in *A League of Their Own* was a combination of a player from Oregon and a player by the name of Mary Baker from Regina, Saskatchewan. The late Mary Baker was a league MVP, player-coach, and the poster girl of the All-American Girls

Professional Baseball League (AAGPBL). She never would have even considered quitting. In *Girls of Summer,* a historic account of the AAGPBL written by Lois Browne, there is a picture of Mary and a description of "Her well-groomed style and dark good looks." One could see why she was considered the poster girl.

Mary was one of many Saskatchewan women to play in the AAGPBL. Ten percent of the league was from Canada, and 50 percent of those were from Saskatchewan. Baker, an all-round athlete, could also throw a pretty good curling rock and ran the Wheat City Curling Club in Regina through much of the 1970s and 1980s.

When I attended the University of Regina, I curled out of Wheat City and would often go down early to the rink with teammate Scott McDougal and have a coffee and chat with Mary. She was a kind soul with a big heart who seemed so wise. Scott and I had no clue that Mary was the Kelley Law of the AAGPBL. It should have come with no surprise since Mary Baker could still turn the heads of most of the male senior curlers in southern Saskatchewan.

There was a picture of Mary in a softball uniform on the wall with a yellowed newspaper clipping underneath the story, but I hate to admit I never took the time to read it. But when *A League of Their Own* came out, my research instincts kicked in and everywhere I looked, Mary Baker's name and athletic moxie came to the forefront. If she would have com-. mitted herself to curling like she did in fastball and baseball, which earned her a place in the National Baseball Hall of Fame at Cooperstown, I have very little doubt that Mary would have left her mark on the curling world. She had the qualities the greatest curler of her era, Ken Watson, possessed and emphasized in his books and speeches.

Ken Watson of Winnipeg, Manitoba, was the king of curling during the same era Mary Baker left her mark in the AAGPBL. The Canadian Press named Watson, the first three-time winner of the Brier, the best curler of the first half-century in Canada. In Watson's curling classic, *Ken Watson on Curling*, published in 1950, he wrote about the "Seven Cs for Curling Success." His book sold a record 150,000 copies. It is still the number-one selling curling book of all-time and one of Canada's top-selling sports books of all time.

Do the Seven Cs still apply over a half century later? Let me refer to NFL Hall of Fame coach Bill Walsh for the answer. Walsh is still considered the most innovative coach the NFL has ever seen. He led his San Francisco 49ers to three Super Bowl championships and laid the foundation for two more to follow after his retirement. Walsh loved to be on the cutting edge of change, yet he valued history as much as innovation; he felt that innovation often came from the study of history.

Many of his principles for building what is known as the *West Coast Offense*, which has become the prototype for the last twenty-five years, came from his study of football in its early days—pre-1960s. His belief is that basic principles/truisms never change but eras or styles will. Walsh fits the motto for Chevy in 1992 when they advertised, "Times change, values don't." What Ken Watson had to say in 1950 with his Seven Cs still applies today as we enter a whole new millennium.

Seven Cs for Curling Success
1.   Compatibility

> When casting about for another player for a team, the questions that cross the mind are: will he fit with the rest of the rink in a friendly personal way? Have we much in common with him besides curling?
>
> —Ken Watson

When one begins to hang around with competitive curlers, you will often here the comment, "Being on a curling team is like being in a marriage." It is understood that compatible relationships are a key to on-ice success. Watson writes a lot about enjoying the game and getting along with teammates. Having fun with your athletic passion can create a positive never-say-die energy among teammates and can foster team chemistry.

Compatibility doesn't mean teammates have to be best friends or that they have to do a lot of socializing together, although that often does happen. Compatibility is when teammates have a clear understanding of the team's overall goals, values, and on-ice philosophy. They know and understand the mission of the team and are committed to carrying it out. Peja Lindholm has had the same core teammates since his teenage years, which has got to be some sort of record in the curling world. He says:

> *We grew up together in the same city, actually the same part of our city in Sweden. We understand each other and our goals, and we now take it a little deeper. To keep our team on the same page, we have included*

our wives or girlfriends in planning out our season because it is not just the four of us affected by our curling anymore. We actually all sign a contract with each other which includes our practice commitment, bonspiels, games, travel schedule, provision for our wives travelling to some tournaments, plus a few other items so that our goals are really understood by each player and our spouses. This helps us keep misunderstandings to a minimum and allows us to focus very strongly on our preparation and goals.

2.   Concentration

Concentration and attentiveness to every shot by every player are necessary. Howard Wood (two-time Brier champion from Winnipeg in 1930 and 1940) is a great skip and a great competitor. When you are standing next to him on the ice, you almost feel a vibration caused by the intensity of his concentration.

–Ken Watson

The dominant last rock throwers on the men's side in the last decade have been Peja Lindholm and Edmonton's David Nedohin. Between them they have six World Championships, three each. Peja is constantly reinforcing to himself the importance of concentration on each and every shot. He values the word *focus* and uses it constantly when talking about the mental game. This is similar to Patrick Roy, the NHL goalie who still holds the record for career wins; he wrote the word *warrior* on the inside of his leg pads to remind himself that warriors always focus on the task at hand.

David Nedohin oozes concentration out on the curling ice. When he threw his last rock in Edmonton to win their team's fourth Brier in five years in front of 16,000 patrons and 1.5 million television viewers, he described to *Edmonton Journal* writer Joanne Ireland what was going on in his mind as he settled into the hack:

When someone asked me if I wanted last rock in the last end, I said I absolutely did. I knew as soon as I let it go it was close. All year long, if there was one shot the guys wanted to give me, it was a draw to win it. And I had just thrown that shot so I knew the leg drive; I knew how it would feel in my hand. All I thought about was about not being heavy.

*I just had to take a few deep breaths. That entire end I had to keep calm-
ing myself down because my heartbeat would start going a little faster.*

Heidi Price was my daughter's second, third, and fourth grade
teacher at Dr. E. W. Coffin Elementary School in Calgary. Students at
the University of Calgary clammered to do their practicums with her. I
used to do some parent volunteering in her classrooms and always
walked out of there having learned something about working with
people and teaching. Whenever the students were getting out of hand,
she would calmly raise her voice and encourage them to "Focus!" If
this didn't work the first time, she would raise her voice a decibel or
two but still calmly and say, "We need **high focus** in here now."
Without fail, these young and energetic students would stop their
messin' around and get back to the task at hand. Concentration and
attentiveness, throwing every rock with a purpose, thinking only about
the process of throwing the rock—high focus are the keys to being a
warrior out on a sheet of curling ice.

3.   Cooperation

Curling is a team game and has no room for the volatile egoist or
the stubborn, untractable player who thinks the game revolves
around him. Teamwork requires the spirit of give and take, consideration of the other fellow, and a willingness to submerge impulsive
individual desires in the common interest of the rink. Cooperation
means confidence in the knowledge that your teammate is doing his
level best and that the other players think likewise of you.

—Ken Watson

Bert Gretzinger of Kelowna, British Columbia, is one of Western
Canada's best skips who has also won a number of WCT events over the
years. As a skip, he has never won the Brier or a Worlds, yet he is part
of the 1994 team from Kelowna skipped by Rick Folk that won both the
Brier and Worlds. Bert has won WCT events both before and after his
Team Folk experience as a skip, but in the mid-1990s, he willingly
moved *down to second* to create what many across Canada called curling's version of the dream team. Throwing third stones was Pat Ryan
and at lead was Gerry Richard.

The high-performance skipping experience of Folk, Ryan, and Gretzinger on the same team may never be equaled. How could three proven skips— regardless of their gaudy resumes—work together and accomplish what they did? This has been tried before with little success, if any. The old adage around curling clubs has always been "you can never throw together three or four skips and have any high-level success." How did these three wily veterans pull it off? One word— cooperation. They put their egos on the shelf and threw their efforts and energy into the goals of the team.

Curling is littered with great individual talents who have had opportunities to advance far in their careers but have never gotten out of their clubs or regions. Some curlers would rather call the shots and have the last word, regardless of the opportunity to play on a better team and then have a shot at Scott or Brier glory. Bert Gretzinger didn't care if everyone knew he was right in his feelings towards the game, he just cared about winning.

Alcoholics Anonymous can teach us about the far-reaching effects of cooperation. AA is far and away the fastest growing self-help movement in the history of humankind. Started in 1935 by two self-admitted alcoholics, the movement is now in over two hundred countries and still growing strong and expanding its self-help base to dozens of other human maladies. How do they do it? One of their valued traditions is simply ***principles over personalities***, which can only work when people have a cooperation mind-set. AA's twelve-step principles are proven truisms that work; but when a step is neglected, the ego steps back in and results in severe regression or failure in the recovery process. AA finds that when the primary purpose of the organization is put first and ego is placed off to the side, everyone benefits and individual lives become that much more productive. Not meaning to overstate the case here, but wouldn't an addict want recovery regardless of the price and wouldn't a championship caliber curler sacrifice his ego if it gave him a shot at a provincial, state, or national title?

4. Courage

The never-say-die attitude or intestinal fortitude. Courage is a difficult quality to define. Sometimes I call it optimism. . . . It is not a physical courage but a healthy mental attitude that refuses to admit defeat even in the face of hopeless situations (and many such arise during a curler's experience).

We all love a man who can come back from behind, or who can get up off the floor and come back for more. This elusive quality is hard to determine in a curler, but if you see any sign of it and he has many of the other qualifications, sign him up. You will never regret it.

—Ken Watson

Arguably the greatest sports team of all time was the famous Soviet Union national hockey team of the 1950s to 1980s, led primarily by the crusty and brilliant Anatoli Tarasov. I have long been fascinated by coaches/leaders of any sport and have read books by both Tarasov and his goalie Vladislav Tretiak, who is one of the few Russians inducted into the Hockey Hall of Fame in Toronto. The CCCP hockey machine felt the primary virtue of the high-performance athlete was courage. Their definition was very similar to Ken Watson's. They had that never-say-die attitude, the willingness to play until the clock runs out or your team has run out of rocks, and determination not to lose your poise.

Tarasov said in his classic book, *Russian Hockey Secrets: Road to Olympus*:

Courage does not mean an unnecessary show of bravado or strength; courage does not mean a constant readiness to pick a fight. Unsportsman-like *or rough play is not a sign of courage, but cowardice. Courage means the ability to stay out of a fight/unnecessary confrontation; real courage calls for self-control and patience. It is the ability to keep a level head even in the most explosive of situations.*

Tretiak devoted an entire chapter to the importance of courage in his book, *Tretiak*. He went onto explain how Tarasov taught that courage has its roots in bravery and how the mature player will not deviate from the game plan unless it's obviously not working (in other words, no panic). Courage does not allow fear to dictate how a player will play because a courageous player will play through the fear or learn to minimize its potential impact. Courage keeps the focus on what you can do versus what fear says you cannot do or what negative things could occur. Courage is maintaining your poise when all around you things seem to be falling apart or the pressure seems too much.

The CCCP of the 1970s were not content to just win World Championships and Olympics if the best North Americans could not take part on a regular basis; they wanted to beat the best and laid it on the line in 1972 in that famous Canada-Soviet series. The CCCP narrowly lost that series but took it as a learning experience to try and get better. Their philosophy of developing courageous athletes took this defeat and caused them to find ways to stay competitive and eventually beat these professionals from North America. It was nine years later in 1981 when the Soviets finally beat the best professionals in a head-to-head world tournament, winning the final game versus Team Canada 8-1.

Curling case studies on courage? Look no further than Al Hackner losing back-to-back Brier finals in 1980 and 1981, and losing a game he had total control in to Kerry Burtynk in 1981. Heartbreak, disappointment, and questions about one's ability to win the big one were all emotions this team felt. However in 1982, Hackner became the first team ever to appear in three straight Brier finals. Would they become the precursor to the Buffalo Bills of the curling scene?

History shows us that Hackner won his first Brier and that his team went on to win the Worlds a few short weeks later. And just for good measure, Hackner and teammate Rick Lang returned in 1985 to win both majors for a second time to go down as one of the most popular and successful Canadian teams in sports history. Watson was prophetic when he wrote, "We all love a man who can come back from behind, or can get up off the floor and come back for more."

5.   Confidence

> Confidence is not conceit or braggadocio (which usually covers up
> lack of confidence) but a quiet, inner conviction that the shot that you
> are about to try can be made and that you can and will make it.
>
> —Ken Watson

I once overheard a newly recruited senior curler at a curling club walk over to a seasoned veteran whom he was trying to model his game after and say, "You know the difference between you and me? When I make my shots I'm surprised, but when you make your shots you expect to. I'm shocked when I make my shots, and you're shocked if you miss."

From my many interviews and Cheryl's observations, we have come to the conclusion that confidence comes from three areas which can be worked on: practice, preparation, and experience.

Cheryl feels that if she is lacking confidence it can be regained very quickly by going down to the rink and practicing. Feeling good about her delivery, making some shots, and getting a feel for the ice back reinforces to her that she can play against any team and have success.

Preparation in covering the bases necessary before a big game or big-time event can involve practice, of course, but preparation is also being comfortable with the venue, being ready for the media, making sure the team is all on the same page, understanding the game plan or plans, and having travel arrangements squared away, just to name a few. Former UCLA Bruins basketball coach John Wooden, New England Patriots coach Bill Belichick, and Green Bay Packers legend Vince Lombardi all concur that if players go into a game well-prepared and focused, normal game distractions and upheavals are easy to deal with and players' confidence levels will seldom be shaken.

There is no substitute for experience. The human mind seems to work best under pressure when we have prior experience in similar scenarios. Keith Wendorf represented Germany at seven World Championships, becoming the first German skip to earn a silver medal at Worlds; he also won two bronzes and lost two tie-breakers. He told a story of losing a German final the year before his first German title in 1978. All he had to do was draw the house on his final rock to win. Keith said his final rock went through the house and off the back bumper because his adrenaline was running so high. Did he learn from this failure? Keith became known as one of the top European skips with his better-than-average draw weight and his ability to perform under pressure.

6.   Competitiveness

Seems to be a determination or desire to excel or the "will-to-win."
—Ken Watson

Watson went on to explain that competitiveness has to do with that nervous, almost nauseous, feeling in one's stomach before an important game. Two-time Brier player (three if you count him being a fifth) Brian McCusker of Regina called it, "appropriate nervousness." Butterflies are common for every high-performance athlete. These butterflies are simply a reminder that we care about what we are doing; it's God's way of causing us to focus on our preparation and talents if we view nervousness as an ally.

Claire Carver-Dias said her coaches on the Canadian national synchro team said, "The key to dealing with butterflies is to get them to fly in formation and not having them fly all over the place causing confusion and doubt."

Tony La Russa has managed pennant-winning teams in both Oakland and St. Louis and is still going strong. In 2004, he was followed around for three baseball games by author Buzz Bissinger who wrote *3 Nights in August* based upon his observations. La Russa looks so cool under pressure, almost nonchalant at times yet says this about his competitive nature: "I'm as nauseous as I've ever been. I have a terrible headache. My head is pounding. I feel like throwing up and I'm having trouble swallowing. And the beauty of it is, you want to feel like this everyday."

The best curlers want to win and tend to be competitive in most, if not all, aspects of their daily lives. Cheryl says her coach Dennis Balderston uses the competitive nature of Cheryl and her teammates during practice sessions. He knows practice needs to have a fun or variation aspect to it, so he will often make up little games for the women to compete in while reinforcing valuable skills. He will bring prizes to the practices such as chocolate bars or coupons for restaurants. Cheryl says it's amazing how serious these meaningless games become.

I'm purposely adding more information under this point than the rest of the Seven Cs because competitiveness can be a misunderstood word for some. Nevertheless, it is a critical quality each member of the team needs to have and to cultivate. Positive competitiveness means that we want to possess something worthwhile or to accomplish something that has meaning attached to it. It is the desire to make a difference regardless of the cost. We just tend to attach this word mostly to athletics, yet it is the quality that drove Mother Teresa to do what she did with her acts of charity and motivates artists like Santana or Rodney Crowell to write music with passion.

Negative competitiveness is not respecting the game or your avocation at its core. It still possesses the same desire to excel or to gain possession of something, but it's done with a selfish spirit or an attitude of poor sportsmanship. Below is an illustration of positive competitiveness with Norwegian great Pal Trulsen.

Pal Trulsen won the 2002 Olympic gold medal for Norway beating Kevin Martin in the final. Pal is one intense customer who always seems to find a way to be in the running at whatever curling event his teams are in, yet he can come across as pretty laid-back with his on-ice persona. I watched him lose the 3-4 quarterfinal game to Team Ferbey at the 2005 Ford World Men's in Victoria, British Columbia.

He had the highest throwing percentage for skips at this Worlds and deserved a much better fate than his fourth place finish. He lost this do-or-die game on last rock to Canada, but what probably won the game for the Canadians was David Nedohin's circus shot in the ninth which tied the game coming home. If David missed his last shot in the ninth, Norway had a three or four point cushion coming home. David played third and sweeps front end stones but threw last rock. After Canada's first rock of the tenth and last end, Pal motioned to David to come closer to him because he wanted to say something. Pal stopped the game momentarily, said something, and shook David's hand for the unbelievable shot he made in the ninth. Pal probably lost a chance to play for the gold medal and, at the worst, earn a silver medal because of David Nedohin.

After the game, I went down to the media area to find the entrance to escape the mad rush of fans heading out to get to their cars. As I turned a corner, I went through an area where very few people had access, and who is headed straight for me but Mr. Trulsen. I wanted to say something sympathetic and clever, which can be so hard to do on short notice. I looked him straight in the eye, and all I saw was the pain of losing and no opportunity for a medal.

All I could say was, "Oh, I just feel so bad for you, you played such a great game. I'm so sorry." He looked me straight in the eye, shook my hand, smiled his famous smile, then put his head down and said, "Thank you." He paused, trying to say something else, then shook his head a bit. I swear I saw a tear in his eye or a lump forming in his throat. He smiled again and walked away. My preacher/social work background was taking over and I wanted to let him vent, but I knew that would be foolish. However, I saw pure competitiveness and class on display like I have seldom ever seen.

7.   Consistency

The steady, dependable player is of far more value to a rink than a brilliant but inconsistent one. Practice and experience help to develop

> consistency, and when self-control and sound judgement are added, you will find a curler who will make a good percentage of his shots in any game he plays.
>
> —Ken Watson

Consistency has to do with what goes on behind the glass as well as what goes on the ice. Behind the glass practice, practice, practice, constantly learning about the mental game and strategy, and trying to make the team chemistry strong has to be worked on constantly. Developing consistency on the ice in actual games, of course, is a huge key to sustained success.

Watson in his book, under the heading of *Consistency*, gave the example of a game he played in his younger days—a twelve end game—where his team was playing a more veteran line-up. He wrote that end after end they would build up ends to break it open, but the opposing skip kept bailing them out. Finally, the opposing skip missed a partial shot late in the game, and Watson's team cracked a five-ender to take control of what he thought would be a loss. He said, "That was a very valuable lesson we never forgot." Consistency is all about hanging in there, being relentless, and never slacking off in intensity.

Sometimes the best lessons learned at a curling rink are the conversations one overhears when changing your shoes, getting ready to go on the ice, or as you leave the arena. One night leaving the arena after a regular club game, I walked past a bantam team that had a practice game versus one of the regular men's teams. I noticed how they hung in there for the first few ends, and then the men pulled away on them and beat them convincingly. One of the dads/coaches was talking to the boys afterwards and said, "What a great lesson tonight. Did you see how that team is relentless in how they played? They never stopped coming after you guys. They never took an end off. Isn't that what consistency is all about?"

The Seven Cs are timeless in their wisdom. They are the mental fundamentals to creating championship curlers. Will they guarantee success? Nothing can guarantee success, but unless one applies himself to the relentless pursuit of the Seven Cs, success will never be attainable. All we can do is put ourselves into position to be the best we can be and see how our curling lives will play out. The odds are definitely in your favor that your game and your team will improve and have more success than previously.

"The relentless pursuit of perfection!"

—The slogan for Lexus and
every high-performance champion curler

Conclusion

"It's a Process of Repetition!"

"Even if you understand the problem, though, that doesn't mean you can correct it right away. It's a process of repetition."

—Ichiro Suzuki,
Seattle Mariners

As you have probably figured out by now, Cheryl and I love quotes. Especially sports quotes or movie quotes. I found this gem while visiting Seattle and taking in a couple of ball games at Safeco Field. I had become an Ichiro fan almost from day one when he arrived in the U.S. to see if he could perform in what he refers to as the best baseball league on the planet. Now, unless you have been living under a curling rock the last few years, you probably know that Ichiro has been the best hitter in baseball since he arrived, and possibly the best outfielder as well.

When I read his book, *Ichiro on Ichiro*, I immediately noticed that he seems to have the curling psyche with regard to how he explains the art of hitting and the art of winning. He is on a lifetime quest to perform at his absolute best as a ball player. Most devout curlers seem to be on a similar quest with their favorite sport.

In *Between the Sheets*, we have tried to put together a book that can point a curler towards excellence and entertain the serious as well as casual fan of the game. Ichiro's quote seems to capture an important truism about putting the lessons of this book to use in creating curling champions. These lessons are meant to encourage and instruct, but they will never come to maximum use unless one commits to the process of repetition, be it in the technical, mental, or motivational part of the game. Learning or being reminded of the lessons we need to do is helpful, but understanding these lessons alone will never take us to the next level of excellence.

> "I have always carried one or two very dog-eared sports psychology books in my curling bag; books that I would refer to over and over again on the road when we were playing. My dream, though, had always been to have a book which focused on the specific sport of curling. Because Guy had that same dream, it has become a reality.
>
> "It is my desire that this book will motivate individuals and teams to pursue excellence in all aspects of their lives. And I sincerely hope to find some well-used copies of *Between the Sheets* in your curling bags as well."
>
> —Cheryl Bernard

Bibliography

Berra, Yogi and Dave Kaplan. *Ten Rings: My Championship Seasons*. New York, N.Y.: HarperCollins, 2003.

Bissinger, Buzz. *Three Nights in August*. New York, N.Y.: Houghton Mifflin Company, 2005.

Canfield, Jack and Mark Victor Hansen. *A Second Helping of Chicken Soup for the Soul*. Deerfield Beach, Fla.: Health Communications, 1995.

Fielding, Betty. "The Body-Brain Connection," *Healthy and Natural Journal*, vol. 7, issue 33 (April 2000).

Gibbs, Joe. *Fourth and One*. Nashville, Tenn.: Thomas Nelson, 1991.

Gretzky, Wayne. "Observations of an Armchair Curler," *National Post* (October 23, 1999).

Jackson, Phil. *The Last Season: A Team in Search of Its Soul*. New York, N.Y.: The Penguin Press, 2004.

Jeffers, H. Paul. *The Bully Pulpit: A Teddy Roosevelt Book of Quotations*. Dallas, Tex.: Taylor Publishing, 1998.

Jones, Terry. "Terry Jones Column," *Edmonton Sun*, April 1, 2005.

Jordan, Michael. *I Can't Accept Not Trying*. San Francisco, Calif.: Harper San Francisco, 1994.

Komatsu, Narumi. *Ichiro on Ichiro: Interviews with Narumi Komatsu*. Seattle, Wash.: Sasquatch Books, 2004.

Levine, Stuart R. *The Six Fundamentals of Success*. New York, N.Y.: Doubleday, 2004.

Levy, Marv. *Marv Levy: Where Else Would You Rather Be?*. Champaign, Ill.: Sports Publishing, 2004.

Lewis, C. S. *Mere Christianity*. San Francisco, Calif.: HarperCollins, 2001.

Lukowich, Ed, Al Hackner, and Rick Lang. *Curling to Win*. Toronto, Ont.: McGraw-Hill Ryerson, 1986.

Lukowich, Ed, Paul Gowsell, and Rick Folk. *The Curling Book*. Saskatoon, Sask.: Western Producer Prairie Books, 1981.

MacIsaac, Angela. "MacIsaac Weekly Curling Column," *Calgary Sun*, April 5, 2005.

Madden, John. *One Knee Equals Two Feet*. New York, N.Y.: Villard Books, 1986.

Maxwell, Doug. *Canada Curls: The Illustrated History of Curling in Canada*. Vancouver, B.C.: Whitecap Books, 2002.

McCallum, Jack. "They're Winning, By George," *Sports Illustrated*, April 5, 2005.

Montiminy, Anne. "Aquatic Athletes." *Maclean's*. Special Olympic Edition, summer 2000.

Penick, Harvey. *And If You Play Golf, You're My Friend*. New York, N.Y.: Simon & Schuster, 1993.

Penick, Harvey. *Harvey Penick's Little Red Book*. New York: N.Y.: Simon and Schuster, 1992.

Richardson, Ernie and Mark Mulvoy. *Curling: Techniques and Strategy*. Toronto, Ont.: McClelland and Stewart, 1973.

Russell, Bill and David Falkner. *Russell Rules*. New York, N.Y.: Dutton, a member of Penguin Putnam Inc., 2001.

Sahley, Billie J. "Amino Acid Brain Boosters." *Diplomate, American Academy of Pain Management*. Pain and Stress Publications, 2004.

Savage, Paul. *Canadian Curling: Hack to House*. Agincourt, Ont.: Sportbook, 1974.

Scholz, Guy. *Gold on Ice: The Story of the Sandra Schmirler Curling Team*. Regina. Sask.: Coteau Books, 1999.

Tarasov, Anatoli. *Road to Olympus: Russian Hockey Secrets*. Richmond Hill, Ont.: Pocket Books of Canada, 1972.

Tiefenbach, Arnie. *Say It Again, Sam: Life In and Beyond the Richardson Curling Dynasty*. Regina, Sask.: The House That Sam Built Publishing, 1999.

Tschirhart, Bill. "Straight, Simple, Silent"; "Brushing 101"; "Stop-Start-Continue"; plus numerous interviews. Articles from the National Training Centre of the Canadian Curling Association. Calgary, Alta.: 2000–2005.

Wassef, Farid. "Stress Less: Live Longer and Healthier." *Alive: Canadian Journal of Health and Nutrition*, issue 271 (May 2005): 44.

Watson, Ken. *Ken Watson on Curling*. Toronto, Ont.: The Copp Clark Co. Limited, 1950.

Wooden, John. *My Personal Best*. New York, N.Y.: McGraw-Hill, 2004.

About the Authors

Guy Scholz

Guy Scholz has many loves in his life—family, faith, writing, his day job, an unfathomable support of the Saskatchewan Roughriders, and, of course, curling. Getting to focus on two at one time with a project like *Between the Sheets* was pure bliss!

Guy's writing resume includes his national best-selling book, *Gold on Ice: The Story of the Sandra Schmirler Curling Team*. He has been a feature writer and regular columnist for *Sweep!* magazine since 1999 and has written for seven different magazines from sports to inspirational since 1989. He has his third book with Nashville co-author Claudia Church titled *Discovering the Masterpiece Within* scheduled for release sometime between 2006 or 2007.

His love affair with curling includes thirty-four consecutive years of much heartbreak (losing 844 games of 2,372 games played since he began recording at the age of twelve), many metaphorical life lessons, moments of joy, and genuine excitement every single time he begins his trek to a curling rink. He is a six-time national clergy curling champion (aka Friar's Briar), has won twenty-five bonspiels, has been on a club champion team on twelve occasions, and has won twenty A-Blocks at the club level, plus sixty-nine consolation events or block wins. His club teams enter provincial playdowns almost every year but that Brier dream remains as elusive as back-to-back Roughrider Grey Cup wins.

Guy currently serves as co-senior pastor with his wife, Carla, at Chinook Chapel in Calgary, Alberta. Curling is his therapy away from the ministry and pastoring is his therapy away from the rink.

> *Nothing flatters me more than to have it assumed that*
> *I could write prose—unless it be to have it assumed that*
> *I once pitched a baseball with distinction.*
> —*Robert Frost*

> *Nothing flatters me more than to have it assumed that*
> *I could write prose and preach well—*
> *unless it be to have it assumed that*
> *I once threw a curling rock with distinction.*
> —*Canadian version*

Cheryl Bernard

Cheryl Bernard is considered by many curling competitors and experts to be one of the top individual shot-makers in the game over the last fifteen years. Cheryl is a two-time Scott Tournament of Hearts participant as a skip in 1992 and 1996. At the 1996 Scott, she finished second in all of Canada to Marilyn Bodogh. Cheryl was also the Alberta mixed champion with Terry Meek in 1993. She has six top-ten finishes on the Canadian Women's Curling Tour and was the 2004 Women's Curling Tour champion.

She has won numerous cashspiels including the Bill Hunter sponsored event in Red Deer in 1996 (which pocketed her team a cool twenty thousand dollars, the largest payday ever up to that stage). In 1999, Cheryl was runner-up at the prestigious JVC/TSN Skins game. Her playdown record is one of the best on the provincial scale; she's won over a dozen Alberta Southern Playdowns berths and made six trips to the provincials—winning two and becoming runner-up on three occasions.

A savvy businesswoman who started her own general insurance agency in Calgary in 1990, Cheryl grew it to an agency with over $5 million in sales before she sold it in 2001. She feels that the lessons she learned in business overlap with curling, especially when it comes to team chemistry, pressure, adversity, work ethic, and consistency.

Active in women's curling in Calgary, Cheryl volunteered on the Autumn Gold Spiel organizing committee for more than twelve years, serving in many roles including chairwoman and investors' workshop co-coordinator. She was also a member of the Calgary Ladies Superleague Executive for many years and has volunteered her time as Women's Players Representative to the Alberta Curling Federation. She is the competitive consultant for the Canadian Curling Association's National Training Centre and is also an executive of the Canadian Women's Curling Tour. In 2005, she was instrumental in joining the women's and men's tours into one body with the creation of the Men's and Women's World Curling Tour.

Cheryl is most proud of the creation and chairing of the hugely successful **Curl for a Cure** annual fund-raiser for the support of the Canadian Breast Cancer Foundation. In the three years of its existence, this event has raised over a half million dollars for breast cancer research. In her message to the participants at the 2005 event, these words from Cheryl capture the integrity of her heart: "I truly believe that everything you do is a statement to the rest of the world of your personal character."

Workshops and Curling Clinics

Cheryl and Guy are available for workshops or curling clinics. For more information, they can be reached at:

Cheryl Bernard
403-701-8886
403-202-1895 (fax)
cherylbernard@betweenthesheetscurling.com

Guy Scholz
403-208-0652
403-701-8737
guyscholz@shaw.ca or
guyscholz@betweenthesheetscurling.com

To order more copies of *Between the Sheets* (or to contact Cheryl and Guy via the Web), go to www.betweenthesheetscurling.com.

This book will still be of no value to the serious curler
unless you consistently apply what's in it!